MAN THINKING

"Man is not a farmer, or a professor, or an engineer, but he is all. . . . In [the] distribution of functions the scholar is the delegated intellect. In the right state he is *Man Thinking*." – RALPH WALDO EMERSON, Harvard Phi Beta Kappa Oration, 1837

MAN THINKING

Representative Phi Beta Kappa Orations

1915-1959

EDITED FOR THE UNITED CHAPTERS
OF PHI BETA KAPPA BY

WILLIAM T. HASTINGS

Cornell University Press

ITHACA, NEW YORK

CORNELL UNIVERSITY PRESS

First published 1962

Library of Congress Catalog Card Number: 62-17816

PRINTED IN THE UNITED STATES OF AMERICA

BY VAIL-BALLOU PRESS, INC.

Preface

THIS third volume of Phi Beta Kappa orations is a representative selection from the many addresses sponsored by the Society, for the most part by individual Chapters, all delivered (with one exception) since World War I. Two previous volumes have been published, the first in 1915 under the editorship of Clark S. Northup, William C. Lane, and John C. Schwab, the second in 1927 under Professor Northup, with an introductory essay by Charles F. Thwing. The introduction to the second volume surveyed the changing character of the addresses during a century and a half, and it is still valid today. The long and highly rhetorical disquisition, loaded with wide-ranging superficial learning, is as dead as the dodo, but, as Dr. Thwing rightly observes, the assumption of intellectual competence and concern of a high order in the traffic between speaker and audience, and of the special responsibility of intellectuals for the stability and progress of civilization, remains precisely the same.

It is particularly interesting, therefore, to note how, in the present collection, the issues of each little day impinge upon and lend detailed color to the addresses as we move from year to year, decade to decade, yet how the basic approach to each day's dilemma remains the same. The public duty of educated men still receives in more than 160 academic cloisters its annually refreshed analysis.

Indispensable help in gathering the material for this third collection has been given by a majority of the Chapters. More than 150 addresses were read, and the 28 chosen for publication represent, it is believed, Phi Beta Kappa at its best.

The editor has greatly profited by the critical judgment of his advisory committee, Dean William C. De Vane of Yale, President Frederick Hard of Scripps, and Professor Whitney J. Oates of Princeton. Each gave careful consideration to all the addresses which survived a preliminary sifting, and there was a surprising agreement, almost complete unanimity, in the final choice.

Phi Beta Kappa is indebted, for permission to publish, to the writers represented in the collection and the Chapters concerned. It is happy also to acknowledge the following specific permissions to reprint:

Mrs. Jacob Zeitlin—Stuart Sherman's "The Gaiety of Socrates."

Hobart and William Smith Colleges—Vincent Massey's "Our Problem and Yours."

Harper & Brothers—a quotation by Vincent Massey from Norman Angell's *The Unseen Assassins* and a quotation by William G. Carleton from Russell Lynes's *The Tastemakers*.

Houghton Mifflin Company—two quotations by Zechariah Chafee, Jr., from Archibald MacLeish's *Poems, 1924–1933*.

Harvard University Press—a quotation by Edgar Sheffield Brightman from R. G. Bury's translation of Plato's *Timaeus*, in the Loeb Classical Library; also a quotation by F. Lyman Windolph from an address by Justice Oliver Wendell Holmes at the dinner of the Harvard Bar Association of New York in 1913; also a quotation by Franklin L. Baumer from Ralph Barton Perry's *The Thought and Character of William James*.

The Michie Company—F. Lyman Windolph's "*Religio Advocati.*"

Cambridge University Press—a quotation by F. Lyman Windolph from A. E. Housman's *The Name and Nature of Poetry;*

also a quotation by Mr. Windolph from Sir Arthur Edding-ton's *The Nature of the Physical World*.

Dodd, Mead & Company—a quotation by F. Lyman Windolph from Chesterton's *Orthodoxy*. Reprinted by permission of Dodd, Mead & Company from *Orthodoxy* by G. K. Chester-ton. Copyright, 1908, 1936, by G. K. Chesterton. Permission applies solely "to publication in the United States and its dependencies."

The Bodley Head, Ltd.—the same quotation from Chesterton's *Orthodoxy*, copyright 1908, 1928, by G. K. Chesterton. Pub-lished by The Bodley Head, Ltd. Permission applies to distri-bution of the book in the British Empire market.

Scripps College—Marjorie Nicolson's "The Romance of Scholar-ship."

The American Scholar, as agent for the authors—John Herman Randall's "The Paradox of Intellectual Freedom," Walter Lippmann's "Education vs. Western Civilization," Theodore M. Greene's "In Praise of Reflective Commitment," Julian P. Boyd's "Thomas Jefferson Survives," and Wilmarth S. Lewis's "The Trustees of the Privately Endowed University."

Randolph-Macon Woman's College—André Morize's "Foreign Cultures and the World Crisis."

Random House, Inc.—a quotation by Lewis Webster Jones from W. H. Auden's *The Age of Anxiety*, copyright 1947; also for a quotation by Douglas Bush from William Faulkner's 1950 Nobel Prize Speech of Acceptance, reprinted from *The Faulk-ner Reader* (Random House, 1954).

Viking Press—a quotation by Douglas Bush from Lionel Trill-ing's *The Liberal Imagination*.

The New York Times—a quotation by Douglas Bush from a news story in the *Times* of November 28, 1950.

Simon and Schuster, Inc.—a quotation by Gerald W. Johnson from *The Open Mind*, copyright © 1955 by J. Robert Op-penheimer. By permission of Simon and Schuster, Inc.

Wake Forest Press—a quotation by Gerald W. Johnson from the baccalaureate address in 1926 at Wake Forest by William L. Poteat, published in *Youth and Culture*, 1928.

Oxford University Press—quotations by Gerald W. Johnson and Franklin L. Baumer from Arnold J. Toynbee's *A Study of History*, Volume X, copyright, London, New York, and Toronto, 1954.

Connecticut College—Franklin L. Baumer's "Religion and the Sceptical Tradition."

Yale University Press—a quotation by Franklin L. Baumer from Carl Becker's *The Heavenly City of the Eighteenth-Century Philosophers*.

The Macmillan Company—quotations by Franklin L. Baumer from Arthur Koestler's *The Age of Longing*.

Antioch Press—William G. Carleton's "The New Conservatism and the Mass Society."

Princeton University Press—Harold W. Dodd's "On the Place of the Intellectual in America."

The Key Reporter—Paul B. Sears's "Physical Law and Moral Choice."

WILLIAM T. HASTINGS

Washington, May 15, 1962

Contents

CONTENTS

x

MAN THINKING

STUART SHERMAN

The Gaiety of Socrates

Being an Extract from the Diary of a Professor Meditating
after a Phi Beta Kappa Dinner on the Lost Art of Banqueting.

MIDNIGHT, May 30, 1915. I have just returned from the Phi
Beta Kappa banquet—sober, as usual, and full of noble ideals.
Quite convinced that I ought to hitch my wagon to a star. Much
impressed, as in 1914, by the necessity of giving up my frivolous
way of life and devoting myself seriously to the career of a
scholar.

Phi Beta Kappa expects every man to do his duty. Sooner or
later I suppose I shall have to speak at one of these dinners myself. I have escaped hitherto; but my freedom in the past dimin-
ishes my chance of immunity in the future. When the good
stories have all been told, when the silver-tongued orators all
have spoken, when the resources of the Committee on Arrange-

Delivered before the Gamma of Illinois, University of Illinois, in 1915.
Published in *Shaping Men and Women* (Garden City, N.Y.: Double-
day, Doran, 1928).

ments are exhausted, my turn will come—and what, in the name
of invention, shall I say? This question disturbed me not a little
this evening, as I glanced across the angle at the speakers' table
and noticed the abstracted expression of the speakers' faces from
the soup onward, and, between courses, their silent rehearsal of
words that were soon to fall from their lips with bright unpre-
meditated felicity.

All Phi Beta Kappa orators, it seems to me as I run over my
acquaintance with them, may be divided into two classes: the
historians and the preachers—the men with a long memory and
the men with a long message. The historians—the older members
usually, those who rocked the cradle of the Society in its infancy,
like Professor Good and Professor Wise—delight us with reminiscences of Phi Beta Kappa as it was forty or fifty years ago—
reminiscences which to us with shorter perspective have all the
freshness of novelty. Theirs is a useful type of speech; for it
impresses upon the minds of our novitiates the venerable antiq-
uity of the organization with which they have just become identified. They will never forget, for example, Professor Good's
impassioned picture of the days when the flowing bowl went
round at the banquets of this Society; nor will they forget his
plea for the perpetuation of traditions. Our younger orators,
on the other hand, those who have not yet sunk into the retro-
spective attitude, those who look not downward and backward
but forward and upward and onward—they sweep the strings
of moral idealism, and urge the novitiates on to high and strenuous
endeavour. In speaking of our younger orators, I am thinking
of Professor Graves, and how his address opened with a solemn
promise not to preach; and how in a moment it branched out
into as many ethical heads as Hydra had or a sermon by Jonathan
Edwards; and how it closed in a glowing peroration on the importance of abiding by our promises.

Now as I shall always be outranked in the field of Society
history by some orator of Nestorian memory, prudence and an

2

ancestral line of New England clergymen point me to the moral disquisition. When my turn comes, I must *deliver a message*. What shall be my theme? PHILOSOPHY THE GUIDE OF LIFE? THE CONSCIENCE OF THE SCHOLAR? THE DUTY OF THE SCHOLAR? THE RESPONSIBILITY OF THE SCHOLAR? . . . Even as I write these words, there breaks upon me a great flood of light, and in the midst of the light is a great interrogation point. The essence of the question is this: Why do all our Phi Beta Kappa moralists exercise their great powers of moral persuasion upon the ninety-and-nine just men that need no repentance? Why do they seek to turn towards scholarly seriousness just those who can by no means be turned away from it? Why should *anyone* think it necessary to rise in this Society and talk to its members about the responsibility of the scholar, the duty of the scholar, the conscience of the scholar? Is not this an attempt to gild refined gold and paint the lily white? To harangue such a society as this, on any such subjects as these, strikes me, just now, as one of a long list of unnecessary things: it is like talking to a life-saving crew about the importance of learning to swim; it is like talking to the varsity football team about the importance of taking exercise; it is like urging a group of sorority girls to take an interest in social life; it is like declaring the value of Greek to classicists, like P. E. More and Professor Babbitt; it is like recommending the Carnegie Foundation or a Company of Deans to "tighten up the screws" or to "humanize the machine"; it is like railing against college presidents at a convention of professorial anarchists like Dr. C—— or our own Professor Freelance. In conscience, duty, and responsibility, the members of our Society live and move and have their being.

If ever I am called upon to speak before the members of Phi Beta Kappa, I shall not urge upon them the virtues for which they are already pre-eminent. I shall rather begin in some such way as this:

Ladies and gentlemen of this ancient and honourable Society:

3

You have all heard the old story about the Phi Beta Kappa poem said to have been published some years ago in the *Atlantic Monthly* by a graduate of Harvard University—that great institution to which many of us owe all that we have and are. I shall therefore repeat it to you this evening. You will remember that the Cambridge poet tells us how in his poetic frenzy a trance fell upon him, and a wonderful vision appeared to him. You will remember that in the vision a little band of Harvard men, all members of Phi Beta Kappa, visit the kingdom of heaven, and inspect the throne, and are granted audience before the Almighty. And you will recall that the visit ended in the completest satisfaction to the visitors—and to the visited. And you will have in mind the last great climactic line in which the author, summing up the impression made and received in heaven by the Harvard Phi Beta Kappa men, says: "And God was pleased with them; *and they were pleased with him.*"

Ladies and gentlemen of the Gamma chapter, Phi Beta Kappa men and women are the same the world over. We who are met here together this evening are the intellectual cream of a great intellectual community. We have been chosen as Gideon chose the three hundred to go up against the Midianites. We have disciplined ourselves to hardness and austerity. We have shunned soft delights and lived laborious days. What pietists call the "temptations of the world" have been no temptations to us. I look around me; and I see heads grown grey in renunciation. I look around at the Dean of Men and at the Dean of Women * and at Dean Tenace * and at Professor Pumps * and at Professor Cleek * and at Professor Brassey * and at Doctor Lofter,* and I say to myself: "Why talk to these great lonely thinkers of husbanding the diamond-studded hours, and eschewing the soft seductions of the dance, the lure of the bridge table, and the green enchantment of the golf links?" What do these things

* Unmarried members are indicated by a single asterisk.

mean to any of *us?* We all, as I have said, have burned the midnight oil. We have sought that excellence which, as the Greeks tell us, a man must wear his heart out to attain. Sitting here this evening, with our golden badges of achievement upon our bosoms and a shade of weariness upon our brows, we represent the accomplishment of a remorseless purpose; we are the embodiments, in the intellectual sphere, of fulfilled desire. What remains to put the last touch upon our perfection? What can we do to keep ourselves, as Matthew Arnold would say, from a self-satisfaction that is vulgarizing and relaxing?

Ladies and gentlemen, when I am in doubt what I ought to think of any movement of ideas or any project or any organization in this community, I turn to that great responsible organ of community sentiment, *'Varsity Daily;* and I inquire what the *'Varsity Daily* thinks of it. What does the *'Varsity Daily* think of the Phi Beta Kappa Society and its banquet? When this great voice of community sentiment reports a banquet of the athletes, or of the seniors, or of the Loyal Order of Hibernians, do we not regularly find its approval of the organization heralded in some such headlines as these?

FEST HALL SEES GREAT REVEL OF SENIORS

Eats and Drinks Abundant

A Grand Time Was Had by All

Now let me solemnly put it to your scholarly consciences, ladies and gentlemen, whether the *'Varsity Daily* has ever admitted that at our annual symposium "a grand time was had by all," or even that "eats and drinks" were abundant? In the cold grey dawn of the morning after, as we open the dew-drenched sheet, do we not rather find ourselves and our activities advertized by some such caption as this?

5

High-Brows Hold Annual Solemnities

Prominent Deans Urge High Standards
in All Departments

O. B. Wise Puts the Punch into
Scholarship

Ladies and gentlemen, I rise tonight to say that the more we plan to put the "punch" into scholarship, the more we should plan at certain intervals, such as this, to take the punch out of the scholar. I mean to mollify and unbend him; to make his wisdom smile; to smooth his wrinkled front; to shake his diaphragm with laughter; and, in short, to subject the tired tendons of his mind to the salutary osteopathy of ridicule. I rise tonight to suggest that the one thing needful to our perfection is a richer tincture of gaiety—gaiety sufficient to make our annual banquet a revel, not a rite, a feast and not a function. If we are to make the key-man who is now playing billiards at the club wish he were here, if we are to make the key-woman who is now dancing at Argentina Hall wish she were here, if we are to make our colleagues who are now viewing the legitimate moving pictures at the Orpheum wish they were here, we must, in one way or another, persuade the public, not merely that "eats and drinks" were abundant, but also that a "grand time" was had by all—a grander time than was to be had anywhere else from the western limits of the Country Club to the utmost shores of Crystal Lake.

In this matter I am in accord with the philosopher Spinoza, who says in his treatise *On the Improvement of the Intellect:* "*It is essential to my happiness,* to try to make many others understand what *I* understand, so that their intellect and desire may entirely agree with my intellect and desire."

I recognize at once that many members of this company may be of Lord Chesterfield's mind, when he wrote to his son that no gentleman ever permits himself to laugh. It is the tenacity with which whole classes of society cling to this rigid principle of decorum that makes it so difficult for the wits of the world to add materially to the gaiety of nations. Thus Molière, who was one of the ablest of wits, says that it is a very serious business making honest people laugh. George Meredith carries on the idea when he declares that all the great humorists have been grave men—permanently saddened, I suppose, by years of effort unavailingly directed towards making their contemporaries smile. The professor in particular is a hard case, as Mark Twain discovered to his dismay when he tried to make the professors at Cambridge cheerful. The professor, I say, is a hard case—which perhaps explains why he seems to live in perpetual fear of losing his character.

The thesis which I wish to advance tonight is nearly the converse of Meredith's. I wish to take up another aspect of the relation between gaiety and greatness. I wish to prove that all great men have been gay men. This will be just a little difficult; because it isn't true. If the whole truth were to be told, many great men, I fear some of them members of our own Society, are now in the fifth circle of Hell. In Dante's Hell, the fifth circle, you will remember, is hardly hot enough to be comfortable. It is the circle to which souls are sent who in life succumbed to spiritual gloom and despondency. There, the poet tells us, "fixed in the slime, they say, 'Sullen were we in the sweet air that by the sun is gladdened, bearing within ourselves the sluggish fume; now we are sullen in the black mire.' This hymn they gurgle in their throats." In spite of these depressing instances, however, there are cases enough of greatness coupled with gaiety to make at least a *show of truth*, which, as every graduate student knows, is all that is necessary to sustain a thesis.

It now becomes necessary to explain the gaiety of greatness and to illustrate it. It is commonly assumed that gaiety is a token of a light nature; quite the contrary is the truth. *The gaiety of the great rises from their sense of surplus power—power more*

7

than adequate to any situation in which they may find themselves.

This power manifests itself in the most exhilarating fashion when serious resolute men, such as we are, who have striven and suffered and achieved, as we have achieved, show themselves able to turn about and laugh at their own achievements, before they press on to new ones. The late William James, much to the horror of his colleagues, who were afraid that he would lose his character, frequently flashed out with that sort of spontaneous unprofessional gaiety. When I heard him speak on philosophy before the Harvard Graduates' Club, a great fresh breeze seemed to rise from his mind, and to sweep over the audience, and blow all the academic dust and conventions out at the windows. He had the power to be a professor of philosophy; and he had also the surplus power to laugh at being a professor of philosophy. I will give you an illustration. "Whatever universe a professor believes in," said William James, as he unfolded the doctrine of pragmatism, "must at any rate be a universe that lends itself to lengthy discourse." There is an example of gaiety rising from power more than adequate to the situation of a professor.

Another American scholar—likewise combining greatness with gaiety, but at our dinners more often remembered for the former quality than for the latter—was Ralph Waldo Emerson. Emerson had sufficient power of goodness to be a Unitarian minister, but he had a surplus power of goodness which enabled him to leave off being a Unitarian minister, and which emboldened him to cry in one of his essays: "Come, let us drink wine, and crown our heads with roses, and break up the tedious roof of heaven into new forms." There is an example of gaiety rising from power more than adequate to the situation of a Unitarian minister.

You will find this superfluous power also in that grim-visaged soldier of God, Oliver Cromwell, of whom a contemporary writer tells us that, in riding to the battle of Naseby, the general drew his horse a little aside from his troops to laugh, thinking how the Lord was going that day to deliver the enemy into his hand. That is a case of gaiety rising from power more than adequate to the situation of a Puritan general.

I think, too, of the surplus power of that great classical moralist of the Eighteenth Century, Dr. Samuel Johnson, who, after an altercation with a friend, sent out peals of laughter so loud that his voice, as his admiring biographer informs us, seemed to resound from Temple Bar to Fleet Ditch. I never allude to that grave melancholy scholar without recalling how from time to time his gigantic gaiety banished his fear of death in hours of golden relaxation.

One night, [says Boswell] when Beauclerk and Langton had supped at a tavern in London, and sat till about three in the morning, it came into their heads to go and knock up Johnson, and see if they could prevail on him to join them in a ramble. They rapped violently at the door of his chambers in the Temple, till at last he appeared in his shirt with his little black wig on the top of his head, instead of a night-cap, and a poker in his hand, imagining, probably, that some ruffians were coming to attack him. When he discovered who they were, and was told their errand, he smiled, and with great good humour agreed to their proposal: *"What! is it you, you dogs! I'll have a frisk with you."*

And the great lexicographer, the author of the *Vanity of Human Wishes,* spent the rest of the night boating on the Thames and "frisking" through the city. Langton left them in the morning to go to a breakfast with some young ladies:

Johnson scolded him for leaving his social friends to go and sit with a set of wretched *unideaed* girls. Garrick being told of this ramble, said to him smartly, "I heard of your frolic t'other night. You'll be in *The Chronicle.*" Upon which Johnson afterwards observed, "He durst not do such a thing. His *wife* would not *let* him."

Here we have an example of gaiety rising from power more than adequate to the situation of a great classical moralist.

I might carry this theme to superhuman heights. If I had the boldness of a Lamb, I might proceed to speak of the "inextinguishable laughter" of the gods. Or I might remind you of those occasions, authenticated by the prophets, when he that sitteth in the Heavens laughs. Both are illustrations of that unimaginable power which is more than adequate to governing the universe. But prudence counsels me to check my adventurous flight below the sublimer levels of gaiety. We shall find it more profitable to confine our meditations to the merciful laughter of mortals.

Ladies and gentlemen, when I meditate on the grim-eyed gravity of modern scholarship, I long to talk with some old scholar's ghost who lived before the Efficiency Experts were born. When I consider most thoughtfully the one thing needful to add the last touch of grace to a Phi Beta Kappa banquet, I think of the invincible gaiety of Socrates. He was the gravest man in Greece; but he was also the blithest. He was the best diner-out in Athens, and every banquet that he attended was a revel. He had the ugliest satyrlike face that the gods ever moulded for one of the children of men; but there was celestial sunlight in his mind. And whether he was discoursing on the divine and the earthly loves at the house of Agathon, or whether he was driving the sophist Protagoras into the intricate net of his dialectic, this superfluous celestial sunlight played about his crooked mouth in a feasting smile that filled the handsomest men in the city with envy and with rapture. And when he made an after-dinner speech, the guests forgot the buffoon and the Syracusian dancing girl provided by their host; and they forgot the vine-crowned goblets of clear wine; for they had drunk the deeper intoxication of the Socratic gaiety; and when he rose to depart, the young men rose and followed him, like bees following the scent of honey, and they went out, walking and talking still, to meet the grey-eyed dawn.

Something like this, ladies and gentlemen, should be the result of a Phi Beta Kappa banquet. I do not despair of the emulation proposed. Though Socrates had a demon, he was not a god. Socrates was a man, such as we are. He was, in a manner of speaking, a professor, such as we are. He sought truth, such as we seek. He had felt poverty, such as ours is. He had a wife, such as ours are. And yet Socrates was gay! His good lady upbraided him, just as ours do; she berated him, no doubt, for wasting his time on his students; urged him to brush his clothes and take her to see the new comedy of Aristophanes; begged him to go with her and call on Mrs. Alcibiades; besought him to *"get in"* with the Pericles circle; scolded him for loitering in the market place; insisted that he should bestir himself, so that they might take the position in Athenian society to which his talents entitled him. But Socrates smiled and pursued his true calling. And when his friends asked how he preserved his charming serenity through the perpetual rainy season of his domestic life, he replied with his victorious and contagious gaiety that to live with his wife was an admirable discipline in virtue. That was an example of power more than adequate to the situation of being Xantippe's husband. And when Critobulus, a very handsome banqueter, gave as his chief reason for self-congratulation his possession of good looks. Socrates cut in with the question: "Why, Critobulus, do you give yourself this air of vanity, as if you were handsomer than I?" That was an example of power more than adequate to the situation of being as ugly as Silenus. And when Socrates was asked what he meant by his boast that he was the wisest man in Greece, he answered, still with that feasting smile, that he was the only man in Greece who knew that he knew nothing. This was an example of power more than adequate to the situation of being—a member of the Phi Beta Kappa Society. It was an example of the power requisite to the enjoyment of a Phi Beta Kappa banquet.

Ladies and gentlemen, other speakers will come after me in later years with a clearer gift than I to preach the gospel of gaiety. I am but a voice crying in the wilderness of our gravity.

I shall be content if of me it is said in the good time to come: "He was not gay himself, but he was the cause of gaiety in others." I shall be content if at our next symposium the Committee on Arrangements acts upon the suggestion which I am about to make.

There is, as the philosopher Lotze tells us, a mystical power in our outward raiment and garniture. When Machiavelli read the classics, he put on his most gorgeous robes of state in order that his mind might the more readily enter into the intellectual splendour of Greece and Rome. When Socrates attended a banquet, he bathed, and put on his sandals, and a fresh robe. If we are to profit by these examples, all the members of our Society, and especially the speakers, will stream into this building at the appointed hour with a kind of festive and processional pomp, each man wearing a scarlet ostrich feather in his hat, and each woman borrowing a hint from our May-day evening celebration. Those who are gay in themselves will express their gaiety in their outward garb, and those who are sullen in their hearts will wear a visor as at a masquerade ball, or they will impersonate for the occasion some dead scholar who was gay. As we enter the portals, the toastmaster in a golden robe leading, and the valedictorian of that year dancing before him to the sound of a flute, the youngest and fairest of the novitiates will strew the threshold with daffodils or such early flowers as the spring affords. When we have taken our places at the board, the fairest of the novitiates, still moving rhythmically about the table to the enlivening strains of the flute, will pin a rose on the coat lapel of every professor, signifying the perfume of virtue; and on the head of every woman who is a doctor of philosophy they will place a garland of red and white roses, signifying the eternal youth of wisdom. Since King George and Lord Kitchener have dispensed with wine, we shall probably never be able to revive the tradition whose lapse Professor Good laments; but we shall pass from hand to hand a great vine-crowned loving cup brimming with liquor potent enough to cheer and inebriate a Secretary of State. I cannot enter into the details of the program; but I am sure we shall have some good speeches on the gayer aspects of science—perhaps some astronomer will tell us about the music of the spheres and how the morning stars sing together. And we shall have some good singing; perhaps some member of the Department of Geology will strike the harp like Caedmon, and sing to us about the creation of the world. We shall have some dancing, too, and some examples of the mimetic art—perhaps some member of the Department of German will give us an allegorical dance, symbolizing the progress of *Kultur* in America. Then the spokesman for the novitiates, in a short and modest speech, will explain undergraduate politics, and tell us how he engineered his election into our Society. Finally, that member of Phi Beta Kappa who has most clearly demonstrated in the course of the year that he has power more than adequate to being a member of Phi Beta Kappa will read a panegyrical poem commemorative of some scholar who though great was gay. And in the rosy dawn of the morning after we shall find, as we turn to our great responsible organ of community sentiment, some such headlines as these:

HILARITY HALL SEES SATURNALIAN
REVEL OF KEY-MEN

Wiseacres Make Wisdom Smile

A Grand Time Had by All

VINCENT MASSEY

Our Problem and Yours

I AM very happy to be with you today. Some of my pleasantest recollections of the time when I lived in your country officially are connected with my visits to colleges. I am not using the word "college" loosely as applied to institutions of learning in a general sense, but I am thinking particularly of those communities, of which Hobart is so fine an example, which have resisted the lure of magnitude which so powerfully influences higher education today, and pursue their corporate search for truth in such pleasant detachment from irrelevant distractions as you enjoy here in Geneva.

I appreciate the honour of the invitation to address a body of students who are about to leave the academic cloisters to venture into the world at a time which challenges their faith in themselves and in what their college has given them. Society has seen few epochs which offer such a test as the one in which we live. I want you to know, however, that I am under no illusions as to the functions of a Commencement Day speaker. He is welcomed, as I have reason to know, in your institutions of learning with habitual courtesy, but this does not disguise the fact that a Commencement Day address is naturally regarded by the

Delivered before the Zeta of New York, Hobart College, June 13, 1932. Published in *Hobart College Bulletin*, July, 1932.

honest-minded student, not as an unmixed blessing, but rather as something to be faced with fortitude—the last inevitable ordeal before freedom is won—freedom from obligatory learning, and shall we say, compulsory inspiration. I am nevertheless grateful for your welcome and the spirit of forbearance which this most hospitable audience reveals to a somewhat apprehensive visitor.

I have suggested as the title of my observations "Our Problem and Yours." We have of course many things in common, you Americans and we Canadians. I need not enumerate them. We have privileges in common, and mutual obligations, and we share many problems which await our respective solutions. But there is one of these most pressing at this time. We not only bear our full share of those ills which beset the world today, but we are forced to reconsider our relation to the rest of society in the light of these difficulties. We are both North American nations, remote as it seemed, from other continents. But the comfortable immunity which geographical distance seemed to give us from the diseases of this sick planet seems now illusory. We have awakened to the fact that not only in war, as we found, but in peace as well, we share in full measure the adversity of other lands. What are the implications of this most obvious fact?

The great depression, either as a theme or by way of allusion, seems almost an inevitable subject in any remarks on public affairs today, be the speaker either facetious or solemn. Sometimes it is hard to know into which category such observations fall. One economist observed not long ago that this present depression is unlike all similar periods in the recent past, and that the only crisis which bears any real resemblance to the one in which we flounder today lasted for four hundred years and is known to historians as the Dark Ages. This can be taken either as a *jeu d'esprit* or as a serious comment to the effect that our current maladjustment must mark an age of chaos and confusion between two distinct eras, just as the Dark Ages bridged a stormy transition between Roman and mediaeval civilization. At all events during the last two years the torrent of words on this absorbing subject has been sufficient, it would seem, to drown both the depression and its victims. Most things on the subject have no doubt been said. Does more remain than to restate old ideas, in different terms, and perhaps with a different emphasis?

I think it well that we should not evade this great depression as a theme so long as we approach it without that depression of spirit which distorts the judgment. Such a condition as exists today, uncomfortable though it may be, is vastly useful in revealing some of those elements in our social and economic structure which were obscured by the whitewash of artificial prosperity. The student of anatomy, we know, can learn much from a human body in a pathological state. So, often, can the body politic be best studied when a period of maladjustment tells us with greater clarity what should be the functions of its organs. After all when the international trade of the world drops in three years to one-half its former volume and we find industrial machinery working at two-thirds of its normal capacity, and the total number of those for whom there is no work in the world is perhaps thirty millions, and when prices have fallen by nearly one-half, and destitution steadily extends in a world of plenty, one can study the defects of our civilization not in terms of academic theory, but as revealed by irrefutable concrete facts.

We have already been taught much. We have learned for one thing that what we are pleased to call our system, if the word "system" can be applied to the negation of it, possesses even under sad mismanagement a persistent vitality. Its very elasticity is reassuring to those of us, and I am one, who believe that capitalism is capable without the loss of its essential virtues of being made to harmonize with the needs of the modern world.

We have also learned that in times of economic stress and strain there is an increased and insatiable hunger for the things for which there seemed to be no time in the frenzied twenties which now seem so long ago. I know that in my own country there is an increased interest in the arts and in the things of the mind which is most significant. The words "spiritual revival" may be too high-sounding a phrase, but when one finds orchestras and dramatic festivals being organized, art schools crowded, discussion clubs humming with activity, one is conscious of the fact that five years ago the "stock-ticker" drowned much that has since become audible.

Is it too much to hope that these lean years may have taught us something else? Has that strange doctrine which elevated waste and prodigality into a solemn philosophy of life been discredited? I remember being told by a manufacturer of motor cars that there were no bounds to the market for his product, because the sale for it could be extended indefinitely by his ability to create discontent with the article as soon as it was sold. We can believe that this may have been good for the manufacturer, but we were more skeptical when we were told with evangelical fervour that this was even the basis of prosperity itself. Buy, waste, buy again! Do we still imagine that wealth is created by the mere circulation of money, that prosperity can be based on a sort of monetary merry-go-round?

But this is a digression. I had intended to speak of something else which the last three years have taught us. They have helped us to isolate the germ which lies at the root of most of our troubles. We have learned the power of that force, so intensified during the war and so unbridled since its close, which robs a sick world of that unity which would be its cure. We can assign plenty of causes to our present ills. We have heard them all *ad nauseam*—war debts, tariffs, reparations, the isolation of gold, the fall in prices. But back of all these interlocking factors—in some cases the reason for them, in other cases merely their aggravation—lies the force of primitive nationalism which we know to be the prime cause of our present ills.

17

At a time when international co-operation is so patent a need the only unifying principle among the nations seems to be what someone has described as the "sacred principle of international distrust." Co-operation being a forlorn hope, national governments in their despair have turned to the very remedies which serve to perpetuate and intensify the conditions from which they suffer. We find ourselves at the present time in a world-wide conflict between twentieth century economics and nineteenth century nationalism. On the one hand society has become, as we know, in a degree unthought of before the war, an economic unit. Science has never moved so fast in the direction of the integration of the world as it has in the last ten or twelve years. The nervous system of this planet is more highly developed and more sensitive than ever before. What happens in one country has more immediate repercussions in another, adversity is more contagious—and prosperity too—than has ever been the case (however little we may recognize the fact). But on the other hand just as knowledge is making the world a closely-woven unit economically, and we are becoming more and more interdependent, we are engaged in doing all that we can to defy this process by emphasizing by every means in our power, economic and military, the political divisions behind which we live. Nations were never so bristling with individualism as now, when their need for co-operation is greatest. If an observer from the moon could see us suffering as we are today from the delayed action of the war, or what is really the continuation of the war with all its consequences of unemployment and political unrest, and if he could see us attempting to remedy this situation by imposing every conceivable artificial restriction on the trade which is our lifeblood, he might well liken us to a doctor who attempts to cure a languishing patient by tying up his veins and arteries. This is all of course very obvious. We know it only too well. Even those who practice such follies in the name of necessity too often recognize sadly how futile and mischievous they are. But the follies nevertheless proceed. Sir Arthur Salter in his brilliant book *Recovery*, which appeared a few months ago, has reminded us that "history records no contrast between an almost unchallenged doctrine and an almost universal practice equal to that which confronts us in the sphere of the world's commercial policies."

Without the restrictions and barriers and hindrances, however well intentioned they may be, which threaten to stifle world commerce today, an economic readjustment might slowly come in our economic system. But as Salter has pointed out, although we have lost the freedom and flexibility of the old "laissez-faire" world in which we lived a generation ago, when there was little to impede the natural action of economic law, we have not gained the compensating advantage of that planned direction in the economic sphere about which we hear so much today. The world, it is true, is full of artificial measures of every description, but these are always taken in the interests of some national unit and are simply born of a spirit of *sauve qui peut*. The water of trade is no longer allowed to find its own level, nor on the other hand is it canalized and directed in one great stream, but is divided into so many trifling rivulets as to evaporate without accomplishment.

All this you may say is self-evident. Or by way of encouragement you may point to the many world conferences now more numerous than ever before, which by their very existence point to a growing realization that world ills can only be cured by world measures. But I confess I am as yet not a convert to the doctrine of salvation by conference. A conference is a means and not an end in itself, and will be effective only in relation to the spirit actuating it. We cannot derive much cheer from some recent international gatherings. For one thing such occasions too often demonstrate the futility of knowledge without wisdom. Too frequently they develop even into a duel between knowledge and wisdom, the knowledge of the specialist and the wisdom

19

which the statesman should possess. How many honest efforts in the direction of disarmament have been thwarted by the equally honest but narrow view of the expert. In this connection it is wisely observed however that "Most men long trained in a special experience have a vision limited by the character of that experience." This is more than true. A military expert labouring to weaken the service in which he believes would of course be an anomaly. For this reason may I suggest that if at a Disarmament Conference naval matters were left to the soldiers, and the affairs of the army placed in the hands of the naval men, some progress could be made in limiting both navies and armies. May I claim some merit for this frivolous suggestion. We must not indeed blame the expert if his functions are misunderstood. It is not his fault if he is asked to lead instead of being used to advise.

A more fundamental problem is presented by the terms of references which our conferences often assemble to discuss. How often are political physicians instructed to deal only with some superficial aspect of the disease, or are ordered to overlook some disturbing symptom. How can we hope for success from a great international gathering which is asked to grapple with the world's ills when essential subjects are carefully eliminated from those interlocking problems which are to be dealt with? If we leave out all embarrassing questions from our consideration and reduce our efforts to avert disaster to something which will offend no one, the formula which will emerge can have little effect. You cannot deal effectively with an earthquake by the application of a mustard plaster.

But who is to blame? Let us not censure the statesman any more than we blame the expert. The latter is faithful to his specialized field of knowledge. The former, I prefer to believe, honestly represents what he conceives to be public opinion. But what is public opinion? It is not something foreign or external. What is our part in forming it? Under an autocracy we might legitimately complain of statesmen imposed upon us by a force not of our making. But if a democracy is true to the definition we hear in political science classes, then democracy possesses the politicians it deserves. You and I multiplied by many millions are responsible. A disturbing thought. I heard the other day of a father who whenever his son was punished at school insisted on receiving a caning at the hands of the unfortunate youth. It was embarrassing to the boy no doubt but was sternly logical. The father felt responsible for his behaviour. Perhaps if we gave ourselves to some form of flagellation whenever our elected legislators did something to merit our disapproval, it might be equally consistent, but let us sadly admit that this meritorious practice might easily absorb too great a proportion of our time. But to be serious, it is surely wiser to be less critical of the politician who is acting according to his lights, however dim they may be, than of a community which fails to give him better light to follow.

We may well be charitable. The statesmen of the world today are grappling with a set of problems never before seen in such a combination, still less on such a vast field. If they seem to our disappointed eyes to be as impotent in contact with these problems as the flies on a locomotive in relation to its movement, let us remember the staggering magnitude of the task which they have on hand. After all, there probably is no one solution for the world's ills, but a thousand little solutions—which if the right spirit prevailed would do more than we know to help us emerge from the slough. And how easy it is to forget the importance of the spirit in our obsession with the mechanism which is secondary to it. We are told that the mechanism of society is ceasing to function. This may be true, but our attitude of mind will be more constructive and distinctly more hopeful if we think less of the machinery than of the motive power, the spirit which should actuate it. The most impressive example of this is provided I believe by the League of Nations. There are plenty of people today who are prepared to say, either in a spirit of vindictive triumph or in sorrowful admission, that the League has failed, that this dream has gone, and they point to its efforts to cope with its great problem in the Orient as an example of this fact if it be one. It is an easy observation to make. The moral authority of the League has, it is true, been challenged successfully, and it has also refused to use the physical sanctions which the covenant authorized it to employ. The principles for which it stood both in Manchuria and at Shanghai seem contemptuously flouted. There have been plenty of references to the fact that the United States is not a member, and melancholy forecasts from this fact have been made. You have not joined the League, it is true, but nothing is more inappropriate or ill-timed than for other countries to urge you that you should. That is your business. You may never become a member. But that as we have seen in the last few months will not impair your effective co-operation with this great body on a self-respecting basis. The essential principles for which the League stands, the collective maintenance of the world's peace, are your principles too. When the League after much vacillation and delay recovered a sense of statesmanship and passed its resolution three months ago which outlawed the spoils of conquest, it embodied a significant principle expressed as it happened by your own Secretary of State not long before. Far from dividing your councils from those of Europe, the League has provided a new point of contact between yourself and Europe. As a mere piece of mechanism it may have fallen short of the ideas of some because that theory which would make it mechanistic, which looks upon it as a superstate, has been discredited; but as the expression of a principle, as an educative force, it will grow stronger despite the reverses which it must from time to time inevitably meet.

Again let me say, it is the spirit that matters and not the machinery. And let us take comfort from the fact that the spirit of international co-operation is as strong as it is, and that, as I believe, it is today growing constantly. There has certainly never been so much interest in the problem before, nor in my opinion such a wide-spread understanding of its meaning. But a theory is one thing and its application another. Some one has pointed out how great is the lag between scientific truth and its popular application, and by way of illustration has said that although for four centuries the educated world has accepted the view that the sun does not move round the earth, there are still communities in educated countries which would deliver a vote to the contrary. So it is, I believe, with this problem of international co-operation. We may recognize this truth but it has not as yet penetrated to the ballot boxes. Our after-dinner sentiments somehow will not keep till the morning after. I was struck by a passage in Sir Norman Angell's last book, *The Unseen Assassins,* in which he says:

The greatest evils which devastate our civilization and at times nearly destroy it are not due in the main either to the wickedness or the evil intention of men; nor to the lack of knowledge, in the sense that we lack the knowledge to release atomic energy, or to communicate with Mars, or cure cancer. Those evils are due to the failure to apply to our social relationships knowledge which is of practically universal possession, often self-evident in the facts of daily life and experience, and to derive from that already available knowledge the relevant social truth.

The problem seems baffling. We profess to know what is wrong with the world today. We seem to be reasonably clear as to what the remedies should be. If for instance you stopped ten men in the street and debated this question dispassionately, they would all probably agree that national selfishness—national myopia—was the root cause of our difficulties. And they would also see the error of a foreign policy based on the jungle law of reprisal. But when the statesman in any country, however enlightened he may be, attempts to apply vision and imagination to this critical problem of foreign affairs, he finds too often that the great inert mass of popular prejudice is too much for him.

23

Men who as individuals are thinking beings can become in the mass the slaves of emotion and suspicion and distrust. This is no new problem in government, but we may well be acutely conscious of it in this present crisis.

In widespread education no doubt lies our hope. Education properly conceived is the light before which the murk of prejudice vanishes. But education, you say, will be too slow to cope with the present crisis. We have indeed far to go before education in the full sense can permeate and transform the mass mentality. But let us look to those to whom education has brought its benefits. From the offspring of our colleges and universities in this present crisis we have a right to ask for aid. What can the educated mind do in these difficult times? I am not of course thinking of the men and women who are satisfied with the acquisition of mere knowledge, but rather those who have learned how to use knowledge—a much more important thing—who have received from the college her most precious gift, a quickened imagination. We have a right and a need to ask for leadership from these. John Smith, A.B., has today a greater task than had his parents.

Nor in these crucial days can we exempt the scholar who remains in the academic world. His function of course is to think, and not to impair his thinking by irrelevant activity. Your intellectual life for instance has been the better here in Geneva for your remoteness from the clamour of the workaday world. But in our disordered society the man of thought cannot wholly detach himself from action. In an ideal state I suppose the scholar would sit in his cloister and think, and the politician would approach him with appropriate humility and after receiving the wisdom from his hands would conscientiously apply it to the practical needs of the community. But as you may have noticed, it does not work in just that way at present. Perhaps such a Utopia would be dangerous. At all events it seems to me that the scholar should be prepared to project himself in some measure from the world of thought into the world of action. It is easy to be rather intolerant of the arm-chair critic nowadays. I know one charming young man who freely, searchingly and sometimes bitterly criticizes modern life and the political leaders of his community. He is honest, intelligent and well-informed, but someone discovered the other day that he had never cast a vote. His influence dropped by several degrees. I would not ask my young friend to be a politician; that is not his role, but it seems to me that comments on our political institutions by persons who have never taken the trouble to find out practically how they work, who have not even exercised their franchise as citizens, or discovered how candidates are chosen, or helped to choose them—such comments are robbed of half their force. I know I am dealing with a subject on both sides of which much can be said. The student's job in life is no doubt to study. But I believe that the international world today would be the better for a greater direct influence on the part of our academic communities. I am perfectly sure that the corporate judgment of the young men and women before me today, for all their inexperience, would be wiser than the collective conclusions of most European conferences. They would probably avoid the rhetoric of the politician, and I hope the jargon of the economist, but their views would inevitably run soundly and surely counter to that nationalistic madness which is gradually bringing us to ruin. In most nations today, in such matters, the student mind possesses both moderation and wisdom. There are countries of course, like China, in the first throes of a militant nationalism where the student represents an intemperate force, but these are the exception. In Japan, I know, student opinion is anti-military. In Europe today the student is the idealist. In the Anglo-Saxon world the international mind is most at home in the university. We need the influence of youth in the international world today, as I think we need to be more generous in the place we assign to youth in all spheres in modern life.

We are of course told that the academic mind is not practical, that statecraft must be left to the practical man. But let us never forget Disraeli's classic definition of the practical man as one who practices the errors of his ancestors. The world has been in the hands of practical men for some time now. The results are not too reassuring. What can be more practical than to realize, as some nations still cannot, that adversity in the international world is contagious, that the international game of "beggar my neighbour" is not a very profitable business in the last results, that the mutual strangulation of commerce is not precisely the foundation of material welfare.

What appeal can be made? The case can be based on the ethical grounds with which we are so familiar. We can strive to break down the false antithesis between the nation and a world of nations. Civilized man refuses to accept any conflict between loyalty to the family and membership in a larger community. In a Federal system, we see no clash between our place in a state or province and our allegiance to a national government. But the ills of the world will not be solved of course until we carry this doctrine of concentric loyalties one step further and refuse to stop short of society as a whole. But it is perhaps well not to limit ourselves to the ethical appeal, however sound it is. The Anglo-Saxon, who is an incurably sentimental animal, often approaches the question of international accord in an evangelical mood, which, on the continent at least, perhaps can defeat the very cause he has at heart. Disarmament and kindred questions have undoubtedly a moral basis, but perhaps if we emphasized the common-sense side of these questions we might make better progress. International co-operation is also, after all, a matter of sound business. An international outlook contrasted with economic selfishness need not be described as being a case of virtue as against wickedness. As a practical matter it represents the long view as contrasted with the short one, and the larger efficiency as distinguished from the less.

There is a stern contest now between the broad vision which can save us and the narrow outlook which can bring us to ruin. Events move swiftly and without control. I think it was your own philosopher Emerson who said, "Things are in the saddle and ride mankind." The sentence carries its own moral. Unless we can learn to master the things which we have created, there is no telling where they may ride us. But a solution, if I may repeat, of this tragic maladjustment of wealth and the social disorders, which are spreading over the world as its consequence, lies in the power of no nation but will rest on international effort alone. That international-mindedness in which I know those of us who are here this morning believe is therefore not simply the toy of the academic idealist, but, I would suggest, is the most sternly practical thing we have before us. Therefore let me say again, if we would be realists in these difficult times ours should not be a "fugitive and cloistered virtue" but rather the valour which sallies forth to meet the adversary of selfishness and blind prejudice writ large on the face of society today. It is you, and those like you, who are passing into the world just now, who give us faith. It will be your task to help restore the faith of others.

ZECHARIAH CHAFEE, Jr.

The Deluge Is after Us

THE trouble with Phi Beta Kappa is that it is an end rather than
a beginning. It is like an inscription on a tombstone, "He did
well," with nothing to do in the future. Our golden key reminds
me of one of those keys which everybody has tucked away in
a drawer, knowing that it unlocks something but you can't remember what it is. I hope that we can consider adopting the
methods of our sister society, Sigma Xi, and gather our new
members into occasional informal meetings where they will have
the opportunity to discuss the contributions which theoretical
investigation can make to the practical problems of life—especially under the confused conditions which now confront us
and will do so for the years immediately ahead.

A woman at the court of Louis XV, who cannot be called a
lady of doubtful reputation because there was no doubt about
it at all, said, "After us, the deluge." Instead I would say, "The
deluge is after us." The flood is on our heels. The question is
whether we can climb fast enough to a rocky summit above the
tumultuous waters that threaten to sweep away serenity in the
present and confidence in the future. This deluge is engulfing
much more than economic prosperity and democratic institu-

Delivered before the Alpha of Rhode Island, Brown University, March
15, 1934.

tions. In critical periods of past history we can see the same spirit pervading widely separated aspects of human life—for example, in the Renaissance, when art, poetry, medicine, philosophy, and government, all broke away from the Middle Ages and adopted new forms with the help of classical learning. So at the present day we find a contemptuous rejection of old standards not only in economics or in politics with the appearance of Fascism, but also in poetry (free verse), painting (cubism), sculpture (obese women), architecture (bedrooms downstairs, dining rooms up, and no windows). We see the new spirit in law with the theory that the decisions of the Supreme Court depend on whether the judges have had grapefruit or shredded wheat for breakfast, and even in chess where black no longer moves out a pawn as of old but jumps his knight to KB3.

Amid such turbulence youth has a great advantage. The experience of age is no longer a handicap against you because it was gained under conditions that have now disappeared. And you new members of this Society are free from the fatigue and strain which the struggles of the last twenty years have imposed upon us. Of the war you remember little more than the whistles on Armistice morning, and though the depression has cost you some hardships, the older generation have done their best in its despite to make sure that bad times should not take away from you the joys of intellectual exploration which they had in the calmer days of a quarter century ago. You cannot conceive what the four years three and one-half months of the war meant to us, and when that horror which seemed never to end was at last over and we thought we could live happily ever after, October, 1929, threw us into an even longer period of trial. When the Abbé Sieyès was asked what he did during the French Revolution, he replied, "J'ai vécu." "I kept alive." We have lived through the depression but the strain has crippled us. We must look to you younger men. It is my hope that a country that was founded by the author of the Declaration of Independence at

29

33 and the author of *The Federalist* at 31 will once more put a large share of its destinies into the hands of young men.

This is all the more appropriate if, like Jefferson and Hamilton, you arrive at manhood during the revolution. And certainly a revolution is what we have now if we are to believe all we are officially told. True I have heard wise old men who remember the panic of '93 or even of '73 brush aside all this talk about great changes. They say that all these watchwords about co-operation instead of competition and the equalization of wealth are old stuff to them. The Greenbackers and the Populists poured out such ideas, yet after business revived the world went on as before. Perhaps this will happen again. If so, I shall not seriously object, for it will be much more comfortable for us who were brought up under the old system. Still tonight I am going to assume that the New Deal is here to stay, that it will give us aces instead of the Yarborough hands we have been dealt so far, and then go on to discuss what this vast reconstruction will mean for you.

You need not fear that I shall embark on controversies over familiar issues. You will not hear anything from me about the boloney dollar or alphabet soup. I am not going to discuss the desirability of killing army aviators *pour encourager les autres,* or whether the forgotten man has been buried beside the Unknown Soldier—one more useless sacrifice. I am going to accept the promises of the New Deal at their face value, payable in gold at 25.8 grains, 9/10 fine, and proceed to consider some of the broader implications of its policies so far as they concern the college graduates of the next few years.

In the first place, despite all this talk about short hours, there will be no short hours for you. Distrust all promises of an existence like that of the islander off Gaspé Peninsula of whom a neighbor remarked, "He doesn't do much in the morning, and in the afternoon he takes a rest." Whatever the future for manual laborers and employees in stores, there will be no thirty-hour week for you. Miss Perkins may strenuously advocate the thirty-hour week for others, but I notice that Miss Perkins works seventeen hours a day, and so does her stenographer. I have no faith in this gospel of salvation by loafing. I still stick by the old tradition that the progress of the individual and the community can only be attained by hard work and plenty of it. I am not arguing for labor beyond the fatigue point when I question the possibility or desirability of a permanent existence far within that period—whatever may be temporarily necessary during the present emergency. At all events hard work must be the fate of those who, like yourselves, hope to guide the policies of the future.

In this connection I want to make two observations. First, there is no real reason to worry about technological unemployment. Although the tremendous advances in science and machinery bring less concentration of work at the manual end, they inevitably increase correspondingly the concentration at the intellectual end. A few men and a few minutes' attention may start and stop machines that almost think between times for themselves, but as the mechanism becomes more intricate it will need more and more men to design it, set it up, keep it in repair, and still more men to design and repair the social and economic organization which must keep pace with the things which it regulates. Let me illustrate this by the improvement of transportation. At the beginning of the nineteenth century one man with the help of two horses could transport a ton and a half of wheat on a wagon ten miles in a day. Now six men can operate a freight train of a hundred cars holding thirty tons of wheat each, or 3,000 tons in all, and traveling as much in an hour as the wagon did in a day. According to this very conservative calculation, it would take 8,000 men in the horse and wagon days to transport as much wheat in the same time as one man can do on a freight train to-day. What has become of the other 7,999 men? They do not ride on the freight train as their ancestors rode on the wagons, but the railroads have provided a multitude of new occupations for them. Wagons needed no switchmen, signalmen, train despatchers, traffic superintendents, railroad presidents, lawyers, or members of the Interstate Commerce Commission, and the wagon driver was much more easily educated than all of these. As manual workers fall off, intellectual workers necessarily increase, and so do teachers to train them. We have only just begun to appreciate another and an almost unfilled need, that for inspectors of the industrial and social organization to tell us whether or not all is well—men of the Stuart Chase type. What I have just said does not deny the temporary dislocation caused by technological unemployment. We cannot shift the same men from the manual end of the scale to the intellectual end, but we can shift some of the children of the manual workers. One of the most important tasks of the college men here will be to facilitate this process.

The other point I want to make in this connection is that if time can be wisely saved for leisure on a large scale, it is a great mistake to distribute it over the whole year, shortening every work day and omitting Saturdays. Instead we should lump much of this leisure into a solid vacation of several weeks. Our example should not be the Gaspé islander, but the college professor. The single holidays we have now are useless enough, at least when they do not fall on Mondays, but a continuous succession of half holidays would be even more wasteful. Suppose that the advance of machinery will make it possible for us to produce all the goods we need and pay a higher weekly wage than now by running a thirty-hour week of five days. Would it not be better to run a thirty-nine-hour week of seven hours on ordinary days and four on Saturdays, and offset the additional 450 working hours obtained by a vacation of nearly three months with pay? In that time whole families, with cheap cars or low railroad fares, could see America and even pay occasional visits to Mexico and Europe. Shorter hours every day will bring business chiefly to the movies and the baseball parks. My suggestion will provide a new market for automobiles, railroads, and steamships. My vision is work for everybody as enjoyable as my own and a vacation equally long.

So much for our first question, the amount of work which the New Deal will involve. Our second is, for whom this work will be performed. It is obvious that with the vast increase of governmental activities made necessary by the New Deal, there must be many more government officials and employees, and the problem of their training, selection, promotion, or weeding out becomes infinitely more important than in the past. This is not the civil service problem as we have known it. I am not thinking of third-class postmasters, treasury clerks, immigration inspectors, or policemen, valuable as they are, where the operation of civil service rules is chiefly negative—to ward off partisan control—but of new civil service policies as an affirmative force to attract the best-trained and best-qualified young men into the posts where decisions are made. Somebody will have to decide how much gold we shall buy, how much cotton we shall plough under, how high prices shall be allowed for shoes and sealing wax and a thousand other things. Unless we give thought at once to the selection of the men who will make such decisions, there is grave danger that we shall be in a general confusion of fluctuating money and foolish or uncertain regulations—a world in which only those undesirable persons who fish in troubled waters are likely to succeed. How can policies be devised so that our ablest college graduates will be attracted toward these new governmental tasks instead of going into law, medicine, or business? It is, of course, true that some of the higher permanent government officials are men of exceptional ability and devotion, especially in the scientific branches of the service, but they were obtained more by good luck than by good management. It was not just for the money that Lindbergh left the employ of the government and went to work for a private firm. Men consider the opportunities for the freest use of their own capacity as well as financial return. I can best test the attractions of government

33

service by asking how many of you undergraduates are now thinking of going into it.

As yet the leaders of the New Deal have not shown that they appreciate the need of recruiting trained men into government service. It is no answer to say that college and law school graduates and professors are now occupying important posts in Washington. They are merely hauled in for the emergency and there is no assurance that they will remain. Some of the most prominent among them have already departed abruptly, and any day for all we know Richberg may follow Acheson back to a law office, and Warren follow Sprague back to a university. The difficult and extensive tasks undertaken by the government under recent legislation cannot be satisfactorily performed unless there is assurance of permanent careers open to talent.

Such an assurance is hardly funished by the fact that most, if not all, of the numerous positions created by the National Recovery Act and the other momentous statutes are outside the scope of the civil service law; or by the action of the new administration last summer in dismissing from the Naval Academy at Annapolis twenty-five civilian teachers out of thirty-three, some of whom had been teaching in the Academy for more than twenty years. The places of these experienced men are taken by naval officers without special training who have been temporarily detailed for that purpose. This was done in spite of the statement from Admiral Sims:

Except for the comparatively few civilian professors, the Academy is therefore, from an educational point of view, essentially an amateur institution. One can readily predict the result if a civilan college advertised that neither the president nor the members of the faculty had any professional knowledge or training as educators, and that all would be replaced every two or three years.

If training is important in any branch of the government, surely it is so in national defense. It is a queer kind of economy that spends hundreds of millions of dollars for new warships and trains the men who'll command those warships a few years hence under a succession of admirals and commanders who run over to Annapolis for brief periods between voyages.

In the current number of *Fortune* is an article on the British and Indian civil service which tells how 1,500 honor men from Oxford, Cambridge, and other leading universities run the British Empire. It is encouraging to notice that until the middle of the last century things were just as bad in England as in this country now, probably worse. Important high-salaried offices were filled with the relatives of cabinet ministers and their noble friends. The reputation of Whitehall for laziness and incompetence was proverbial. "Heavy swells with long whiskers lounged in late and left early." Their replacement by brilliant young university graduates was largely the result of the work of two men— Thomas Babington Macaulay, an historian, and his brother-in-law, Sir Charles Trevelyan, the ancestor of historians. Efforts in the United States like theirs may have equal returns.

The examinations for the higher civil service positions in England and India are not practical like our civil service examinations for the rank and file of government employees. Outside of certain prescribed topics like English, current events or economics, a science, and a language, one can choose any five subjects he wishes among a list of sixty, ranging from algebra to zoology. The candidate answers questions like this: "Write a congratulatory ode to the gas, light, and coke company on the completion of a new 250-foot gasometer." "What is actually known, as a result of tests or experiments, concerning the mental differences between the sexes?" "If you were given an entirely free hand to fix school teachers' salaries, explain on what principles you would act and what sort of figures you would fix."

This absence of practical considerations is no drawback. A practical man, as Disraeli said, is one who practices the errors of his ancestors. When unfamiliar and constantly changing conditions have to be faced by officials, definite information is far less important than the habit of rapidly applying general principles drawn from a wide background. A study of the *Republic* of Plato makes it easier to understand the distorted ideals of national socialism in Germany. We never know what precise information will be necessary for the future. My grandfather in 1850 wrote from Pittsburgh to his uncle in Providence about a new medicine called "rock oil" which had been discovered twenty miles away by a man boring a deep well to obtain salt water for the manufacture of salt. This man's observation that the water was a little greasy led him to fill a tub and let it stand. The oil soon came upon the surface and he then built cisterns to save the oil. Soon it was recognized in the neighborhood of Pittsburgh as among the best family medicines, and my grandfather sends two dozen bottles to his uncle with the recommendation to stand before the fire and give himself a good rubbing with the oil for rheumatism, besides taking a teaspoonful once or twice a day. Who could have prophesied that this petroleum would one day involve the most complex questions of geology, physics, and mathematics in its extraction, would call for probability formulas in the regulation of automobile traffic, and eventually bring about regional planning demanding a knowledge of history, geography, economics, and architecture? Such theoretical subjects furnish a training essential for men who will have to recommend decisions of momentous character under unforeseen circumstances.

I am not urging that we blindly swallow the British system whole. The article in *Fortune* might say more of its limitations, though it does quote one of the leaders in the English civil service as saying, "There is a danger that this terrific examination may attach an undue importance to brains as such. You do not want everybody to be so terribly clever that they complicate things and look down on their neighbors." Some matters that we should have to consider carefully in adapting British methods to our needs are these. The British system has a surviving aristocratic bias and perhaps gives too much advantage to wealthy young men. And when we see what some of the leading English political thinkers like Graham Wallas have to say about their civil service, we find serious adverse criticisms. Wallas, for instance, says that there has been no real reconsideration of methods since the system was founded in 1870. He points out the danger of what the French call *paperasserie*, undue preoccupation with paper rather than with faces and voices and things themselves.[1] The British system does not include local government, a very important point for us. The need for trained men is not limited to the federal service. Whether or not the New Deal wipes out state lines, as it sometimes seems likely to do, the United States are too big to be governed entirely from Washington, and many of the most vital governmental activities must be carried on either by the states or by regional divisions like those of the Federal Reserve System. The problem of removal of unsatisfactory officials will surely be serious with us. A civil service system too often becomes a wall to keep incompetents in and not to shut them out. Finally, there is the problem of popular support for the new organization of trained officials in the federal and local governments in this country. Its introduction would not be an antiaristocratic measure as in England, but in a sense antidemocratic. The average American citizen is easily made suspicious of what he doesn't understand, and care must necessarily be taken to avoid making him feel that the change I am suggesting merely enables a new bureaucracy to entrench itself.

Notwithstanding these difficulties, it does seem possible to attract college graduates into government service by methods somewhat like those used in England. A recent address by Presi-

[1] Graham Wallas, *Human Nature in Politics* (Boston and New York: Houghton Mifflin Company, 1909), pp. 267–268.

dent Roosevelt indicates that he is beginning to think of this aspect of the New Deal, and his thoughts are usually followed by rapid action. At all events it is an essential part of any program of radical measures to consider the personnel who will carry over those measures into actual life. The most advanced thinkers in England, like Laski, are constantly occupying themselves by asking what kind of men they want in the government service and how they can best obtain them and develop their abilities to the fullest possible extent after they have been obtained. If we can succeed in answering such questions for our government service, we ought not to stop there. It is equally important that the men who make decisions on behalf of large corporations like the railroads shall not be chosen by haphazard or by pull. The telephone companies have already adopted a policy of appointing and encouraging college graduates, and we may hope for similar opportunities in the other large businesses of the country.

After considering first how long college graduates will work and secondly for whom they will work, I now come to the last question, for what they will work. They cannot expect great pecuniary rewards. If the measures of the New Deal are to be carried out, as I assume, nobody will be able to get something for nothing. The actually disabled—the aged, the sick, and the men crippled in the war—will be taken care of better than they are now. But if the government is to end unemployment, shift those on unprofitable farms to fertile land, and assure a living wage to all, it simply cannot afford to hand out presents to unwounded veterans. It must be remembered that the proposed equalization of wealth will soon remove the fortunes which pay surtaxes and large estate taxes, so that the New Deal itself will lessen the revenue at its disposal. And like the unwounded veterans, the rest of us will be obliged pretty much to abandon all hope of windfalls. Accidents of birth and speculation will

38

play little part in the future. Whether we work for the government or not, there will be no large profits and no large legal fees. To quote Wallas again:

We are nearly all of us officials now, bound during our working days, whether we write on a newspaper, or teach in a university, or keep accounts in a bank, by restrictions on our personal freedom in the interest of a larger organisation. We are little influenced by that direct and obvious economic motive which drives a small shopkeeper or farmer or country solicitor to a desperate intensity of scheming how to outstrip his rivals or make more profit out of his employees. If we merely desire to do as little work and employ as much leisure as possible in our lives, we all find that it pays us to adopt that steady unanxious "stroke" which neither advances nor retards promotion.

The indirect stimulus, therefore, of interest and variety, of public spirit and the craftsman's delight in his skill, is becoming more important to us as a motive for the higher forms of mental effort, and threats and promises of decrease or increase of salary less important.

In the past we have been afraid of the equalization of wealth because it seems to mean leveling everyone down to an unsatisfactory standard of life. However, if the equalization of wealth is to mean leveling up, as we are told by the advocates of the New Deal—and you may remember that I assume all they say is true—then it is a very different matter. Suppose that it were possible for everyone to enjoy the opportunities which we consider essential for the enrichment of life. Perhaps it is possible. Already books and pictures and music which were once the monopoly of the rich are open to all through public libraries and art galleries and the radio. Lessened pecuniary rewards will not be so disappointing if we have satisfactory work and can also obtain intangible rewards of effort outside our work. One of the most important of these will be the long vacations of which I have spoken, and these will be even more necessary in the future than in the past. As labor shifts from contact with things to contact with abstract ideas, as it seems likely to do, we must obtain the indispensable contact with things in some other way. There is a danger in being engrossed wholly with symbols—entries in ledgers and on cards that are the symbols of things, and more abstract conclusions which are only the symbols of these symbols. Like the mythical Antaeus we shall lose strength without contact with the soil. In our small way we are like the bankers after the Civil War who developed the West without leaving their offices in New York.

> It was all prices to them: they never looked at it;
> why should they look at the land: they were Empire-Builders:
> it was all in the bid and the asked and the ink on their
>   books. . . .
>
> When Crazy Horse was there by the Black Hills
> His heart would be big with the love he had for that country
> And all the game he had seen and the mares he had ridden
>
> And how it went out from you wide and clean in the sunlight.[2]

Perhaps one of the greatest satisfactions of the promised future will be the opportunity to roam at will through vast stretches of scenery redeemed and protected by government from the devastations of modern industry, so that we may see it as it was in the beginning.

After the deluge, us. We shall be here when the world settles down again, but what sort of world will it be? Perhaps all my visions of this evening will prove only an airy fabric and things will be much as before. Even after Noah's deluge, there wasn't much change from the time before the flood when the earth was corrupt and filled with violence. The tower of Babel and Sodom and Gomorrah were hardly an improvement, and almost the first thing Noah himself did after he left the ark was to get

[2] From "Wildwest" by Archibald MacLeish, in *Poems, 1924–1933* (Boston and New York: Houghton Mifflin Co., 1933), pp. 174–175.

drunk. Perhaps we shall just muddle through back to the days of bull markets and nationwide strikes. Still the deluge may have swept too much away for us ever to return to familiar scenes.

There's no way back over sea water

Nor by earth's oaks nor beyond them:
There is only the way on:

.   .   .   .   .

You had best—trusting neither to
Charts nor to prophets but seamanship—

.   .   .   .   .

You had best—if you ask me—
Sail on by the sun to the seaward

Till you come to a clean place
With the smell of the pine in your faces and

Broom and a bitter turf
And the larks blown over the surf and the

Rocks red to the wave-height:

.   .   .   .   .

On by the open sea
To a land with a clean beach

An unplowed country
Pure under cleansing sun

.   .   .   .   .

And begin it again: start over
Forgetting the raised loaves and the

Fat cows and the larders . . .

.   .   .   .   .

And launch ship and get way on her
Working her out with the oars to the
Full wind and go forward and

Bring yourselves to a home:
To a new land: to an ocean

Never sailed: not to Ithaca:
Not to your beds—but the withering

Seaweed under the thorn and the
Gulls and another morning. . . .[3]

[3] From "1933" by Archibald MacLeish, in *Poems, 1924–1933*, pp. 186–
194.

CHRISTIAN GAUSS

The Scholar and
His Country

I DEEPLY appreciate the honor you have done me in inviting
me to come to Tallahassee and welcome another college and
a new group of scholars into Phi Beta Kappa, that society whose
only purpose has ever been to promote scholarship and truth.
To discharge this errand thirty years ago was an unalloyed pleasure to the Phi Beta Kappa orator, who was bound only to find
new and, if possible, more telling phrases in which to express
his congratulations to the fortunate neophytes. Today I cannot
feel that the privilege of your speaker can or should be like
that, and without wishing to trouble you on what is after all
a day of rejoicing, I feel that the function of him who welcomes
you into this fellowship is far more like that of an army chaplain
who offers a prayer to whatever gods there still may be, before
his little company enters into battle on an immensely extended
front. In this twilight of our time, our congratulations must be
muted. It is no longer fitting that we shout our huzzas, wave our
flags, and return to our easy life with the self-satisfaction of

Delivered at the installation of the Alpha of Florida, Florida State College for Women, now Florida State University, March 5, 1935. Published
in *Bulletin Florida State College for Women*, XXVIII. 4 (1935), 7–22.

43

empty victories already won. Let me hasten to add that a Phi Beta Kappa speaker today would, like that army chaplain, be recreant to his faith and trust if he showed the white feather and in weary defeatism surrendered to his fears. There was, in the age of chivalry, a beautiful ceremony, held often on the eve of battle, when a page who had faithfully served his apprenticeship finally received his armor and accolade and was dubbed soldier by one of his elders. As I see it today, your position is no longer that of persons about to take their positions above the conflict, but of members of a church or company militant about to enter battle. Let us warn ourselves, however, that this is not the time or place to be too pompous, or solemn overmuch.

Let us begin by contrasting as realistically as possible our situation with that of our predecessors of what are sometimes called the gay nineties. Many a man is still alive who remembers those famous days and years. Let me confess that I am one of them. Let me contrast for you our conception of the scholar then with what must be your conception of the scholar today. In those less troubled years, and I refer you to any file of our newspapers, the word "academic," which had in Plato's time a high significance, had come to be synonymous with words like "futile" and "harmless." Scholars were living in a garden of Eden, and we were for the world at large the personification of innocence. Even the big business man of that day did not fear the scholar. That redoubtable Treitschke, of whose mailed fist doctrines we were to hear so much after 1914, had not yet for us become the type and exemplar of the German professor. The professor was still, for the crowd at least, an engaging, rather amusing fellow, like Browning's Grammarian earnestly discussing *hoti* and the enclitic *de*. Into such harmless logomachies rode he his hobby-horse and won his pewter spurs. The stock example of the scholar for the average American was the good old German professor with the long gray beard who having returned to his home on a rainy night, after an inconclusive seminar far from

44

all practical concerns, abstracted, absent-minded, entered his quiet bedroom, tucked his soaking umbrella carefully into bed and then stood himself upright and dripping into a corner and remained there for the rest of the night. With only a touch of comic exaggeration, in those days, the life of the scholar could still be conceived of in those terms. It was an untroubled life that impinged little upon the concerns of our busy world and it was, let us confess it, a little remote. Stripping all this of its caricature, let us get down to what in our country we call the "brass tacks" of the situation and find out, if we can, why it was that the professor had become something like that.

When later historians examine the various phases of nineteenth-century intellectual endeavor, I am inclined to believe that they will find that in the main it was not really so much scientific, in spite of Darwin, as it was archeological. Even Darwin's *Origin of Species* was primarily concerned with the sequence in time in which biological phenomena had occurred, and that is of course an essentially historical problem. Without minimizing the great work done by scientific pioneers, the really upsetting discoveries in physics, chemistry, and mathematics were to come in that next century in which you had the perhaps doubtful honor to be born. The immense mass of nineteenth-century research was along historical and above all archeological lines. We of the nineteenth century were resurrectors of dead civilizations. We added an immense number of facts to the world's previous knowledge of Greek, Roman, Persian, Chinese, Hindu civilization. We started the vogue for the antique and I believe for antiques. Our colonial ancestors were not interested in antiques. They could still make good furniture themselves.

History became for us an exceedingly interesting museum of changing customs, costumes, and institutions. We were a century of excavators and dug up, so that the sun might once again shine upon them, the sites of buried cities like Troy, Nineveh, Sardis, Herculaneum, and Pompeii. The great triumph of the scholar was to come upon a temple or tomb long overwhelmed by time and give it again exactly the form and features that once it had. We pushed back history into the prehistoric and discovered remains of men, some of whom had lived hundreds and thousands of years ago in Java, . . . in the Neanderthal, and in the caves of France and Spain. Scholars were often told by their teachers that they must draw no personal conclusion, pass no judgments; that they must accept the facts with a Buddhistic submissiveness. Theirs not to reason why. It was their sole responsibility, in Michelet's famous phrase, "integrally to reconstitute the past," and the scholars of the nineteenth century, with infinite patience, reshaped for us the interesting panorama, rich in local color, of all past times. Behind it all there was no clarion call to action. Why should there have been? Ours, we believed, was a sure, set world. Other nations might still stumble in the dark, but to Americans life, liberty, and the pursuit of happiness had been guaranteed forever.

Perhaps we shall find that so much preoccupation with what was dead had itself a deadening effect, weakened and broke down the scholar's sense of responsibility to the social order of his own time. Not infrequently, historians, like Renan, gave way to a sense of weariness which expressed itself in what we have come to call the "dilettante" attitude. As one of his disciples was to say, in these long cycles of thousands and thousands of years there had been tyrannies, monarchies, republics, empires. In politics, in morals, in religion, there was no conceivable error by which man, at some time or other, had not managed to live. Time seemed to have secreted civilizations, as the liver secretes bile, and in this perplexed historical, panoramic welter, what did the individual count for anyway? It had its discouraging side, let us admit it. To sit in your library and decipher curious forgotten inscriptions was an exacting but highly satisfying occupation for scholarly leisure, yet here and there a man was troubled by one phase of all this immense archeological enterprise upon which scholarship was engaged. Man had lived on this planet half a million years. Generations had succeeded each other on every continent, but what was to become of our sense of the significance and value of the individual human life? What did one man's life, even the scholar's life, matter in so immeasurably extended a succession of biological, geological, and historical epochs? With this increased sense of the long, long time the world had lasted, what difference did it make what Susie Smith or Johnny Jones did or did not do in his or her brief day? Could it make any difference to this world so vast in time and space, whether he or she, one of billions who had inhabited or did now inhabit this earth, yielded to the desire or lust of a transitory moment which in the twinkling of an eye would itself become frozen into this incalculably immense archeological past? The scholar too might very well accept, and occasionally he did, the doctrine of *laissez faire*. How infinitesimal in this perspective becomes one man's or one woman's little sin. With a new and far more distressing sense of its significance, he or she could repeat Horace's:

> Vitae summa brevis spem
> Nos vetat incohare longam.

How great is the sea and how small my ship!

Not so often, to be sure, in America did this mood come upon us, for round about us there was still an immense activity. Of our own republic, the foundations were secure; we had after all come upon the scene in the fullness of time. Here we had declared that all men should always have the blessings of life and liberty, and we fondly believed if we pursued happiness desperately enough we would finally catch up with it, and few of us ever seriously doubted that the rights could ever be denied to us or to our children's children. If occasionally some such doubt like the passing shadow of a cloud on a sunny day crossed his mind, in the main the American scholar lived an untroubled

47

and a happy life and accepted a philosophy which left him and his world in peace. Let me tell you in concrete form just what all this meant and the form that it took in our own universities.

As a still living member of that perhaps now discredited generation, I can remember the untroubled satisfaction with which we entered upon our graduate studies. I have no desire to criticize any individual, least of all to cast any reflection upon a teacher whose memory I shall always cherish. The scholar, he told us, must be intellectually honest. That, and we should shout it from the housetops, is still true, has always been true, and must remain true *in saecula saeculorum*. But he used to tell us, and his advice was repeated in a hundred seminars, that there was only one thing that the great scholar should aim to do. He should add to the sum of truth. Now this implied that if our scholar was, for instance, an Egyptologist and discovered in the Egypt of Roman times an as yet unexcavated house or tomb and found there by chance an unmouldered papyrus and deciphered its reading correctly, he was entitled to the scholar's crown. To the scattered facts already known, he had added one more. That this might conceivably be a valuable service, none will deny, but something has happened in the brief but crowded years between. Let me say of my old master that he was the soul of scholarly consecration, of devotion, and of modesty. There may have been an error in all this, but it was neither his devotion nor his consecration, nor least of all his modesty, that can be held responsible for the troubles which now threaten to overwhelm us.

It is the privilege of the orator to omit from his presentation discordant details, and let me admit that the course of true scholarship, like the course of true love, perhaps even in our own blessed land and in that seemingly blessed time, never did run quite smooth. But even after we have made our discounts, we know that in your time this conception of the scholar can no longer hold. You have passed your latest college years in a time when the professor, the scholar, is no longer regarded as harmless. Even here in your academic shades you have perhaps heard the phrase, "brain trust." On many campuses, in many Wall Street offices, those are fighting words. Brains, ideas, are dangerous. Clearly our conception of the scholar is no longer that of our absent-minded German who innocently put his dripping umbrella to bed. At least you will agree with me that we live in other times and with other manners. The very things which the scholar held most precious, his freedom of speech, his freedom of inquiry, are threatened even in this land of the free. Whether we like the New Deal or not, so far as the scholar is concerned, he has been projected into a new dispensation.

We have said some things in dispraise of the nineteenth century. In the hope of being equitable, let us distribute the blame somewhat more evenly over the centuries and include our own, the twentieth. In your century, then, the twentieth, clearly something has happened. Scholars lost not only their nineteenth century innocence, but, alas, their modesty as well. Here, to continue blaming, and I realize that as a humanist I am treading on thin ice, let me say that in my humble opinion the responsibility for this loss of scholarly modesty and the beginning of all our woe lies in large part with our colleagues, the scientists. Let me add that I have known many admirable scientists who were fully as modest in their pretensions as we humanists long since have been compelled to be. But in general, if you read the addresses of some of our ablest leaders in science of a few years ago, you will find there a tone of aggressive confidence in their own powers which modern men had not heard since the days of the revolutionary *philosophes* of eighteenth century France. These scientists were telling us that if we only left the field to them, allowed them to push out the frontiers of knowledge, they would quickly bring us all into the promised land. They would make us all healthy and wealthy and wise. Under their guidance life in the new scientific world would become a paradise. As

49

every stone the mason lays tends to lift the level of the wall, so every discovery of the scientist raises the level of human life. It was thanks to them, they told us, that we had radios, transoceanic telephones, and all the wonders of technology. They sometimes failed to add that it was thanks to them that we had poison gas, long-range guns, technological unemployment, and T.N.T.

We are beginning to realize that the role of the scholar is not a passive one. The discoveries of the scientists, of scholars working in their laboratories, have changed our modern world in far more fundamental fashion than we with our innocent conception of the scholar's role could ever have dreamed. Scholars in science have revolutionized our ways of life, our methods of transportation and communication, above all our methods of producing what we once called goods, and have brought us to the verge of this revolutionary age. Old systems of political and economic belief once satisfactory and seemingly permanent have been weakened or destroyed. In this new age the scholar in the humanities and the social sciences can no longer remain an idle dreamer and continue merely to resurrect the past. He must again establish sanctions which will once more make life stable and secure, lest all the advances of the scientists prove our undoing.

But let us not blame it all upon the chemists, physicists, and technologists. Even the dullest politician knows that our world in this heyday of scientific discoveries became strangely and unaccountably unstable, and in the dismal years of the war and the depression old civilizations and kingdoms collapsed. The discoveries of the historians and the political scientists which the nineteenth century had regarded merely as interesting additions to the sum of truth became suddenly alive. So it was, for instance, with the theories of Karl Marx. Ideas in politics, economics, sociology, ceased to be decorative playthings, little archeological additions to the sum of truth. They became menacing forces.

Governing classes, that for centuries had been in the saddle, might be suddenly dispossessed and deprived of all that they and their fathers had earned, not by great armies but only through the force of an idea.

At certain times evidently the work of the scholar might act as a catalytic agent to political and social orders, which previously had only undergone the very slow and imperceptible processes of change. This is what the ruling powers today in Germany, Italy, and Russia have already learned. Hitler and Mussolini and Stalin are paying scholars a far higher compliment than the innocent nineteenth century professors ever dreamed of paying themselves. We know that in these lands enquiry and scholarship are no longer free. The scholar, these new rulers of Europe tell us, is dangerous, is a threat to social stability and must be forced to bow to the regime in power. Distressing as all this may be to those who once believed they lived in ivory towers, it contains a truth which our nineteenth century masters had overlooked. Truth and knowledge are not, as they once believed, a sum. They are not added to by the slow accretion of new truths, and the discovery not only of the physical scientist or the social scientist, but also of the humanist, is not merely one more embellishment, one more flourish added to the picture that past generations of scholars have painted. In our eagerness to make new discoveries, to add to the sum of truth, we had forgotten the commonplace—knowledge is power, truth a dynamic force. In the light not of what our teachers or books have told you, but in that fiercer and more brutal light in which you yourselves have lived, you sense this, you know this fundamental truth. It is not new forces, new discoveries, that we need so much as it is a larger life of the spirit. And what you blame us for not having taught you and what I know you will teach your pupils if you become teachers and scholars is this: There is in this world no such thing as an isolated truth, an isolable bit of knowledge, and there is no truth worth dwelling upon which in some way does not minister to the richer life, toward man's mastery over fate and circumstances.

We have spoken of the long, long time the world has lasted; some of the scientists say perhaps five billion years. That is a staggering interval. Many have used, and I have repeated, the phrase, the twilight of our time. Let this not discourage you. If the earth has lasted five billion years, we may assume that it will last as many more and that for you and me this is an ageless world. A country's youth and age, its vigor or its decrepitude, depend only on the spirit of those who inhabit it. What we need in America is not only a New Deal or a new era, but a new spirit. As we look over our past, in spite of our immense scientific progress from one point of view, our technological achievement, it seems as though on the spiritual side we have been going down hill; and one lesson those patient nineteenth century scholars, those excavators of the past, had discovered: civilizations die when their ideals wear out, when the spirits of men weaken and flag. How does this stand with us? A long diminuendo: Declaration of Independence, Land of the Free, Asylum for the World's Oppressed, The White Man's Burden, The Full Dinner Pail. To fill all the world's gaping dinner pails is no longer a sufficiently stimulating adventure for the spirit of America.

You who have the priceless gift of youth must and can revivify the spirit of our country. Never has the earnest young man or woman lived in a time richer in possibilities, in invitations to high emprise. If you will take it so, the twilight of our time is the morning and not the evening twilight. It is the lark and not the nightingale that you are hearing.

Thank God, therefore, that you are living in a time when the scholar is no longer innocent and harmless, when truth is not a sum, but a force, when ideas have become again the greatest power in human history.

If, then, there is one thought I would leave with you, it is this.

52

You have learned long since that you no longer live in the untroubled days of Tennyson's Princess. You are not merely sweet girl graduates with golden hair. It is not for you who today take over the responsibilities of scholars to continue to dream nineteenth century dreams. It is not for you to listen in sheltered seclusion to

> The moan of doves in immemorial elms,
> And murmuring of innumerable bees.

The scholar is not relieved of his responsibility when like the soldiers of Manfred he adds his stone to the monumental mound upon the grave of the dead, no matter how great and deserving they may have been. You live in a troubled time, in a distracted America, and your responsibility is not to the past, but above all to your country and its future. The function of the scholar is to think longer and less selfishly than others, to help lead his fellows to the *good* life. Now that the day of kings and hereditary aristocracies seems to be past, if democracy is to endure the scholar must lead—if the people are not to continue to fall a prey to the demagogues and the political witch doctors. By leader I do not mean that man or woman who flatters the crowd and joins in the clamor, but the man or woman who, desiring the good life for all his kind, is willing to suffer that the truth may prevail.

Scholarship today is not a matter of intellect only. That was the unforgivable blunder of our older time. Do not repeat our error. No one today can discharge the full responsibility of the scholar unless he or she has also something akin to religious fervor, something within him that makes him realize that his own life is bound up with the common weal.

Let me, then, in closing congratulate the Florida State College for Women [now Florida State University] upon its entrance into Phi Beta Kappa, that formal fellowship of scholars; and let me, in the name of your college, your friends here assembled, and your country, congratulate those of you whose distinguished records have won you the honor of membership. And as we wish you Godspeed upon your soon dividing ways, let me remind you once more that the scholar of today cannot be satisfied by amassing empty information; he must realize that the forces that shape the future are in his hands. He must desire the good life and with something approaching the crusader's fervor must strive to bring it ever more within the reach of his own country and his own time.

EDGAR SHEFFIELD BRIGHTMAN

Three Conceptions
of Culture

IF false prophets are those who say, "Go up and prosper," and
true ones are those who say, "I saw all Israel scattered upon the
mountains as sheep that have no shepherd," then true prophets
abound today. The hopes of yesterday have grown old and become tarnished; the hopes of today are boastful but uncertain.
Spengler's philosophy of decline fits the mood of the present,
as does the otherworldly theology of Barth, based on the despair
of everything earthly. One more war, we hear, and our culture
will be at an end. Jonas Cohn has said that civilization is dying of
its own beauty. Culture is being used to destroy culture.

At such a time it is fitting to ask what culture is. Certain uses
of the word need not detain us. We shall not be concerned with
culture in the anthropological sense, which identifies it with the
mores of a society. Much less shall we be concerned with its
use in biology to describe the development of microorganisms.
We shall not even pay much heed to its etymology, although it
is suggestive to bear in mind that *cultura* is derived from *colere*,
to till or cultivate. Rather, we shall start by defining culture as

Delivered before the Alpha of Rhode Island, Brown University, February 24, 1937. Published in *Philosophia* (Belgrade), II (1937), 146–158.

the value which cultured people prize. This is much like the definition of mathematics as what mathematicians talk about, but it will do as a preliminary pointer.

People who are generally regarded as cultured manifest certain fairly constant traits. They possess a comprehensive taste resulting from a broad education, a generous interest in all arts, sciences, literatures, religions, philosophies, as well as in all races and all nations. A cultured man is to be distinguished from a narrow specialist. The education of the specialist, we say, is not cultural, but utilitarian, vocational, or professional. Culture is broad and inclusive.

Let the proposed definition stand for a moment. Under scrutiny, in these times, its aspect is pleasing but irrelevant, for it contains no explicit reference to the social situation in which we find ourselves. In fact, it points rather toward the much-mentioned Ivory Tower than toward a solution of the problems of humanity. Its air is rather one of "there is much to be said on both sides" than of "there is something to be done" about either. In short, while it may correctly describe the content of a cultured mind, it is silent about the function of culture in society. But our idea of the social function of culture is certain to react upon our idea of its content.

At least three views of the function of culture have been held. Although the sacred number three smacks of the Hegelian dialectic, not to say the Trinity, it is proposed with no claims of completeness or of metaphysical sanction, but only with the hope that it may be a step toward clarity. In short, the first view is that culture is contemplation of the eternal; the second is that culture is contemplation of the past; and the third is that culture is a remaking of the future. If someone asks why the present doesn't figure here, the answer is that the present doesn't tarry long enough to develop a culture. It is merely the *ave atque vale* which the future cries to us as it rushes into the past. Every real present contains past and future. Further, it is clear why the choice is between contemplation and action. In so far as culture is directed toward the eternal or the past, only contemplation is in order; nothing can be done to alter them, however much they may be reinterpreted. On the other hand, the future cannot well be contemplated with any assurance; it is the realm of ends, the field for action. If eternity and the past give us necessity, the future gives us possibility.

I

A great tradition—perhaps it is more correct to say the great tradition—of culture, both Occidental and Oriental, has been the first-named in the triad, that is to say, the idea that culture is contemplation of the eternal. Our Occidental culture took its inception from Plato more than from another source. It is to Plato's founding that we owe the blessed word "academic," which is at least a step-sister of "cultural" and points to the rock from which our culture is hewn—not far from the Acropolis. Plato was one of the first of men to achieve a self-conscious conception of culture, or, as he called it, education ($\pi\alpha\iota\delta\epsilon\iota\alpha$). In the *Gorgias* (470E), Polus the Sophist and rhetorician is represented as conversing with Socrates. Polus asks in amazement: "Then doubtless you will say that you do not know that even the Great King is happy." And Socrates replies: "Yes, and I shall be speaking the truth; for I do not know how he stands in point of education ($\pi\alpha\iota\delta\epsilon\iota\alpha$) and justice." This statement contains no definition of culture, but it shows its place as a central value.

Plato does not need to restate his conception of culture in each dialogue, for every one of his readers knows where the center of gravity of Plato's interest lies and what he means by knowledge, education, or culture. It is knowledge of the realm of Ideas or Forms. The aim of life is "to soar upwards and carry that which is heavy up to the place where dwells the race of the gods." It is to partake of the divine, which is "beauty, wis-

57

dom, goodness, and all such qualities." It is to seek "the colorless, formless, and intangible truly existing essence, . . . visible only to the mind," "the real eternal absolute." Plato exhorts us "to look at the light itself." He speaks of "the contemplation of things above," "the soul's ascension to the intelligible region." There can be no doubt where Plato's interest lies. The supreme good of existence for him, and the soul of all culture, was the contemplation of the eternal Forms and Essences, and a turning away from the things of sense and time to the objects of pure thought and of eternity. The light that is in the cave is darkness and shadows; the true light of the sun is the only real light, and it is eternal. Plato was both mathematician and mystic, as Pythagoras before him had been. Plato's "keep out" sign over the entrance to the Academy read: "Let no one ungeometrical enter here." If his influence in Neo-Platonism was far more mystical than mathematical, his view of true culture as contemplation of the eternal was thereby made only the more vivid.

The Platonic ideal reappeared in Aristotle. The life of moral virtue, says Aristotle, is "happy only in a secondary degree," whereas "the happiness that belongs to the intellect is separate." The student "needs no external apparatus." "Happiness," he concludes, "is some form of contemplation." So, too, the Stoic, with all his emphasis on the human will, aimed above all to discover the eternal laws of nature and to live in conformity with them. "Whatsoever is good for thee, O Universe, is good for me."

The rise of Christianity brought much that contrasted with the Hellenic ideal. Yet from the start the contemplation of the eternal was given a prominent place in the Christian scheme of values. "Blessed are the pure in heart: for they shall see God." "Hallowed be thy name." "The things which are seen are temporal; but the things which are not seen are eternal." If this vision of the eternal was present in primitive Christianity, and if in the Gospel of John a mystical relation to the eternal, technically called "eternal life," became the very essence of culture, how much more was it present in the later development, when first Platonism and later Aristotelianism became assimilated to Christianity. The combination of intellectual apprehension and mystical experience of the eternal which was the heart of Platonism was also the heart of developing Christianity for centuries. Contemplation of the eternal deity was the ideal of perfection for the scholastics. John Calvin saw in time no more than the exemplification of eternal decrees, and he proclaimed as the chief end of man "to glorify God and to enjoy him forever." Historical Christian culture has related human life to the eternal. When the God-intoxicated Jew, Spinoza, viewed all things under the aspect of eternity, through an intellectual love of God, he was but expressing the great tradition.

The majesty and persistence of this great tradition of culture may be illustrated by two quotations, one from its Greek birth and one from its Christian maturity. Plato, in the *Timaeus* (29A), writes:

If so be that this Cosmos is beautiful and its Constructor [God], it is plain that he fixed his gaze on the Eternal: but if otherwise (which is [our] impious supposition), his gaze was on that which has come into existence.[1]

Here Plato sets forth his view of the priority of the eternal in value and in reality. And Descartes toward the end of the Third Meditation sets forth the ideal of contemplation, in spirit quite identical with that of Plato:

For just as faith teaches us that the supreme felicity of the other life consists only in this contemplation of the Divine Majesty, so we continue to learn by experience that a similar meditation, though incomparably less perfect, causes us to enjoy the greatest satisfaction of which we are capable in this life.

[1] Translation by Rev. R. G. Bury, Loeb Library edition (London: William Heinemann, Ltd., Cambridge: Harvard University Press, 1935), pp. 51–52.

Indeed, Descartes, with his desire for seclusion and his motto "Bene vixit qui bene latuit," exemplifies the culture of the eternal as opposed to the temporal even better than does the Greek who saw in time a movable image of eternity and who wrote *The Republic* and *The Laws*.

It would, however, be an error to suppose that the view of culture as consisting in contemplation of the eternal was confined to philosophy and religion. The same ideal has hovered over the progress of science. Mathematics and logic, the cornerstone of science, are the source of the eternal truths so dear to the founders of modern mathematics, Descartes and Leibniz. Even modern experimental science with its inductive method, which seems committed to observation of what Plato despised—the phenomena of sense—and to the facts of time as distinguished from supposed eternal Ideas, nevertheless reckons with time only as a variable and is never satisfied until it finds a law which is always true for all cases. Pure science, then, is seeking the eternal, too. Thank God, says the conventional ideal scientist, I have discovered a truth that has no practical application. It has been said that the physicist will never be satisfied until he has found a single formula that will account for every motion in the physical universe. The reign of scientific law is the reign of the eternal. A culture which seeks invariant principles, as our scientific culture does, is still engaged in the Platonic quest.

It is not far wrong to say that the contemplation of the eternal represents the predominant cultural tradition from Hellas until the end of the eighteenth century, that is, from Plato to Kant. Pythagoras and Parmenides set the pace for Plato and the centuries. Here is a cultural heritage of dignity and noble worth, and one which has much in common with the lofty philosophies and religions of the Orient. For them, time is Maya and illusion; for them the goal of culture is the achievement of Nirvana through the noble truths of Buddha, or the discovery of the eternal principle, the Tao, of Lao-Tze.

The social effects of such a culture are manifest in the history. That it develops individuals and groups to spiritual heights is certain; but it is undeniably, in the first place, an aristocracy. Whether Plato's Guardians, or the elect of St. Paul and John Calvin, or the church *ultra quam nulla salus*, or the specialists of modern science, an aristocratic class of those who have access to the eternal verities is developed, who possess something from which those in other classes are excluded. Secondly, it is an otherworldliness, which tends to turn away from the visible to the invisible, and to substitute knowledge of the eternal for attention to the temporal. Thirdly, it is much more effective as social criticism than as social reconstruction. In the light of the eternal, it is easy to see what is wrong with the City of Man, but it is not correspondingly easy to see how to build the City of God on the site of fallen Rome.

II

With the coming of the nineteenth century a new conception of culture was dawning, the historical. Historical influences had, of course, always been at work on culture; and histories had been written. The Renaissance had turned to Greek sources, it is true, yet not from an objective interest in historical fact, but because the Greeks had what was for the men of the Renaissance a new view of truth and values, setting the meaning of life in a new perspective. The culture of the Renaissance was not yet historical, although it was moving beyond the otherworldliness which had led Dante to call Boethius "the blessed soul that exposes the deceptive world to anyone who gives ear to him." [2] Until the nineteenth century history had been written either for practical purposes, as in legal and governmental records, or for moral, religious, or patriotic edification, as in the histories of the

[2] The translation is by H. R. Patch in *The Tradition of Boethius* (New York: Oxford University Press, 1935), p. 1.

Hebrews, the Greeks, the Romans, down to the historical writings of Voltaire and Hume. History was regarded, accordingly, as an exemplification of the eternal Ideas. The superscription over all history was *Haec fabula docet,* or "So also will the Lord do unto you. . . ." The culture of the eternal as distinguished from the culture of time is well embodied in the famous saying of Kant to the effect that "history serves only for illustration, never for demonstration." It is instructive that the thinker in whom the transition from the eternal to the historical took place in its most profound and widely influential form, namely Hegel, was able to effect that transition only by including all historical process and development within the timeless and eternal Absolute.

But Absolute or no Absolute, Hegel was the herald of a new moment of culture. Before Darwin and Marx, before the Tübingen School and Mommsen, he saw that life and culture could be understood only in the light of its historical development. Indeed, he viewed eternity itself under the aspect of history. For Plato's "Time is the moving image of eternity," he substituted in effect the principle that eternity is the static image of time. Partly under the influence of Hegel, but even more because the time was ripe for such a view, there arose a new objective interest in historical truth. The nineteenth century is usually regarded as the era of natural science; but from the point of our present analysis, the growth of scientific interest may well be regarded as a continuation of one aspect of contemplation of the eternal. The new principle in culture came not so much from natural science as from history. Historical culture is not essentially contemplation of the eternal, but contemplation of the past. Regardless of values or supposed eternal Ideas, regardless of the effect on religion or morality, the true historian wants to know the facts exactly as they were. The nineteenth century began to develop a historical conscience and with it a culture of the past. It was a time of the onward march of evolution, the objective historical study of institutions, of ideas, of religions, and of morals.

That this represented a real change in the dominant culture is hardly to be questioned. The contemplation of the eternal was a philosophical and religious culture; contemplation of the past is a scientific culture. It was scientific in a special sense, for, despite its proclamation by Hegel, it soon came to be more independent of philosophy and religion than even natural science. After all, mathematical physics always remains cosmic in its scope and, by virtue of its use of mathematics, akin to the eternal; whereas history expects to find few, if any, eternal laws. "A thousand types are gone: I care for nothing, all shall go."

The new historical culture, consequently, is a cult of factual objectivity. In its pure form its motto is: "All people need is to know the facts." In its spurious form, the motto reads: "All people need is to know the facts and then they will do the right thing." But this notion of a right thing that springs full-armed from the head of fact is a lingering uncritical intuition left from the culture of the eternal, and reference to it is indeed spurious within the scope of purely historical culture. The pure doctrine of this view of culture appears rather in the maxim that no historian is to pass a moral judgment, or in the statement that evolution does not necessarily imply progress. Something of the sort may have been in the mind of Charles Peirce when he said: "I must confess that I belong to that class of scalawags who prefer, with God's help, to look the truth in the face, whether doing so be to the interest of society or not."

This view of culture as contemplation of the past without fear or favor or interest represents a great stride forward in humanity's sense of fact. But who can deny that it brought with it a corresponding loss in the sense of value? The eternal essences included among themselves the eternal values; but historical objectivity acknowledges no value save the one value of loyalty to the facts. The contemplation of the eternal and the contemplation of the past are not only important types of culture, but also, it is fair to say, essential constituents of the fullest and ripest culture which has grown up out of the experience of the race. Yet the one gives us values apart from life and the other gives us life apart from values. On the whole, the scholarly tradition in America has cast in its lot with the older view, that of contemplation of the eternal.

Both of the two views of culture thus far considered are socially defective. As we saw, contemplation of the eternal tends to be aristocratic, otherworldly, and critical rather than creative, in the actual social situation. Is the culture of historical objectivity a more effective social instrument? By its indifference to any scheme of values, it is a sort of attack on aristocracy in the interests of a democracy of fact. By its concentration on the facts of history, it is an attack on otherworldliness. By its objectivity it avoids all *a priori* criticism. Thus it possesses merits which are lacking in the older view. On the other hand, because of its very virtue of objectivity it lacks any standard of value, any criterion of progress, or any goal for human endeavor. As a social culture, the ideal of the nineteenth century was no better than the older ideal.

A culture that will be adequate to the whole of human nature as a social phenomenon must include contemplation of the eternal and of the past. But it will not be sufficient merely to add these two together. Socially they have two defects in common. First, they are both cultures of contemplation, whereas man is an active being and a culture of the will must supplement the culture of the intellect, however we solve the knotty problem of the relation of intellect and will. Secondly, neither of them faces the future, whereas all of the hopes and actions of man are directed toward what is yet to be.

III

Is a new synthesis possible? Are we on the way to a culture the soul of which is action? Mere action without contemplation would plainly never produce culture. A culture of action would therefore have to include all that the eternal truths of reason and the historical truths of fact could contribute. But, seeing that all life is movement, the culture that may be growing is a culture for the sake of action wherever action is relevant and possible. It is a knowledge of the eternal and the past for the sake of a better future. Will the flux of Heraclitus, the activity of Leibniz, the process of Hegel, come into their own? Humanity has sought to escape from this task of mastery. The contemplation of the eternal was, after all, an escape; it was the flight of the alone to the alone, as Plotinus called it, not a transforming of the temporal process by action. The contemplation of the past is, in a different way, also an escape from the responsibility of defining ends for human action and of remaking society in accordance with those ends.

The attempt of culture to escape from the task of will is no minor incident. It is the essence of the religion of the Buddha, who regarded all desire and will as evil. It reappears in the nineteenth century as the philosophy of Schopenhauer. For Schopenhauer, although all the cosmos is one will, will is evil. Further, for him, time is unreal and there is no future in the metaphysical realm. The only salvation from meaningless striving, pain, and ennui is to learn the art of contemplation so completely that will is conquered and desire is dead. Only in escape from the world of action is true culture, true satisfaction, to be found. A not dissimilar conception is portrayed by Santayana. All the value of life for him is situated in what does not exist in space and time at all—the realm of essence, which spreads infinite variety before the imagination and is a complete release from action.

Buddhism, Schopenhauer, Santayana, as well as the recent interest in the timeless neutral entities of neo-realism, the relations of symbolic logic, and the Neo-Platonic mysticism of a Dean Inge, all are aspects of a culture of contemplation.

But meanwhile there has been growing up another culture, sometimes in crude and irrational form, a culture which demands action. It was true to say that Christianity has much in common with the contemplation of the eternal; but it is also true to add that Christianity is a call to action. "By their fruits ye shall know them." "If any man willeth to do, he shall know." It was true to say that science aims at eternal laws, but it is also true that she uses the active method of experiment. The third view of culture is therefore a culture of action, a remaking of the future, that is, making a future which shall be different from what it would be had man not acted. It is, of course, true that man has always acted with reference to the future; but it is not true that such conscious reference has been the animating soul of culture. The Egyptian pyramids and temples survived, but they were built for the eternal, not for the human future.

For better or for worse, we are now committed to a culture of the future, the attempt not merely to dream or to define Utopia, but to realize it in Moscow and Rome, Berlin and Washington. This new conception of culture was developing contemporaneously with the culture of contemplation of the past, during the nineteenth century. It was illustrated in Christianity by the birth and growth of the modern missionary movement. It received one of the most typical formulations in the famous words of Karl Marx's eleventh thesis against Feuerbach: "The philosophers have only interpreted the world differently; the main thing is to change it." Here is the battle cry of a movement from the culture of contemplation to the culture of action. The harsh hands of Nietzsche laid hold of the old eternal tables of value in order to destroy them and make way for new standards and a new type of humanity. Geography and the spirit of adventure combined in America to produce the life of the pioneer and the later amazing growth of capitalistic enterprise, both of which are, in a sense, the deification of action. American pragmatism was an expression of this spirit in philosophy, as Walt Whitman was in literature. Tolstoi's rejection of formulas about the Good, the True, and the Beautiful, with his social view of art, places him in this same movement. He insisted that "art, like speech, is a means of communication and therefore of progress, that is, of the movement of humanity forward towards perfection." The World War jarred the complacency of our previous culture and brought us down to earth. The culture of today —whether Fascistic, Communistic, capitalistic, or democratic— is a culture of acting and of planful remaking of the human future.

If this is the view of culture to which the present age seems committed, it is the task of those who are presumably the leaders of culture to make sure that the new view shall not lose the benefit of the older insights. Are there any eternal truths in logic, in mathematics, in ethics, in religion? If there are, they must be accorded their place in the human future. Is it possible to know objectively the facts of past history? Only in so far as it is can we diagnose the ills of the present and prescribe for the future. One of the most solemn tasks of the cultured man of today is set by the current tendency to legislate eternity and the past out of existence in order to build the future in a vacuum created by the present. Such a culture cannot possibly survive. On the other hand, any tendency to avoid the remaking of the future is equally doomed to failure. Man is an active and purposive being and any view of culture which omits this fact omits the essence of human personality and of society, namely, activity toward goals. Man has moved thus far more or less blindly. Only a few have formed plans for the development of society, and they have been unable to carry them out because of the dead weight of opposition and indifference, as well as the material and economic conditions which they confronted.

More and more individuals are now beginning to see that culture is, after all, what its etymology asserted, namely, the cultivation of human life. The view is spreading that culture means intelligent participation in the remaking of society and the cultivation of a better world order. In the eighteenth century, Voltaire in *Candide* ventured a look at the world about him and found so much of evil in it that he sought escape in the maxim, *Il faut cultiver le jardin* ("We must cultivate the garden"). Today we may well adopt the same maxim, but in a different sense; for the garden to be cultivated is all humanity.

It would be absurd to maintain that this culture of the social will is an utterly new idea in our times. It is not the intent of this exposition to hold that our age has discovered an unheard-of principle. What is intended is to assert that the emphasis on action, which has risen and fallen more than once before in human history (notably in the Roman Empire), has now become a predominant mood with more world-wide insistence than ever before, and to add that any conception of culture which ignores the practical demands of the age for the remaking of the social order is doomed to extinction.

One of the soundest philosophical insights of the past was Kant's doctrine of the primacy of the practical reason. Unfortunately he developed it only meagerly. His *Critique of Pure Reason* was a weighty tome, his *Critique of Practical Reason* relatively slender. Nevertheless he perceived that the practical reason, the rational moral will, was the supreme good-in-itself, and that all descriptive science—all of what we have called contemplation—was in the service of the good will. In this sense, Kant, although we have taken him as a representative of the culture of contemplation, anticipated the culture of action. It is to be regretted that Kant did not develop his insight more fully. But he may have seen the time coming when man's knowledge would so exceed his goodness as to threaten destruction to all culture unless the moral will asserts its supremacy. Today we confront either a remaking of the future or an unmaking of civilization.

The new view of culture, as we have seen, is essentially practical; it looks to a culture of action and so of will. What, then, is the task of the scholar? Is he to lay aside his classical aims and ideals in order to undertake the task of building a new social order? To use the jargon of the day, should he go Rotary? Far from it. This would be to betray not only the mission of scholarship but also the cause of the future society which is dimly shaping itself in the mind of the world. The primacy of the practical reason does not mean the abandonment of reason. The moment the will ceases to be rational, it ceases to be significant. The scholar dare never cease his allegiance to the eternal values discovered by the intelligence of the past. But it is possible that some scholars need to enlarge their conception of culture, not merely by adding the contemplation of the past, as, it is safe to say, most have done, but also by perceiving the incompleteness of contemplation without social action. Social action is taking place inevitably all around us. Will it be action guided by thought or by what Kant called "blind empirical groping"? The future will decide.

A final question and our discussion is completed. What part will America take in this new culture of action? There are three possibilities. She may possibly develop her genius for action to such a degree that she will become the world's leader in the new culture—although the exclusive leadership of any one nation seems both improbable and undesirable. Or she may withdraw from co-operative participation in world affairs, surround herself by a wall of flame, shutting out the goods and the Good of other nations, thus adopting the theory of Fichte's *Closed Commercial State;* and there are those who would prefer this mode of action. Or, again, she may see the opportunity for genuine international co-operation and direct her policies toward making her contribution to the international culture of the future in a world in which the value of every race and nation is recognized, and in which a democratic harmony will be achieved. Here too the future will decide.

HERBERT AGAR

A Program for the
Citizens of a Democracy

FRANCE is now celebrating the 150th anniversary of her Revolution, the 150th anniversary of the Declaration of the Rights of
Man and the Citizen. As M. André Siegfried has pointed out in
a current issue of *Foreign Affairs,* that celebration is not the perfunctory thing given over to the politicians' speeches and the
after-dinner speeches that it would have been a few years ago. It
is a renewal or an attempt at a renewal on the part of the French
people of their deepest feelings—an attempt to return to some
of the excitements and moral purposes that characterized 1789
and the principles of 1789 when they were first born into our
world. And it asks us to remember the obligations which are imposed upon citizens by those principles.

"The Rights of Man," so called by the people that first conceived them, were obligations imposed upon society to conduct
itself in a certain way so that all men should be able to enjoy
hard-earned privileges. But they were obligations imposed upon
society. As time passed, and as the excitement of the first generation of people who conceived those rights in terms of obligations
cooled, the rights of man have been taken more and more as a

Delivered before the Alpha of Massachusetts, Harvard University, 1939.

71

kind of perfunctory promise that man shall have these privileges no matter how he behaves.

In other words, the rights of man have descended from being a statement of high moral purpose into being a statement of second-rate sociology. And because of that descent, I want to suggest to you that democracy and freedom and all the good things associated with that original statement of the rights of man are on the decline all over the world. And they will not be saved and that decline will not be stopped unless we're capable as citizens of re-examining the obligations imposed upon us by the ideas we profess and doing something toward living up to those obligations.

Let me give an illustration from my own job of journalism as to what I mean by saying that the rights of man have descended from being a statement of high moral purpose into being a promise that people can have privileges no matter how they behave. The freedom of the press derives from the concept that one of man's basic rights is his freedom of thought and of combative argument. The people who wrote into our Bill of Rights a special privilege for the press did not do so because they had any affection for journalists or for publishers. As a matter of fact, they thought journalists were a pretty scurvy lot. They did it because they hoped that if journalism were given this privilege, with the promise that the State would never interfere, journalism might help mankind to become free. It might help the citizens of our country to know what was happening, to exercise their reason; it might be one of the major aids to adult education. The obligation so to conduct itself as to promote adult education is implicit in the giving of this right or this privilege. Journalism, as you all have probably noticed, is the only private business mentioned by name in the Constitution of the United States, the only business given a special privilege which no other business has. The government will keep its hands off and allow it to go ahead without interference. Again I remind you that that wasn't done because people liked journalists. It was done because people thought maybe journalists could contribute something to the common well-being of mankind.

Therefore I want to make a few suggestions as to practical deeds that we, as citizens of the United States of America, can and must do if there is to be any democracy by the time our generation comes to die. I'm not suggesting this is by any means an exhaustive list. I'm suggesting that it is futile and vain to teach the generalities—to tell a man that he has a grievous duty and that democracy will perish unless he performs it—unless you follow with some suggestion as to what that man can do. I'm sure we can all do a great many more and a great many better things than I'm going to suggest; but I think that these things at any rate are necessary and possible, although they may be irksome and difficult. Democracy will not be dragged down because of wicked people at the other end of the earth. It may be dragged down because of our own mental and moral sloth—we, the citizens of the countries trying to be democratic.

The first duty I suggest to you is this (and it sounds extremely trite when I say it, but I'll try to put some thought content into it afterwards): that we, all of us, must make a very great effort to do two things steadily—first, to keep clearly in our minds what is the tradition under which we live. What is this thing that we call "Americanism" and which we are constantly saying is so much better than Communism, and Fascism, and so on? And second, to know what is happening. What is the idea and what are the facts? In so far as we are capable, we have an absolute obligation to know what is happening and to have a clear idea what we mean when we use such words as "democracy," "liberty," "freedom." When the ordinary politician or the ordinary journalist talks about democracy, he isn't saying anything at all. He is just making a soothing noise which he hopes will keep you quiet while he gets on with his talk. There's no thought content in the word as it is normally used. And when

73

the American reads his daily paper, I suggest to you that in that paper he tends to leave out the awkward and inconvenient facts—and that already, by the knowledge which the managing editor of the paper has of his reader's prejudices, a large part of the awkward and inconvenient facts have been weeded out before the paper ever gets into print.

Let me give you an illustration. I was down in San Antonio, Texas, for ten days this spring. Now San Antonio happens to be the town, so far as I know, in the entire Western world, or at least west of Poland and the Balkans, which has the most atrocious slums. It's all on a small scale, I grant you. There are 90,000 people living in this slum district of San Antonio, living under conditions wholly unfit for man and unfit for any except the most hardy animals. I'm not going to disturb you by giving you too many details; but I have never seen anything in Western Europe at all comparable to the conditions in San Antonio.

While I was down there Mrs. Roosevelt happened to come to town; and naturally, whenever she comes to town, she's interviewed. In the course of her interview Mrs. Roosevelt mentioned the fact that San Antonio has the highest tuberculosis rate of any city in America, which is putting it extremely politely, as I'll tell you in a minute. But the Chamber of Commerce of San Antonio, the newspapers of San Antonio, the leading citizens (or at least such as I saw during my few days' stay there), were all outraged at Mrs. Roosevelt's saying that, not because it wasn't so, but because she shouldn't have said it. One man said it wasn't true; he said to me this was an outrage because San Antonio did not have the highest tuberculosis rate in the United States, it only had the second highest. Nobody seriously attacked Mrs. Roosevelt's facts; but they all agreed that it was an outrage to state the facts. It's an outrage to tell the truth.

Under those circumstances, you can't have a free society; you can't have a democracy. If we're such mugs that we don't want to know what's going on around us, what chance have we of solving any of our problems or of meeting any of our obligations? San Antonio happens to have been a great deal worse than Mrs. Roosevelt said. San Antonio has the highest tuberculosis rate of any city in the world except Shanghai, and the highest venereal disease rate of any city in the world except Shanghai. I've never been to Shanghai, but it must be a troublesome town.

A completely disgraceful situation exists in a considerable section of San Antonio, which has great placards over the roads as you drive into it saying, "San Antonio the Beautiful." That's a symbol of the way we're treating our country today. We don't want to know the facts. I think maybe we in the South are slightly worse than you in the rest of the country; but I'm not sure. It may be that the South is a little more fantastic in saying that you are betraying the South or in some way attacking her fair name as soon as you try to bring out into the light any of the serious things that are going on in our country.

I choose one small example, but I think it's a fair example. And I say to you that it is impossible to expect a free society unless we the citizens are willing to have the intellectual hardihood to know what's going on. Side by side with knowing what is going on, we've got to know what we really want to have go on. What is the ideal? Not in vague terms, not just in saying how wonderful "Americanism" is or how grand it is that we're a democracy whereas other people have horrible governments like the Russians and the Germans. But what is it really that we want to have happen? What do these words mean? Again, just as an illustration, I want to tell you what in my mind the word "democracy" means as a minimum. And I think it is necessary for us to go through the whole long list of the words which we use to describe our tradition and know precisely what we mean by them, each one of us, singly. We may differ with our neighbors, and we can dispute with our neighbors, and we can learn from our neighbors. But if none of us know what we mean, we're all just making noises, and we'll never get anywhere.

What is democracy, and what does it impose upon us? In order to try to describe it, you have to break it up into three parts and start with the moral affirmation on which the democratic creators built—a pure act of faith as unprovable as a man's act of faith which says that he believes in God or believes in the immortality of the soul; an unprovable act of faith which you make or you don't make according to your temperament and desires. But if you do make it, it imposes a lot upon you. The act of faith you can describe inadequately by saying that at the end of the eighteenth century, about 150 years ago and around the time which the French are now celebrating, there came together in the minds of a number of people in the Western world, in France and in this country, two great ideas which fused and made our modern form of the democratic dogma.

One part of that tradition was the old Christian statement that the brotherhood of man applied to this world, here and now; not a theological pronouncement about what we trust will happen to man after he has died and gone to heaven or to hell but a statement of the nature of man and his relation to his fellowman in this world; a statement that the things which bind men together are infinitely more important here in this world than the things which separate them; a statement that it is therefore an obligation so to conduct society as to make it possible for this brotherhood of man to find some expression in the secular world. The second part of the dogma, the second stream of tradition which came together with that other stream to form what I call the "modern democratic idea," is the eighteenth century rationalist tradition of the reasonableness of man, the also unprovable assertion that man is the kind of creature who through the use of reason can elevate his status in the world, his moral status and his economic status and his whole position in the world. In other words, man has a special relation to his fellow man which is described in the Christian tradition as the brotherhood of man; man is also a person who can use his reason to elevate himself, and this is expressed in the eighteenth century rationalist tradition. Put those two things together and you get the moral affirmation on which democracy rests. Nobody is under any obligation to accept that affirmation any more than anybody is under any obligation to believe in God.

But if you do believe in God, it has a very serious effect on you—on you and your life. And if you do believe in the democratic tradition, it will have a serious effect on you and your life. One reason that it doesn't have a more serious effect on the lives of a great many American citizens is that they don't believe in it. But the time has come to decide whether we believe in it or not. For a long time it didn't seem to make much difference whether we lived up to our great faith or not. But now we're on the edge of a world disaster. Now we're seeing what happens to man, and what sort of a future he will have, if we neglect this tradition which we have inadequately served. We also have a horrid picture of what may happen to us; and because of that, I think, we're moving into an era where we may take our tradition with seriousness. If we do, it is an imposing tradition and it will make life inconvenient in many ways.

You cannot assert those two dogmas that I've been talking about, in the world in which we live, without having to dedicate your life to trying to alter and ameliorate many of the circumstances in this world. If you make that daring affirmation of democracy, you assume the burden of trying to move our society in a direction where the brotherhood of man will have more chance of being expressed and where the life of reason will have more chance of being lived. I suggest that the United States of America has kept its part of the bargain fairly well and that the press has kept its part of the bargain fairly badly—that the press was supposed to do a special job in addition to the ordinary salesman's job of producing what the public likes in an attractive package and at a reasonable price. Journalism has to do that too, obviously, or journalists would all go out of business. But, in

77

addition, there is an extra something which the press is supposed
to do in the way of service to mankind—or why should it have
this privilege? That extra something is to go out of its way, to
spend lavish money, in order to give space to what people would
prefer not to hear. If our world finally goes down hill, one of
the reasons will be the failure of the press to live up to this
obligation.

Now you've had one symbol, one illustration, coming from
my own job. You can carry this through all the rights of man
and all the civil liberties conferred upon us by our Constitution.
Wherever you find us not living up to the obligations implicit in
the privileges which we have been given, you can be pretty sure
that those privileges are in grave danger of being withdrawn. The
reason they have been withdrawn over so large a part of the world
in the last twenty years is, I suggest, that the people of the so-called
democratic societies were not living up to their obligations. We
cannot save democracy by conquering the outside enemies of
democracy every twenty years in a world war. The only place
where we can save democracy is within ourselves, by making
it worth saving, by trying to live up—as democratic citizens—
to the obligations which we assume. I would remind you that
the hardest thing on earth to be is a citizen of a democratic
society; this is probably why history shows so few democratic
societies that have endured. The easiest thing is to be the citizen
of a tyrant state, of a military autocracy. This is probably why
the tyrant state is the oldest and the simplest and the most often
repeated form of government throughout history—the form of
government which man is returning to today, having failed to
live up to the obligations and difficulties of a free society.

Most people in our country would probably agree with these
generalities. But inevitably, if you say such things, the reply
is, "Yes, but what can I do about it? What is it that I, the citizen,
can do?" That is perhaps the reason for the hopelessness and
cynicism which have overtaken so much of the democratic

world. The plain citizens in the democracies can't find anything to do which they feel confident will help. Now in the tyrant states that's taken care of. You are told, "Do this, do that." You are given all kinds of praise for doing this and doing that—so long as you do it promptly and without making any complaint. You are told what to do, you are told what your duties are; and that's one of the most restful things in the world. One of the reasons why men will finally in despair accept slavery is that, along with the slavery, they can get the comforting feeling of having been told what their duty is and that they're good boys and girls after they have done it. We who have dared to be free have got to find that comfort for ourselves; nobody can give it to us—because if we are not good enough to find it, by that fact we have ceased to be a free people. When we turn in desperation and ask somebody to "tell" us, we have sold our freedom; we consort with a Hitler.

If we succeed in elevating ourselves to the point of knowing what we mean when we talk about the American tradition, of knowing what we mean when we talk about democracy, we have begun the lonely task of adult self-education. I can illustrate what I mean by referring you to the history of one of the few parts of the world where democracy has been reborn in the last few generations.

Sixty-five years ago in Denmark the Danish people began to say to themselves: "It is intolerable that we should be living under these conditions. We don't like it; we want to move towards a free society. How are we going to do it? We can't do it by calling in somebody from above to impose freedom upon us. If we're ever going to have it, we've got to have it because of our own work." Therefore they began to educate themselves. They began to try to learn what was happening in Denmark. They began to meet together in groups, hundreds of them all over the country, to discuss, to debate, because they believed in the democratic process. They believed that if people, working towards a common end (no matter how much they disagree with one another) will meet together, will debate, will discuss—that out of that can come the formation of a policy which might even save Freedom. Well, it saved Denmark, and it spread from Denmark to the other Scandinavian countries and helped to save them. It has made them the freest, and probably the happiest countries to live in, in the world today.

On our own continent, up in Nova Scotia, spreading out from one university all over northeastern Nova Scotia and out into the islands, a similar movement began thirty years ago, which is beginning today to show remarkable results. It began in exactly the same way: citizens getting together and saying we must learn, we must know, we must understand. There is no other hope for democracy. All men of good will are trying to go in the same direction. They disagree with one another as to how to get there. Yet by getting together to debate, to discuss, to learn, they do learn from one another how much each of them still has to learn. Those are the only processes by which democracy has been saved, anywhere in the modern world.

I see no reason why similar processes shouldn't save democracy in our country. But it's hard, and it's irksome, and to many people it seems very foolish—the idea of getting together with other people to discuss things. It sounds foolish or socially ignoble. Nevertheless, if we the citizens of America don't get together among ourselves to discuss some of the major problems of man, if we don't make ourselves better equipped to find answers to some of the major problems of men, there is no reason to assume that democracy will survive in this country. Before giving you some examples of what I mean by that last statement, I would say this—that one of the hopeful things that we can learn from the few places in the modern world where democracy has repaired itself, where democratic citizens have done their job, is that when you begin this kind of study, one of the startling facts that emerge is how much the citizens, even in their modern, advanced, complicated, technological society, how much the citizens can do for themselves. Take Sweden, which, although a tiny country, happens to be divided up economically very like our own country and is a small-scale model. The amount of capital devoted to one sort of industry and another in terms of the advancement of technology, the amount of capital devoted to agriculture, the division of the population in terms of occupations, is not very dissimilar in Sweden and in our own country. The Swedes discovered when they really got to work with adult education, with educating themselves, that a very considerable area of their economy could be taken charge of by the citizens. Having got together to debate and learn, it was not a question of simply forming themselves into pressure groups to get the government of Sweden to do this for them and do that for them; at least 50 per cent of the process was learning that citizens, even in a modern advanced technological society, can elevate themselves by their own activities and without calling in the outside aid of the government. The lesson which we who want to preserve our free society can learn from Sweden and the other places where this has been tried is helpful and hopeful.

Let me give you an illustration of what I mean by saying that we the citizens have simply got to learn more, that we are not good enough at the moment, that we are incapable of forming policy because we are too ignorant to form it. I'll give you two examples of what I mean: one in terms of domestic policy and one in terms of foreign policy and world crisis. It seems to me obvious that the greatest failure of this country during the last ten years is the failure to do anything of any sort whatsoever about unemployment. In 1929 to 1933, and until today, we have failed completely to deal with the problem of unemployment. It went up to maybe fourteen millions at one point, and it went down maybe to nine millions at another point, and it may be somewhere between ten and eleven millions at the moment. It's an interesting fact that we don't even know what our unemployment is at any point. We are the only "democratic" nation in the world that does not know. We have never taken the trouble to count the unemployed to find out. But at any rate, those are roughly accurate figures. At no point have we ever done anything to change things drastically. All we tend to do is to get excited, to abuse one group or another group, defending the group we belong to and expending a great deal of emotion. We don't know the facts—yet we've got to learn. Who is going to learn? Let us—you and I—learn. Unless we take pains to do so, to put ourselves in a position where we can at least judge suggestions that are being made with some reason and some wisdom, we are just pushovers for a tyrant state. We are just sitting around twiddling our thumbs and waiting for a strong man to come along and say, "You mugs, this is the answer, and I'm going to make you take it." That is the only alternative to our doing something about it ourselves.

Now in regard to the world crisis. Here we are, bumbling along after years and years and years, and having it still perfectly fair to say that the United States of America has no discernible foreign policy. Not only have we no foreign policy, but we can have no foreign policy until we the people of America make up our minds what we think are the vital interests of our country. Go to the State Department and ask them what they can do about this or that. They will reply, "We can't make any definite statement yet; we can't lay down any line of policy till we know what the people of America think are their vital interests." Go to our armed forces and ask them whether they can do this and that. They will say, "We can't answer any of those questions till we know what the people of America are going to make a stand on, among all the vital interests of America." We've got to decide that. We can't wait for a Mr. Hitler to come and tell us what our vital interests are. But we haven't decided it yet. We don't know. It isn't possible to say whether our Army and our Navy are big enough, or too big, or too little, because we have no idea what they're expected to do. We don't know whether our foreign policy is directed towards reaching the ends we want or not, because we don't know what the ends we want are. The fate of the world may depend upon the position that America takes in regard to today's struggle for power. And America can take no position because the people of America have no idea what they want. I say again, that is not good enough. But it will go on being true until all the world maybe goes to ruin unless we start taking the trouble to think. Nobody can take that trouble for us. If we do not take it, it will not be taken. If it is not taken, democracy will not work. If it does not work here, it will not have a chance to exist anywhere.

If we could imagine the citizens of our country doing as people in other countries have done in the very recent past and are doing today, if we could imagine the citizens of our country doing these things that I am talking about—learning what nihilism means, learning what is happening, trying to apply new knowledge and thus new moral stature to specific problems, really working, really studying, really participating—if we could imagine all that happening, we would then be in a position to perform what seems to me the third necessary duty of citizens who want to have a democracy. That is to insist that the tone of our politics be improved. The cynicism which is being imposed upon the American people today, and especially the young people, is something which no country which wants to remain free can accept.

Let me give you some examples of what I mean. First I say that all of us have got to learn to have some respect for the opinions of our opponents. And I add, sadly, that at this moment we have almost no respect for the opinions of our opponents. It doesn't make any difference what side you take it on, whether it's a group of so-called advanced thinkers meeting together and abusing the "economic royalists," or a National Chamber of

Commerce meeting in Washington and drawing up resolutions which suggest that every one that disagrees with them is both half-witted and blackhearted. Whichever side you take you find this same complete intolerance of the point of view of the other people. It isn't something that we can afford to have, and it isn't something that we need to have.

The mechanism of the national nominating convention we may be able to use if we choose to. We can purify it and make some sense out of it, or perhaps we can scrap the whole thing. It is just created *ad hoc;* it has no position in law. We can have a more dignified way (maybe "dignified" is the wrong word), but we can have a more sensible way, a way with some responsibility and authority, of choosing our presidential candidates. We can have that if we want it. If we don't want it, again it is going to be too bad for democracy. I'll remind you finally of one thing, and then I'll quit.

In 1928 Will Rogers went to the White House to call on Calvin Coolidge, who was then President, and he asked President Coolidge how it was that he, Coolidge, kept so young and healthy-looking in a job which had killed a good many Presidents and had destroyed the health of a great many more. Coolidge replied that he did it by avoiding the big questions. Will Rogers published that in his little daily paragraph and the American people laughed. They thought it was very funny, good old Cal, a typical Coolidge crack. He keeps his complexion and his health by avoiding the big questions. Well, Coolidge, as he so often did, put into a few words a national mood. We the American people had been avoiding the big question for many years, and eighteen months after the President of the United States made that crack America landed in the ditch. One of the chief reasons she landed in the ditch is that we had been avoiding the big question all those years. And we haven't got out of that ditch yet. And we won't get out of that ditch ever, and democracy won't recover ever, unless we stop avoiding the big questions.

Side by side with that remark of Coolidge's (which I think might have been spoken by the American people as a whole in 1928), side by side with that, let me remind you of what Carlyle wrote in *Heroes and Hero Worship*, when he tried to describe the common quality of those great men who in his opinion were so great that they changed the course of history. The only thing he could find true of them all was that they were people who found it impossible to turn their backs on the major questions of their age.

The great Fact of Existence is great to him. . . . Though all men should forget its truth, and walk in a vain show, he cannot. At all moments the Flame-image glares in upon him; undeniable, there, there! I wish you to take this as my primary definition of a Great Man.

Is this not also true of a great nation? Should we not be ashamed of ourselves for avoiding the great questions, for asking not to be told the bitter truth, and for applauding a President who boasted that he did not choose to face the facts? Our facts, today, are more terrible than those with which Coolidge was asked to deal; therefore we turn our backs upon them more firmly than did that weak and inarticulate man. Therefore is our democracy in danger.

JOHN HERMAN RANDALL, Jr.

The Paradox of
Intellectual Freedom

IN the chronicles of history, 1939 will stand as the year in which
Americans discovered their priceless heritage of intellectual freedom and organized to defend it. This deep concern, it will be
recorded, was not confined just to those with so virgin an experience as to preserve a shameless enthusiasm for ideas. It was
not limited to newly-educated seniors enduring the trials of
Commencement addresses, nor to that group of liberal journalists
and writers, popular preachers, and open-minded professors for
whom the happy blend of knowledge with irresponsibility has
earned the name of "intellectuals." Its appeal was so great and
so widespread that it replaced "peace" as the football of the
politicians of the Left and promised a new meal-ticket to the
statesmen of the Right. Indeed, "intellectual freedom" was one
of those blessed discoveries, a symbol that could unite Americans
against all that was wicked, depraved, and incomprehensible in
the goings-on of other peoples. Deans ventured to speak of it
to alumni. Droves of college presidents issued manifestos in its

Delivered before the Delta of New York, Columbia University, 1939.
Published in *The American Scholar*, Winter, 1939–1940.

86

favor. Bankers underwrote it. Dorothy Thompson explained its implications. Even Phi Beta Kappa came out for it.

So it seems we are all for intellectual freedom these days. I fear no dissent—unless it is "cultural freedom" you prefer, and then your deviation is both dialectical and inevitable. We might find it hard to explain just what it is we are all for and just how we are going to defend it. But at least there is no doubt what we are all against. Our warm indignation, to be sure, has so far been neither notably intellectual nor particularly free. It might well lead to more impressive results had we a better understanding of its objects and were it a little freer from entanglement in the toils of our various party politics. But though they be not too effective, our emotions are at least generous and our platforms ingenious. More questionable is the fighting psychology, the sense of war to the death, that blinds so many of our hearts and heads. For it is a fact, sad but inescapable, that the most earnest and righteous battle leaves no room for the inquiring mind. Those who would save freedom of thought by taking up arms must first lose it. This fact is worth pondering. It brings some inkling of understanding to the tragedy of those we despise. And it suggests that we think a little more deeply before in the delight of fighting those we hate, by declaration or by deed, we lightly sacrifice the freedom we yet have.

So today we need no pep-talk to rouse our fighting spirit, no mere waving the flag of intellectual freedom. That flag we are already resolved to defend, to the last drop of blood of the last Frenchman or Briton. Nor need we seriously consider whether it were a real service to intellectual freedom to shoot off—or to starve off—all the Germans, Russians, and Japanese. Many of them are doing abominable things we should like to see stopped; and one stick is as good as another to belabor them with, if we must. Hence I do not propose to speak of those we hate, or to use a popular symbol in the present fashion, whether to glorify American complacency or to hurl anathemas at peoples once mighty in the faith who have fallen from grace. It may be naive to assume that those nowadays so eager to serve "intellectual freedom" mean anything at all by it. But I judge the reason it is so effective a symbol for releasing our anger and mobilizing our hatred is just that it does stand for something we think we love. And it is that something I want to examine.

What do we really mean by intellectual freedom? We all agree it is a priceless blessing. You and I will never give it up. But it is exceeding hard to defend, far harder than our leagues and declarations would have it, and exceeding easy to sacrifice the substance in fighting for the name. And it is still harder to discover what it is, or rather, what it would be if we had it; for it needs little reflection to realize that, far from being a familiar American heritage, freedom of the mind is hardly yet a landmark on the American scene.

I am not talking of that collection of legal rights and liberties we group together as freedom of expression or of that set of ill-defined conventions and aspirations we dignify as academic freedom. Of them Americans have indeed a precious heritage, confined to be sure within shifting limits decent and indecent. We do well to guard them jealously, and still better to organize to defend them and to extend them. For it is not enough to preserve them in the clear-cut and familiar cases: only the unremitting struggle to apply them in those new situations in which their observance is not yet habitual and recognized can keep them from slowly dissolving away. It still costs us great effort to maintain the liberties of men whose ideas are so unconventional as to be un-American, or whose tactics are so unaccustomed as to be unmannerly. The best of us, I fear, share something of the feeling of the Texas editor who boasted "In our town everybody has complete freedom of speech, except the radicals." And it goes without saying that only the most vigorous organization, political and professional, can effect this defense and extension. In times of rapid change, when feelings run high and ideas are rightly taken seriously, men with the best of intentions as well as men with the worst strike out at those they fear.

The rights to discuss and communicate ideas are indispensable conditions of intellectual freedom; without them the mind withers and dies. But they scarcely make up what we mean by free intellect itself: that, alas, is not so easy to obtain or defend. A society where anybody can say whatever comes into his head is not necessarily a society of free minds. He who has ever suffered at a public forum knows the gulf between free speech and free thought. The former our human courts and judges can measurably secure; the latter the good Lord himself has been unable to guarantee.

Now there are many sound and excellent reasons for granting the utmost freedom of expression even to those who seldom or never think. Blowing off steam has its points over blowing up the government; it is more satisfying to the blower and much less upsetting to his neighbors. Those who can talk and play politics don't have to conspire; and so deans sleep of nights because college faculties never rebel. A man with something on his mind, though the burden be infinitesimal, still keeps his self-respect if he can get it off his chest. But the chief reason, I take it, we so profoundly cherish our liberties of expression is that we desperately hope that out of them may emerge something of a genuine freedom of mind. And often the miracle happens: from the discussion and inquiry of average men there come an intelligence and a wisdom that Fuehrers might well envy. Those perpetual miracles, our modern schools, can do the trick with surprising success. By sheer freedom of expression, it seems, and without teaching anything at all, they can turn out extraordinarily competent products who need only to learn something to be first-rate stuff.

No, were our liberties of expression not the soil in which to cultivate a freedom of the mind, they would scarcely deserve our passionate defense. They would then be mere useful devices, born of the wisdom of experience, for smoothing over the frictions of social living and keeping men's passions below the boiling-point. We could still question the prudence of nations that sacrificed them to other ends. Mindful of the wisdom of Talley-rand, that you can do everything with bayonets except sit on them, we could with some patience await the event. We might even wonder whether on the drug of propaganda one cannot also sleep. But were the enterprise magnificent enough—did it really promise to abolish the age-old fear of insecurity and want —we might well be tempted to pay the heavy price. We too might listen, as so many have of late, to that ancient counsel of the disillusioned men of Athens, to grant intellectual liberties only to them that know—until they know too much. The temptation is all the stronger since today it is so clear that without security from want a free mind can never be a sure social possession.

A "free mind" indeed! Are we men, or are we only liberals? Are not those right who tell us "intellectual freedom" is a con-tradiction in terms? Can it mean anything but freedom to im-pose our ideas on others? Speech, discussion, yes, even teaching —we can understand how by ceaseless care they may be made relatively free. But how can mind, how can what we think, how can knowledge of what is so, possibly be free? How can our thought hope to escape the passions and prejudices, the ignor-ance and the interests, in which it is inevitably rooted? And does not any measure of success involve in turn a surrender to the compulsion of truth? Does not the very nature of thinking lie in bondage to its human origins and in submission to the rigorous conditions of its validity?

When we speak so hopefully of defending the mind against external and artificial restraints, we are forgetting internal and natural bonds far more pervasive and inescapable. The wisdom of a century of psychologists, social scientists, and historians might have taught us what slaves we are to our fellows and to our past.

Our most daring thoughts, we know, ripen in the long tradition and accumulated knowledge of our society; our feelings and our opinions are rooted in the thousand social habits and attitudes that make us what we are. Our institutions, our class, our group, our profession—these limit and shape our mind at every turn. Our most original innovators are linked most closely with their predecessors; even our boasted pursuit of what we like to call "free inquiry" is so dependent on a fragile chain of scientific tradition, so exposed to every wave of popular feeling, that it is the first victim of any social shock. And then we fancy we are intellectually free—we who can so easily explain the historical sources, the emotional roots, and the class bias of any man's ideas!

No, as every freshman knows, and as any psychologist or economist could tell him if he has forgotten, the freedom of thinking cannot mean sheer detached independence. No man can hope to achieve it in isolation from his fellows. A free mind is born only of a society that has carefully built up the institutions and conditions needed to generate it. Whatever intellectual freedom may be, it is clearly a social before it is an individual possession, the product of a complex and delicate cultural fabric. Unless all the institutions of that society, from lowest to highest, are so ordered as to foster it, no mere guarantee of civil liberties will suffice. Where they are not, the most untrammeled academic freedom will never free us from the academic mind.

That is why to pursue intellectual freedom involves us at once in every other social problem, so inextricably that really to achieve it we should need to have solved them all; that is why our most valiant efforts to "defend" it by itself, our unending protests against crude legal and external restraints, take us so short a way. For it is no family heirloom for Americans to guard proudly and complacently: to come within hailing distance will take a drastic revolution in all our attitudes and institutions, a revolution to make our reddest radical programs pale into pink. We shall need enough patient and sustained work to satisfy the most constructive conservative and all the hard struggle the most determined radical could wish. We shall have plenty of time to abolish economic insecurity and clean up war before our college faculties are societies of really free minds.

Yet we Americans have made a fair beginning at the foundations. Just because the structure is so delicately balanced and takes generations to rear, we must be ever watchful lest some seductive solution to a pressing ill send what we have crashing to the ground. We have seen how easy it is, under the imperative compulsion of an immediate goal, to wreck overnight all that a great nation had built up for centuries. With the example of Germany before us we should be slaves indeed if because we too must organize the life of our body economic we too should blast the life of the spirit.

If in its origins thought cannot hope to be free—if it is so deeply rooted in the social and cultural soil in which it grows that not in independence of his age, his society, his class, or his education but only as they too are "free" can a mind become free—surely then it is to the fruits of thought that we must look for thought's freedom. Not in the limitations and relativities whence thinking springs but in what it does and what it brings— in the operations of free inquiry and the knowledge it discovers —there if anywhere lies emancipation. "Ye shall know the truth and the truth shall make you free."

But despite the Evangelist we are not yet come to the end of our quest. We have rather arrived at the central paradox of intellectual freedom, with which the greatest minds have wrestled and failed to agree. For in its very nature, it has seemed, the last thing intellect is or can hope to be, is free. The fruit of intelligence and knowledge is not freedom. It is power, or it is understanding; and neither leaves the mind with any unfettered choice. For power is no liberator: it rather sets conditions and obligations of its own from which there is no escape. The more power we possess to do what we can, the more we are bound to conform to those conditions and to observe those obligations—and the more inexorably intelligence is compelled to seek what they are, and how what that power can do must be done. And the compulsion of understanding, though less harsh, is no less ultimate. For to know what is, and why it must be so, may indeed win us release from the vain endeavor to do what cannot be done; but in abandoning the illusion of external power we are none the less bound to be what we are and to do what we must. Neither with the power to do, nor with the understanding why, can the mind find independence of circumstance or hope to legislate its own career. The knowledge that is power makes us slaves of the responsibilities of power. And the knowledge that is understanding can set us free only by convicting us of powerlessness to alter what we are and must be. We are caught in the cruel dilemma: if knowledge be power, it brings no freedom; if knowledge bring freedom, it is at the price of impotence.

From St. Augustine down the keenest intellect has without avail rung the changes on this dialectic of freedom. The classic solution seeks victory in the defeat itself: it finds the mind's freedom to lie in its very bondage to the conditions of its power, in complete surrender to the command of rational necessity. Perfect freedom, it concludes, can be no other than perfect obedience to perfect law.

In two ways men have tried to break through the chain; at best they make the surrender somewhat more palatable. Francis Bacon turned away from perfect law and sought a new kind of knowledge, the knowledge that is power over the world's processes, the busy intelligence of the craftsman and technician extending the bounds of human empire over Nature to the effecting of all things possible. Surely the more things we know how to do, the greater our freedom! But Bacon realized that Nature to be commanded must be obeyed; and a society that has more than fulfilled his prophecies of human power has drawn ever tighter about itself the web of bondage to technology, until what we must now do to maintain our control over Nature has robbed us of all freedom to do anything else, or to choose another destiny. Intelligence, the power of knowing how, has brought us untold riches and untold responsibilities; it has taught us what must be done and how we must do it. But it has not made us free.

Spinoza identified knowledge with a far different power, the power over ourselves and our passions. For him knowledge was not intelligence, not knowing how, but rather understanding, knowing why—in the end, sheer intellectual vision. Men are free, not when they are doing what they can but when they see why they are doing as they must. They are freest of all in the vision of themselves as parts of the great Scheme of things: knowing themselves at last for what they are, in the very under-standing of their impotence to be otherwise they are released from bondage to any desire to be so. We have the power to do what we must and to accept our own destiny. Spinoza had ample precedent for calling this power "freedom"; but that did not make it any the less an impotence and a necessity. His many successors—idealistic philosophers, social scientists, psychol-ogists, and historians, all those who have contributed so mightily to our understanding of man—have transformed it from a thing difficult as it was rare to something we can now teach to every freshman. And this understanding of human nature and human society, the knowing why, the vision of what it means to be a rational animal, has for many brought acceptance and peace and for many others bondage to some great social ideal. But it too has not made us free.

On the one side lies the bondage of understanding and vision, the bondage of impotence; on the other the bondage of intel-ligence, the bondage of power. Where lies freedom of the mind? With him who understands why, with the artist, the poet, the social scientist, the historian? or with him who knows how, with the engineer, the technician, the administrator and executive, the politician? Despite our philosophies of power, we have traditionally answered, freedom is possible only for the impotent. By a "free mind" we have meant one detached from all obligation and responsibility; to its emancipation, power has seemed fatal. It must feel no sense of urgency in values, it must not know how to do anything—or if it should, the doing must be quite useless. We still call those studies which give a vision of human nature the liberal arts, and that discipline which fails to teach men how to do anything at all a liberal education. Both the impotent who understand and the powerful who know how have had good reason to encourage this prejudice. The impotent have found consolation in their freedom and the powerful have found safety in the impotence of the wise.

But it should be clear today that neither those who know why without knowing how, nor those who know how without knowing why, can claim to be free minds. It is this very divorce between understanding and intelligence, between vision and power, that has made possible the destruction of intellectual freedom where it has been destroyed. This was the tragic guilt of German culture at its best; let it be our warning. For our education also is disastrously divided. So long as we too are content to graduate able technicians without understanding and well-educated men who know how to do nothing, all our defense of freedom will be a losing struggle. With experts who are illiberal and short-sighted, and intellectuals who are irresponsible and unintelligent, we cannot hope to win. Unless vision be married to intelligence there can be no freedom of the mind. The Chicago prophets of intellectual celibacy cannot make us free.

Knowledge is power, and power is bondage—that wisdom cannot be gainsaid. But our mistake has been to take all bondage as the utter destruction of freedom. And we have made the mistake because we have assumed that freedom is a single thing, one and undivided, which we must possess whole and entire or not at all. If that assumption be true, then intellectual freedom is indeed a paradox that drives us to make freedom and bondage, power and obligation, one and the same. This dialectic may satisfy our philosophies of freedom, but it hardly fits our needs. But we can escape it if we realize that freedom is not general but specific and determinate: it is release from one kind of bondage the better to assume the yoke of another. It can never mean the escape from all obligation. Freedoms and obligations are both correlative and plural, and each is at once a freedom from this and a submission to that. Knowledge itself is both an emancipation and an exchange of bondages: it frees us from the slavery of ignorance for the service of the conditions and responsibilities of knowing. Without losing its determinate nature, thought can never be wholly free; nor can it be wholly bound without ceasing to be thought.

But if freedoms be indeed many and not one, we have managed to transform the historic paradox into a problem—the problem of securing the greatest range of specific freedoms, each with its own insistent commands. And our task has ceased to be to strive for a forever-unattainable goal of ideal and complete freedom; it is rather to multiply and strengthen the manifold freedoms of the mind. They are various and conflicting; they display incompatibilities that may well prove ultimate. To balance them and adjust them to each other in the shifting pattern of social change is a never-ending process calling for ceaseless effort; for now one suffers and needs renewed emphasis, now another is slighted and needs bolstering up. But to balance and adjust them is the proper task of a rational animal. To harmonize the freedoms and the obligations of thought is an end for our education to aim at and for all our work of social reconstruction to keep in mind.

And so it's not so strange that we should be calling on intellectual freedom when we really mean we'd like to stop Hitler, or wish they would teach more Latin, or are just trying to pay the rent. Those are all good things to do, and it is the very nature of freedom to consist in that kind of specific fight. But once we've invoked it in some pressing need, we've let ourselves in for more than we've bargained for. We're committed to all the other freedoms of the mind as well. And that's a large order—larger, I fear, than most of the valiant defenders of intellectual freedom today are willing to fill. I'll pass over the college presidents, and the radical politicians. Take Dorothy Thompson. Aren't there some important freedoms of the mind even she hasn't got around to remembering? And aren't we all today infected with acute Thompsonitis? This epidemic disorder is caused by a too exclusive diet of headlines; the only cure is a more varied intellectual fare.

And it would help to remember that understanding has its freedoms, and that intelligence is a matter of rigorous obligations. As it is, I'm afraid we've got them quite turned around. We've been boasting too long of the freedom of intelligence; little wonder many have fled to the Word of God, which does not chatter, or to the dialectic of history, which speaks in deeds. And we've been content to shudder and glory in the bondage of understanding: we who know it all today all know the worst, and we have never raised a finer crop of irrepressible conflicts and inevitable dooms. As every columnist can explain, and does daily, if the Nazis don't get us the Communists will, and what's left will be polished off by the axis of Trotsky, the Japs, and the national debt. Now that's really no way to preserve intellectual freedom. That's not even slavery—that's just plain insanity.

Yes, we need the emancipation of real understanding: we sorely need to cultivate the freedoms of the mind. Most of all we need the freedom from the provincialism of the present, the freedom won by communion with the things that endure. There are the great achievements of mankind, in art, in thought, and in deed, that almost atone for its manifold follies, and liberate us from a too narrow preoccupation with the problems of the passing present. There is the priceless record of human experience in all its variety of greatness and weakness, that vision of the rationality and the animality of human nature that justifies the claim of the humanities to be truly liberal arts and makes them a necessary part of the furniture of any free mind. There is the lesson of other cultures and other civilizations that there are many forms of social organization under which men can lead a richly satisfying life—a lesson that can reconcile us to the price we must pay for the changes our power has made necessary. There are the eternal visions of religion, the past's chief avenue of escape from the insistence of the moment; they still have their power of deliverance, if religion be no mere social work or sentimental politics but the human seeing of God. And there are those ingenious schemes for fitting the puzzle of history together whereby the Marxian can regard Fascism as the last stage in capitalist decay and even the Republican can understand the New Deal.

We need too that freedom from the tyrannous fear of the future that comes from the vision of history itself: the vision that sees men forever engaged in conflicts and insistent problems, each new one, though it seem today a crisis in the universe, but one more incident in a long series, with an endless chain yet to come—the vision that reveals comedy as more ultimate than tragedy, and takes mankind beyond the tragedies of men. "It is five minutes to twelve," we are told; "it is later than you think." No, short-sighted little man, it is still long before dawn. We need patience—the patience that is not cast down by a few failures, that does not demand that every problem be solved at once but is willing to try and try again. It is the impatient, who know the answer and cannot wait till others have learned it too, who are responsible for the intolerance and brutality and fanatical temper of today. We need to face remorseless change as itself an enduring fact, to be accepted, understood, and worked with as intelligently as possible, not as a cosmic crisis in which by a last supreme effort we must finally vanquish the Devil and usher in the Kingdom of God or perish in the attempt.

And we need freedom from yearning after the impossible and from despair at the limitations of our power. We cannot set the world to rights overnight, we who can barely look to our own ills. We need freedom to discriminate, clearly if regretfully, what we can reasonably hope to do from what we must renounce. We cannot keep the Japs out of China. We cannot save the Germans from Hitler. We cannot give order and peace to a Europe that cannot yet help itself. It is bondage to romantic illusions to think we can. And it were worse than bondage, it were disaster, to lead another sentimental crusade for these generous but impossible ends. In these harsh times there is much we might do, yet with that we have still to make a beginning. We dream of ending the menace of Hitler, yet for his tragic victims we have made not a single move to set our gates ajar. We who would save the world will not even do what we can. Till we have made the sad renunciation of the impossible we shall not be free to do what we must.

For in the end all the freedoms of the mind are but a sterile and a bitter bondage if they fail to free us to obey the commands of intelligence. There is no need to belabor so insistent and so obvious a fact. You know and I know the problems that must be met. In a world in which we can and do exercise so marvelous a power over Nature, those problems are set for us by that power itself. If we are to exert it, if we are even to live with it, we know what must be done. If we have thought at all, if we have submitted to the conditions of inquiry and surrendered our minds to what has been discovered, we already know how to do much that must be done. What we do not yet know is how to enlist the cooperative support of men in doing what we know how to do. We do not yet possess the political intelligence to persuade men to use the intelligence we do possess. There lies the most insistent problem of all. There is the real obstacle to intellectual freedom today. For it is our ignorance and our failures in political techniques and methods that are causing all our other freedoms to falter. To work upon this problem of developing political intelligence is the first obligation of all the intelligence we can muster. To give up in despair—to fail to see that political skill is itself a technical problem, to which inquiry can bring an answer, to deny that men can ever be intelligently persuaded to use intelligence, to drug them with passionate hatred, to coerce them with brute force—whatever the trappings and the glory, that is not power but slavery. And that is to abandon all hope of intellectual freedom. We should thank God that in America we have made a beginning with political intelligence, and that we are already free enough to work intelligently for the freedoms of the mind.

F. LYMAN WINDOLPH

Religio Advocati

I HAVE wanted for many years to have an opportunity to address a group of young men about to graduate from college and take their places in the life of the world. The reason lies in the vividness and permanence of an impression made on me by the addresses to which I listened during the formal process of my own education.

In the course of that process—which you will recall that some cynic has characterized, let us hope with more wit than accuracy, as the casting of imitation pearls before real swine—I listened perforce to the usual number of Commencement orations, baccalaureate sermons, and other addresses of the sort delivered on occasions such as the one which brings us together tonight.

As I look back over the lapse of years, it seems to me that my attitude as a listener was all that my teachers could possibly have desired. I was aware, acutely aware, that my ignorance on a great many subjects was abysmal; and I was eager for enlightenment. The questions which puzzled me were chiefly of two sorts—those about which the difficulty was intrinsic and which seemed to me (though I hoped mistakenly) to be in-

Delivered before the Beta of Virginia, University of Virginia, June 10, 1939. Published by the Michie Company, Charlottesville, Virginia.

soluble, and those which, though involved in complexity, mastered the fund of information which was actually available. In the first group were included those fundamental questions which have engaged the attention of the great philosophers of all ages and which, as it seems to me, are too often passed over by the philosophers of today—whence life comes and whither it goes; the secret at the heart of the paradoxes of time and space; the nature of that imperious necessity which drives water about the great business of seeking a lower level; the mysteries of growth and form, whereby my body, though changing from instant to instant, continues to present itself in a likeness which my friends can recognize; the significance of those seemingly happy accidents by which trees are invariably green and the sky blue—and a hundred other questions of like moment which are thrust, willy-nilly, upon every man and woman born into the world and which contribute so largely to what William James has aptly called "the wildness and the pang of life."

You will notice that most of these questions may best be stated in sentences beginning with the word "why." The Commencement orators to whom I listened never answered them and indeed seldom referred to them. Instead, they answered a variety of questions of the second group, questions beginning with the word "how" rather than "why"—*how* water flows down hill, for instance, but never *why* it flows down hill—and for a time I was inclined to ascribe my resulting disappointment to nothing more significant than a run of bad luck in the selection of Commencement speakers.

Now I wish to present myself to you as one who was an ingenuous youth—that *iuvenis ingenuus* who survives, at least in name, wherever college diplomas are still written in Latin—but not as one who was altogether a fool. You will understand, therefore, that I did not suppose that the scholarly gentleman who addressed me on the evening on which I was initiated into the Phi Beta Kappa Society would, in the course of an hour's discourse, present for my consideration a complete solution of the riddle of the universe. I did think, however, that he knew more about the solution than I did, and that if he could only be gotten on the right track he would be able to remove a part of my perplexity. As matters turned out, he never did get on the right track—and though I did not fully understand the reason then, I do understand it now. The first law of scholarship is humility; and in telling you the reason, I am presenting to the initiates of this evening not the least important item in the esoteric lore of our society. The speaker to whom I listened a generation ago did not give me the answers to the great questions which I had in mind because he did not know the answers. Neither do I know them; neither does any man.

Another point deserves to be mentioned. I think we are inclined to assume too readily that age necessarily, or at least usually, brings wisdom to its possessor. Too often it is true, as Shakespeare noticed, that

> We worldly men
> Have miserable, mad, mistaking eyes.

Like everyone else, we spend a third of our time "in a mysterious state which we do not understand and which we minimize and normalize under the name of sleep." We spend most of the rest of our time in the business of making a living. Sometimes this business becomes so engrossing that we forget the underlying problem of what we are to do with our lives when our livings have been made. Young people seem to me, on the whole, more courageous, more clear-sighted, more sensitive, and more disinterested than older people. If my own opinions have changed in the course of my life, I think I may not take it for granted that they have invariably changed for the better. In short, if you ask me to address you on the occasion of my hundredth birthday, I hold it to be no more than a foolish convention to suppose that you will certainly listen to a wiser speech than this one.

This illustration will perhaps justify my mentioning a personal matter which, in the nature of the case, can be of very little interest to anyone but myself. It so happens that this is my fiftieth birthday. I was graduated from college on June 9, 1908, and I was admitted to the bar on June 19, 1911. It follows that I have been a human being for fifty years to the day, a bachelor of arts for thirty-one years and one day, and a lawyer for twenty-eight years less nine days. My purpose tonight is to present to you some of the convictions which have been borne in upon me as a result of that experience. In doing so, I am not unmindful of the advice which Cromwell addressed to the Presbyterians in Scotland— "I do beseech you, in the bowels of Christ bethink you, that ye may be wrong." I have already indicated that I think the admonition is sound, but I am resolved not to be too much cast down because of it. After all, fallibility is the inertia against which every man moves when he undertakes to speak at all. If none of us spoke except upon certain knowledge, we should all be silent; and if even a working degree of certainty —certainty, as the lawyers say, to a common intent—were one of the requisites of an acceptable Phi Beta Kappa address, the list of eligible speakers would, I suspect, be smaller than it actually is.

I

First of all, then, I believed in my youth, and I believe now— less vividly perhaps, but with an ever-increasing sense of matured conviction—that magic is abroad in the world. I referred a few moments ago to our human origin and destination, to time and space, to form and growth, and to some of the properties of the physical world. You know, however, that all of the magic is not included in this enumeration.

"Poetry," said Professor Housman—who was in his own right a true poet as well as a famous scholar and critic—

Poetry indeed seems to me more physical than intellectual. A year or two ago, in common with others, I received from America a request that I would define poetry. I replied that I could no more define poetry than a terrier can define a rat, but that I thought we both recognized the object by the symptoms which it provokes in us. One of these symptoms was described in connection with another object by Eliphaz the Temanite: "A spirit passed before my face: the hair of my flesh stood up." Experience has taught me, when I am shaving of a morning, to keep watch over my thoughts, because, if a line of poetry strays into my memory, my skin bristles so that the razor ceases to act. This particular symptom is accompanied by a shiver down the spine; there is another which consists in a constriction of the throat and a precipitation of water to the eyes; and there is a third which I can only describe by borrowing a phrase from one of Keats's last letters, where he says, speaking of Fanny Brawne, "everything that reminds me of her goes through me like a spear." The seat of this sensation is the pit of the stomach.

Perhaps it is unfair to wrench this passage from its context in the noble essay on *The Name and Nature of Poetry* in which it appears. The symptoms described are doubtless more violent than come to most readers of poetry, but the emotion giving rise to the symptoms would have been classified by James as a "rudimentary mystical experience" and, at least in a modified form, is familiar to nearly everyone.

There is a story about Emerson attending a performance of *Hamlet*. When the actor playing the title role came to the lines in the first act—

> That thou, dread corse, again in complete steel
> Revisits thus the glimpses of the moon—

the attention of Emerson was so forcibly arrested that he sat through the entire performance without hearing another word. In the essay from which I have already quoted, Housman said that the seventh verse of the forty-ninth Psalm in the Book of Common Prayer—"But no man may deliver his brother, nor make agreement unto God for him"—was to him so moving that he could hardly keep his voice steady in reading it; and added: "That this is the effect of language I can ascertain by experiment, the same thought in the bible version, 'None of them can by any means redeem his brother, nor give to God a ransom for him,' I can read without emotion." In somewhat the same way the lines which bring to an end the second scene of the fifth act of *King Lear*—

> Men must endure
> Their going hence, even as their coming hither;
> Ripeness is all—

seem to me the greatest and most memorable lines in English poetry, though I should not find it easy to answer an inquiry as to the precise qualities in which their greatness consists. If you were to press me, I should have to make the answer of St. Augustine to the question, What is time?—"I know when you do not ask me."

The illustrations which have been given are all from the field of poetry; and this is natural enough since it happens that I know more about poetry than about the other fine arts. You are aware, however, that the same sort of rapture—I am not sure that this is the best word but I mean more than ordinary aesthetic pleasure—is to be found by some persons in special combinations of line and color and by what I suspect is a larger number of persons in special sequences of musical sounds. The music of a violin has been defined as the noise made by scraping hairs from the tail of a horse across the entrails of a dead cat. The definition is completely accurate so far as it goes, but you will never get a musician to admit that it tells the whole story. The chemist may analyze the horse hair and the catgut, just as the physicist may count the vibrations producing the noise and just as the physician may measure the pulse and blood pressure of violinist and listener. As every true scientist knows well enough, these are descriptions, not explanations. The magic itself can neither be measured nor explained. I am persuaded that it is real magic, and that as often as we experience it, we stand on the very threshold of the door which, if we could push it ajar, would reveal in an instant the awful simplicity of the secret of the world.

II

In the second place, I believe that human life and human beings are of more than delusive importance. We have frequently been admonished in recent years to avoid the arrogance into which our ancestors fell by supposing that they lived in an egocentric universe. I pass over the fact that there is a sense in which everybody lives, and always will live, in an egocentric universe, just as every observer sees, and always will see, an egocentric rainbow. The purpose of the admonition is, however, to remind us that there was a time when even educated people believed that the earth was not only the center of what we now call the solar system, but was the center of the entire cosmos; and that the sun and moon had been set in the sky by the Creator for no other purpose than to provide light for the inhabitants of the earth. At a later time Carlyle, seeking to preach humility to his readers, was at pains to point out that in the "Palace of the Eternal . . . our sun is but a porch lamp." It now appears that this figure of speech is absurdly flattering to the sun. The sun is not a porch lamp in a palace; it is a grain of dust so small that its size in relation to that of the palace can only be expressed in figures which, for all practical purposes, are incomprehensible. Indeed, if the entire solar system were destroyed, as perhaps it will be during the course of this address, it can hardly be said that the structure of the palace would be changed.

Now I think it almost unnecessary to say that I do not question any of those facts. I suggest, however, that we have been too ready to suppose that there is some necessary connection between size and importance.

In the year of my graduation from college I read with a sort of instinctive sympathy the passage in *Orthodoxy* in which Gilbert K. Chesterton paid his respects to the modern love for "expansion and largeness." Said Chesterton:

Herbert Spencer would have been greatly annoyed if any one had called him an imperialist, and therefore it is highly regrettable that nobody did. But he was an imperialist of the lowest type. He popularized this contemptible notion that the size of the solar system ought to over-awe the spiritual dogma of man. Why should a man surrender his dignity to the solar system any more than to a whale? If mere size proves that man is not the image of God, then a whale may be the image of God; a somewhat formless image; what one might call an impressionist portrait. It is quite futile to argue that man is small compared to the cosmos; for man was always small compared to the nearest tree. But Herbert Spencer, in his headlong imperialism, would insist that we had in some way been conquered and annexed by the astronomical universe.[1]

Twenty years after this passage was written Professor Eddington published his book, *The Nature of the Physical World*. In the course of it he considers the possibility of the existence of life on some of the planets in our solar system, such as Venus and Mars. These, he thinks, would fail us if we were on a house-hunting expedition, but he reminds us that "there remain some thousands of millions of stars which we have been accustomed to regard as suns ruling attendant systems of planets." It seems to him "a presumption, bordering almost on impiety, to deny to them life of the same order of creation as ourselves"; yet in the end he dares to commit the presumption and denies the life. He concludes as follows:

[1] *Orthodoxy*, pp. 110–111.

A further point arises if we have especially in mind contemporaneous life. The time during which man has been on the earth is extremely small compared with the age of the earth or of the sun. There is no obvious physical reason why, having once arrived, man should not continue to populate the earth for another ten billion years or so; but—well, can you contemplate it? Assuming that the stage of highly developed life is a very small fraction of the inorganic history of the star, the rival earths are in general places where conscious life has already vanished or is yet to come. I do not think that the whole purpose of the Creation has been staked on the one planet where we live; and in the long run we cannot deem ourselves the only race that has been or will be gifted with the mystery of consciousness. But I feel inclined to claim that *at the present time* our race is supreme; and not one of the profusion of stars in their myriad clusters looks down on scenes comparable to those which are passing beneath the rays of the sun.[2]

I present this claim to you for no more than it is worth—for no more than an evaluation of probabilities by a distinguished astronomer. I do not mean to labor the point, but if the claim is sound—if, as we face each other this evening, "our race is supreme"—I cannot escape the conclusion that the ideas of our ancestors about human preeminence and human dignity were less egregiously wide of the mark than is sometimes made to appear.

Let us be chastened by our realization that ten billion years ago human beings did not exist and that in "another ten billion years or so"—I like these loose astronomical numbers—they will have ceased to be. But in the meantime let us not be too much impressed by dimensions and distances. It has been wisely said that the size of the stars is less wonderful than the fact that man has measured them.

That human life and human destiny are of real—I do not say of paramount—importance is indeed taken for granted in all art and in all scholarship. It was taken for granted by the great and

[2] *The Nature of the Physical World*, pp. 175, 178.

forgotten artists and artisans who built the cathedral at Chartres and who, as Henry Adams tells us, were content to place some of their most beautiful work where it was unlikely that any human eye would ever see it. It has been taken for granted by the countless scholars of the past—men like Browning's Grammarian who

> Gave us the doctrine of the enclitic De,
> Dead from the waist down.

It is taken for granted by the equally self-effacing scholars of today who in a hundred universities such as this one are devoting their lives to minute and laborious tasks in the faith that as each task is completed "one stone the more swings into place" in the growing edifice of truth. For all such men, living and dead, the appropriate epitaph must be found in the often-quoted lines of George Herbert—

> Who sweeps a room as for Thy laws,
> Makes that and the action fine.

May I say parenthetically that I am afraid that not all the work done in our graduate schools comes up to this standard. Not long ago I read of a professor in an American university who read a paper before a conference of psychologists entitled the "Origin and Nature of Common Annoyances." In the first instance this scholar noted 21,000 kinds of annoyances, which, after deducting duplications and "spurious annoyances" (whatever they are) were reduced to 507. To this residue of 507 the author was able to assign grades—26 marks for "hair in food," 2 for "the sight of a bald head," and 24 for "cockroaches." I am inclined to doubt whether the nature of this paper was such as to add anything to the edifice of truth. Moreover, I cannot refrain from adding that I do not agree with the conclusions announced. Hair in food as compared to cockroaches (at least if they are not in food) annoys me in a ratio much greater than that of 26 to 24, and it is perhaps a fortunate circumstance that the sight of a bald head does not annoy me at all.

Before leaving this branch of my subject I propose to touch on a possible objection—if for no better reason than to show that I realize that such an objection may be made. I have spoken of human life and human beings as important, and I may be asked what I mean by the word "important." I cannot attempt to answer this question within the time at my disposal, but I can at least suggest the direction in which I believe the answer is to be found.

It has been said in the past by disinterested and high-minded men and it will be said in the future by men equally disinterested and high-minded that the universe in general and life on this planet in particular must be regarded as the results of what may best be described as an accident within an accident—a major and cosmic accident in the first instance and a minor and terrestrial one in the second; that there is nowhere in the universe intelligence, purpose, or plan; that the only meaning in beauty is that the number of people who have derived pleasure from looking at the Parthenon is greater than the number of people who have derived pleasure from looking at the average New York tenement house; and that the only meaning in morality is that, for various and recurring reasons, tribal customs harden into prohibitions and taboos.

Now I do not accept these assumptions and I use the word advisedly—I think they are assumptions. But if I did accept them, I agree unreservedly that the word "importance" is stripped of any practical significance. Without the concepts which the assumptions negative—without a universe containing somewhere within it both intelligence and purpose, without standards, without what Plato would perhaps have called absolutes—I agree with the Macbeth of the fifth act—

> Life . . . is a tale
> Told by an idiot, full of sound and fury,
> Signifying nothing.

There is one depth below the cosmic pessimism which I have just attempted to describe. If you are engaged in the study of epistemology, you may have concluded that the human mind is an instrument incapable of correct thinking. You may perhaps have come to the state of mind of the disciples of Pyrrho, who doubted whether they doubted. You may even have come to the state of mind of the Chinese philosopher who said that he had once dreamed that he was a butterfly and that since that time he had never been able to decide whether he was a man who had dreamed he was a butterfly or a butterfly who was in the act of dreaming he was a man.

Upon these doubts I propose to make two comments—the one subjective, the other empirical and founded upon the lessons of history. The subjective comment is that if my mind is incapable of correct thinking, I question whether it is capable of passing judgment on its own incapacity. The historical comment is that whenever men begin to doubt whether they doubt, or to doubt whether they are men or butterflies, the barbarians are at the gates. If the doubters were wise, they would welcome the barbarians, if only in the interest of a reinvigorated certitude. There is, I believe, no instance of a healthy barbarian who was uncertain whether he was a man or a butterfly.

III

In the third place,[3] and finally—by a transition which seems to me so obvious as to be almost inevitable—I believe in America. I have expressed certain convictions about the dignity of man and about scholarship and art. In the long run all of these ideas are no more than illusions except upon a single condition. That condition is liberty. All history shows that it is a sound tradition

---

[3] A small part of what follows is based on certain chapters in the author's book, *The Country Lawyer: Essays in Democracy* (Philadelphia: University of Pennsylvania Press, 1938).

which affirms that the cornerstone of all liberty is political liberty.

Let me assure you that no man deprecates more than I do a flamboyant type of patriotism. We Americans, indeed, live in the vicinity of too many glass houses to permit us to indulge in the indiscriminate throwing of stones. During all or most of our national existence we have been too much preoccupied with material advantages. Our peace of mind and our national security are vexed by problems—economic, racial, and social—which we have solved inadequately or failed to solve at all. We have wasted our resources with a callous indifference which is worse than prodigality. In these connections and in a hundred others we have left undone those things which we ought to have done, and we have done those things which we ought not to have done.

But there is health in us. Through the medium of a common language we have established over half a continent the factual basis without which democracy cannot exist—a working degree of unanimity about great matters and a willingness to compromise about small ones. Over the length and breadth of this vast territory we have extended and developed the special sort of democracy which our fathers set up. During the course of a century and a half we have, I think—and I speak deliberately—brought liberty and opportunity to more persons than have enjoyed them during any like period of time since civilization began. I will go a step farther—for the time being, at least, the preservation of liberty on this planet seems to me to rest very largely in our hands.

In the light of that responsibility, let us not deceive ourselves by the comforting assumption that, as a result of some constitutional miracle, we have placed ourselves beyond the reach of arbitrary power—an assumption which is as offensive to the theory of politics as it is offensive to common sense.

It is true enough that the Congress of the United States is without power to inflict "cruel and unusual punishments"; that the President of the United States may not, by arbitrary fiat, attack the lives or property of his political opponents; and that if either of these usurpations were attempted, the act of usurpation would be declared void by a decree of the Supreme Court. But the Congress, the President, and the Supreme Court are no more than organs of the government, endowed with constitutional powers and subject to constitutional limitations. Since the days of the Medes and the Persians no people has been so foolish as to suppose that there can be such a thing, in logic or in fact, as a law or a constitution which cannot be amended. If a constitutional provision set up the Supreme Court, a constitutional provision can strike it down. If the Constitution itself was lawfully adopted, it can be lawfully repealed. The first axiom of politics is that in every sovereign state there must be somewhere absolute, arbitrary, and unlimited power, and that from the exercise of this power neither the subject of a despotism nor the citizen of a democracy has any lawful protection or can take any lawful appeal.

Not long ago Mr. Douglas Jerrold, an Englishman with Fascist sympathies, said that there was nothing within the competence of dictatorships which was not also within the competence of democracies, and that the only reason we do not persecute Jews in the democracies is because we do not wish to do so. Mr. Jerrold was well answered in an American periodical that while it is no better than a truism to say that the American people could persecute Jews if they wished to do so, the difference between the America in which we are living and the Germany of Hitler is that in Germany Hitler can persecute Jews whether the German people wish to do so or not.

It is a real difference, which turns not on the existence of absolute power, but rather on the source of it. "All power," says the Constitution of my own state, in words which fairly express the political philosophy underlying the Constitution of the United States as well, "is inherent in the people and all free governments are founded on their authority and instituted for their peace, safety and happiness. For the advancement of these ends they have at all times an inalienable and indefeasible right to alter, reform or abolish their government in such manner as they may think proper." "The people," said John Marshall in *Cohens* v. *Virginia,* "made the constitution, and the people can unmake it. It is the creature of their will, and lives only by their will. But this supreme and irresistible power to make or unmake, resides only in the whole body of the people; not in any subdivision of them." It is not, therefore, on the variety and richness of our natural resources, however impressive; it is not on the achievements and sacrifices of our fathers, however memorable; it is not on any paper constitution, however justly revered—it is on the tolerance, the wisdom, and the courage of the whole body of our people that the future of democracy and liberty depends.

There is a story about a priest and a minister who had served together as chaplains during the World War. On the day of their discharge the priest said to his friend: "I am afraid that before the war I had a bigoted prejudice against Protestants. I have lost all of that prejudice. We may never meet again but I shall never forget you. As often as I think of you I shall take pleasure in realizing that you are serving God in *your* way, while I am serving Him in *His* way." I think it is a perfectly tolerant statement. The essence of tolerance is not doubt, but charity and a sense of fair play. The ways of the dictators are not our ways and their thoughts are not our thoughts. I have no wish to minimize the sharpness of the issue which exists; still less have I any wish to compromise it.

To speak of tolerance at Jefferson's university is, indeed, to carry coals to Newcastle, but I am tempted to add one observation with which I feel sure that your founder would be in full accord: if the premises of democracy are ill-founded, "Chaos is come again." But if they are not ill-founded—if, to use the words of Jefferson himself, "freedom of discussion, unaided by power" is "sufficient for the propagation and protection of truth"—it is both illogical and stupid to dissipate our energies and belie our principles by the persecution of those propagandists, whether Communist or Fascist, who, under the protection of the federal Constitution, are attempting to sell their political wares in our markets. Some of you will remember the words of Gamaliel. He was speaking of men who taught what seemed to be so revolutionary a doctrine that certain of their countrymen took counsel to slay them. He said,

Take heed to yourselves what ye intend to do as touching these men. For before these days rose up Theudas, boasting himself to be somebody; to whom a number of men, about four hundred, joined themselves: who was slain; and all, as many as obeyed him, were scattered, and brought to nought. After this man rose up Judas of Galilee in the days of the taxing, and drew away much people after him; he also perished; and all, even as many as obeyed him, were dispersed. And now I say unto you, Refrain from these men, and let them alone: for if this counsel or this work be of men, it will come to nought; But if it be of God, ye cannot overthrow it; lest haply ye be found even to fight against God.

Gamaliel was a conservative. The fact that he was a conservative at that particular time and place shows that he lacked vision. But he was a good democrat for all that, and his doctrine is our doctrine.

I have said that I believe in America. That belief is the justification for even longer views.

On February 15, 1913, Mr. Justice Holmes, who was both a great patriot and a great jurist, addressed the Harvard Law School Association of New York. He concluded as follows in words which seem to me extraordinarily prophetic:

For most of the things that properly can be called evils in the present state of the [world] I think the main remedy, as for the evils of public opinion, is for us to grow more civilized.

If I am right, it will be a slow business for our people to reach rational views, assuming that we are allowed to work peaceably to that end. But as I grow older, I grow calm. If I feel what are perhaps an old man's apprehensions, that competition from new races will cut deeper than working men's disputes and will test whether we can hang together and can fight; if I fear that we are running through the world's resources at a pace that we cannot keep; I do not lose my hopes. I do not pin my dreams for the future to my country or even to my race. I think it probable that civilization somehow will last as long as I care to look ahead—perhaps with smaller numbers, but perhaps also bred to greatness and splendor by science. I think it not improbable that man, like the grub that prepares a chamber for the winged thing it never has seen but is to be —that man may have cosmic destinies that he does not understand. And so beyond the vision of battling races and an impoverished earth I catch a dreaming glimpse of peace.

The other day my dream was pictured to my mind. It was evening. I was walking homeward on Pennsylvania Avenue near the Treasury, and as I looked beyond Sherman's Statue to the west the sky was aflame with scarlet and crimson from the setting sun. But, like the note of downfall in Wagner's opera, below the sky line there came from little globes the pallid discord of the electric lights. And I thought to myself the Götterdämmerung will end, and from those globes clustered like evil eggs will come the new masters of the sky. It is like the time in which we live. But then I remembered the faith that I partly have expressed, faith in a universe not measured by our fears, a universe that has thought and more than thought inside of it, and as I gazed, after the sunset and above the electric lights there shone the stars.[4]

Young gentlemen, on what I hope is, for you at least, a memorable occasion, I bid you welcome to membership in the Phi Beta Kappa Society.

[4] *Collected Legal Papers* (New York: Harcourt, Brace and Howe, 1920), pp. 296–297.

MARJORIE HOPE NICOLSON

The Romance of Scholarship

FROM the undergraduate point of view, I am sure, the title I
have chosen will seem either irony or paradox. At your age you
should and do know a good deal about "romance," but one of
the last things with which you are likely to associate it is "scholarship." "Romance" is a light, a charming word. In spite of teachers
whom you admire and respect, "scholarship" is likely to seem a
heavy word. The layman has inherited from literature, particularly from satire, a picture of the scholar as a pedant, an elderly
man (usually with thick glasses) spending his life in a dusty
library, reading books which only a bookworm has visited before
him, a man, as has often been said, who devotes his life to knowing more and more about less and less, perhaps like Browning's
Grammarian:

> He settled *Hoti's* business—let it be!—
> Properly based *Oun*,
> Gave us the doctrine of the enclitic *De*,
> Dead from the waist down.

Delivered before the Alpha of Michigan, University of Michigan, in
1940; originally given at the Barnard College semicentennial and subse-
quently at Scripps College in 1952. Published in *The Humanities at
Scripps College* (Los Angeles, 1952).

I am told that Browning is a forgotten poet today. My own college generation was enthusiastic about him, and I am quite sure that some of my undergraduate feeling about the scholar as a learned pedant came from "The Grammarian's Funeral":

> So he gowned him,
> Straight got by heart that book to its last page;
> Learned we found him.
> Yea, but we found him bald too, eyes like lead,
> Accents uncertain. . . .
> Back to his book then; deeper dropped his head:
> *Calculus* racked him:
> Leaden before, his eyes grew dross of lead:
> *Tussis* attacked him.

One need not understand Browning's classico-medical puns to get a clear picture of the Grammarian. But even in youth I realized that that old scholar was a symbol of something else to the disciples who carried him to his grave on the mountaintop, chanting the exultant last lines:

> Here's the top-peak; the multitude below
> Live, for they can, there;
> This man decided not to Live but Know—
> Bury this man there. . . .
> Loftily lying,
> Leave him—still loftier than the world suspects,
> Living and dying.

In spite of what the world believed, the Grammarian *lived* and lived richly. But it is not that type of scholar with which I am primarily concerned, but with lesser fry like myself, as I set out on my task to try to show you that "scholarship" is not all baldness and spectacles and old age and great erudition. There is no one of your teachers who does not know that scholarship is *adventure*—even more, that it is often *fun*.

Many years ago I set out on my first great adventure which

opened up to me a world of enchantment. I had taken my doctor's degree at Yale and had been teaching at Goucher and studying at the Hopkins, when I read in the newspapers about a new foundation established by Senator Guggenheim in memory of his dead son: the Guggenheim Foundation, which offered fellowships for foreign travel and study to young scholars. Today fellowships and scholarships are common, and foreign study and travel within the reach of many. It is not uncommon for undergraduates to spend "the Junior Year Abroad"; every year hundreds of young men and women just out of college receive Fulbright Fellowships; and other great foundations—like the Rockefeller, the Ford, the American Council of Learned Societies—offer all sorts of opportunities unheard of in my generation. I could not believe what I read in that newspaper announcement, and I still did not believe it when I ventured to apply for a fellowship. The competition was less keen then than now, but it was still with a feeling that it was all incredible that I read the letter saying that I had been appointed. I wonder whether you can imagine how it seemed to me: in those days Guggenheim Fellowships paid twenty-five hundred dollars—more than the total annual salary I was receiving as an assistant professor. It was all incredible and overwhelming, and even when the letter-of-credit arrived, I still felt there must be some mistake. "This could not be I!" We have become so accustomed to the vast generosity of foundations today that there are some who take such generosity for granted: someone owes them a living, someone owes them a fellowship. I myself have never forgotten, and I hope I shall never forget, the fact that the Guggenheim Foundation owed me nothing—and it gave me everything that was to matter in my professional life.

I had been to Europe once before. As a tourist I had seen the cities and the countryside, paintings and sculpture, cottages and cathedrals. This time I saw all these again, to be sure, but most of my time was spent in buildings which the tourist seldom sees

—libraries. The tourist, to be sure, usually visits the British Museum if for nothing else than to see the Elgin Marbles. But the path of the tourist ends where that of the scholar-adventurer begins: at those swinging doors marked "FOR READERS ONLY." Long before the tourists arrive in the morning, even before the great outer doors of the Museum open, the scholars begin to congregate on the steps, each eager to be the first arrival in order that he may claim the seat he feels his own—and woe betide any unwary casual reader who happens to take the seat of a "regular reader"! I can see them yet in my memory—the motley crew of early-morning scholars of my own *wanderjahr*, some of them familiar to generations of Museum readers. Some of your teachers will remember them as vividly as do I. There was, for instance, the elderly Negro (his hair was grizzled in my time) who, rumor said, had never missed a day at his desk in fifteen years, during which time he drew out daily the same pile of books, all on elementary arithmetic. There was the very corpulent priest who, we knew, was compiling a bibliography, who seemed never to read books but only to read their titles in those great folio volumes which constitute the catalogue of the British Museum. Evidently he was as nearsighted as he was tall, so that he bent double over the volumes. He has gone down in history in an amusing caricature of "a reader finding his way through the catalogue by sense of *smell* only!" My own favorite was a demure little elderly woman in bonnet and shawl who might well have been a returned missionary of the Victorian era. She carried an old-fashioned reticule, and every-hour-on-the-hour she drew out a flask from which she gulped a satisfying draught of something that certainly was not tea.

One could understand the little bonneted woman better as the winter days set in, the Museum daily colder, the pea-souper fog outside settling into the reading room so that the domed roof was obscured, spoiled Americans shivering as they looked forward to teatime when they might feel a momentary warmth.

But there was not one of us reading there, I am sure, who did not feel the romance of that place even in the worst possible weather. Sometimes I would stop my work, flexing my fingers which were stiff with cold and cramped with copying, to think of that great host of readers of the past who had preceded us— for the library is far more venerable than the present building, which was a century old when I was working there. I thought of Lamb and Coleridge, who had used some of the books I myself was using. On more than one occasion I had found those characteristic marginalia of Coleridge, in the writing of which he enriched the library by breaking all library rules. Where, I wondered, had Karl Marx sat when he was developing the ideas which were to revolutionize the world far more than we realized in the 1920's. Surely even Marx must have been grateful for the wealth of the British Museum. Around me in dim recesses which I had never penetrated stretched, I knew, some fifty-five miles of shelves, bearing more than three million volumes of that fabulous library. For a time I was content with the treasures I was finding in books. Later I was to discover even greater romance in the great manuscript collection of that library.

Is there, I wonder, any greater charm to a lover of the past than is found in manuscripts? Nothing in my undergraduate or graduate training had prepared me for the excitement that was to come as I began to discover and piece together the correspondence of men and women who had lived nearly three centuries before.

The subject on which I was engaged was of little importance to anyone except myself—"scholarly" projects usually are not! I was seeking the correspondence of a minor philosopher of the seventeenth century, Henry More, the Cambridge Platonist. Many of his letters were in the British Museum—that much I knew. I shall not forget my shock when a volume of his manuscript letters was laid before me. I opened them eagerly—only to realize that I could not read a word of them! At no time in my graduate training had I ever worked with manuscripts, and my knowledge of different "hands" was only theoretical. The "Elizabethan hand," for example, is as unintelligible at first glance as is German script, and while More himself did not write an Elizabethan hand, his predecessors—equally necessary for my purposes—did. I had to stop and put myself to school all over again, studying until at length I could decode those handwritings. When I came back to my manuscripts, I discovered that the real trouble with Henry More's writing was one I shared—for my correspondents speak acrimoniously about what President Neilson used to call my "interesting but entirely illegible writing." Not only was Henry More's writing almost illegible, but —thrifty as he was—he wrote all over the margins of his pages, and sometimes turned the paper upside down and wrote between the lines. He had another habit which I shared until he cured me of it—he seldom dated his letters, other than to write "Monday" or "Wednesday," so that his letters were in no logical or chronological order, but had to be dated by internal evidence, with blood, sweat, and tears on my part. Gradually, however, his hand became as familiar to me as that of any of my friends; gradually, too, order began to emerge from the chaos of his letters, and I could begin to surmise the richness of the story I had discovered. Here was a tale of Platonic love between a philosopher and a noble lady who were perhaps the last people in history who really understood what "Platonic love" meant. Here was a story of adventure and travel, of discovery of things but even more of ideas, bringing together on a broad canvas poets and philosophers, Quakers and charlatans, spiritists and scientists: William Harvey, discoverer of the circulation of the blood; Sir Theodore Mayerne, who introduced calomel into England and was the physician of three kings; scientists such as Robert Boyle, Thomas Willis, Isaac Newton; philosophers such as Descartes, Hobbes, Leibniz, Cudworth; Quakers such as William Penn, George Fox, George Keith; not least, one of the most universal characters of an age of universality, Francis Mercury van Helmont, alchemist, chemist, philosopher, adventurer, and the original Scholar Gypsy. Always in the midst of them, the center of the whole group, was a great lady, a woman who suffered from an incurable malady all her life, yet wrote an original philosophical treatise praised by the leading philosophers of her day, the Lady Anne Conway.

It is not the story that is of importance, however. What I remember best is the excitement of the chase, as I sought throughout England for the missing letters that would complete the story I could only guess from the one-sided correspondence with which I started. It was then that I came to understand the excitement and the adventure of the scholar's life—which often seems so drab and dull to the world outside the library. It was then, too, that I discovered the frustration, the hours of toil that seemingly led to nothing, the dead-end streets ending in a sign: "Turn back; no passing here." Let me give you an example. I started with known letters of Henry More, which he wrote to others; but what of the letters others wrote to him? I knew he had kept them—particularly those of Lady Conway—for they were mentioned in his will. But I could find no record of them in any library catalogue. Since he spent his whole life as a Fellow of Christ's College in Cambridge, it seemed as if some of his papers should be there—and there I started that part of my search. The librarian of Christ's was an elderly man who felt little need of a catalogue—since his memory *was* the catalogue. He assured me peremptorily (for he did not approve of women-scholars, particularly American barbarians) that there were no More manuscripts in the Christ's College Library. For four months I sought to track those manuscripts down, going to Somerset House to read wills, studying old catalogues of sales of books and manuscripts, using every device I could think of to find those missing links. At last I tracked some of the papers down to the beginning of this century, at which time they had been in the possession of someone named Robinson, of whom I knew nothing except that he was a clergyman. I wrote to dozens of clergymen of the name of Robinson, and finally after many weeks discovered that the person I sought was a very distinguished gentleman indeed, Dean Armitage Robinson of Wells Cathedral. Eagerly I went to see him. Had he by chance purchased any letters written to or by Henry More? He had, indeed. Breathlessly I asked what had become of them. "Oh," replied Dean Robinson, "naturally I put them where they belonged— in the library of Christ's College!" Four months after I had begun my search I was back right where I started. The librarian still insisted he had no such papers, but his insistence was surpassed only by my persistence. I found my dust-covered papers where they had fallen on a shelf behind some old folio volumes. I had no reason to regret the lost time, which was not wasted, in part because I had learned by practical experience much that I could never have learned in a classroom, in part because the chase had led me from library to library throughout the length and breadth of England and had all been fun and excitement.

I wish there were time to tell you many of those adventures that made the whole experience exciting, but I must deliberately limit myself only to one or two. I wish I could take some of you with me to the Public Record Office in London, that great repository of all State Papers. For years it was the natural Mecca of students of political history, but only in my own generation has it become a haunt of students of literature. It was there that Professor Leslie Hotson discovered the legal papers which finally solved a three-hundred-year-old mystery which might be called "The Strange Case of the Death of Christopher Marlowe." I remember vividly the paper Professor Hotson wrote for *The Atlantic Monthly* in which he described his emotions late one afternoon when after a search of many months he held in his hands a legal document which gave the clue to the mystery of the death of the great poet-dramatist who was killed in a tavern brawl. Just as he started to read it the bell rang, indicating the end of the day at the Public Record Office—a sound as final as that of the Trump of Doom. Without having had time to read the document, out staggered the professor, afraid to walk along the streets for fear he might be hit by a car or bus before he knew the answer to the puzzle, afraid even to go to bed that night since, as Mark Twain said, most people die in their beds, spending the longest night of his life waiting until the Record Office reopened in the morning. Morning came at last and with it the end of a chaper and the end of a search and an answer to the problem that had teased scholars for nearly three centuries.

The Public Record Office is not imposing. Indeed at first sight it seems very small in comparison with the reading room of the British Museum. The press of scholars is to be there early enough to get near the fire which heats the chilly rooms. At high rostrums stand scholars working in early fields whose materials come in long rolls—like gargantuan ticker tape. The manuscripts used by workers in fields like mine come to the reader in "bundles"—just bundles tied up in strong butcher-paper, wrapped with cord that always seems perversely to knot itself in fancy sailors' knots. One opens the bundle with growing excitement: certain political papers, one knows in advance, will be there, for they have been "calendared" (that is, published in brief digest form in the *Calendars of State Papers*). It is not for the "calendared" papers that the literary student looks, but for all sorts of other documents which may or may not be there, far more interesting to us than the political papers. Let me give you an example. The father-in-law of my Lady Conway, the first Viscount Conway, had been twice Secretary of State. I knew from the *Calendars* that many of his political papers were in the Public Record Office; it was my hope that included with them might be letters and documents of a much more personal nature.

I was richly rewarded, for in bundle after bundle I found the personal letters of a most charming and amusing gentleman who corresponded with a host of people, who seemed to have known everyone worth knowing in his day, who was a gourmet, and who had an eye for the ladies. Here were his order books, kept by a steward who ordered from abroad all sorts of gifts for the ladies, every kind of delicacy that could be imported. My Lord Conway liked the rich foods he ordered so lavishly; that was clear, for as the food-orders grew, so too did Lord Conway, as I discovered when the steward noted that the tailor reported he must make his Lordship's breeches two inches larger than before. Lord Conway's was an impish humor, as his correspondents knew, and his personal letters sparkle with wit and irony. Among his correspondents was Sir Walter Raleigh's son, Garew, who had been with his father in the Tower during the imprisonment. On one occasion the younger Raleigh sent Conway a bundle of old medical recipes which he said had been his father's, and on another occasion he mentioned having in his possession many "verses and other discourses" of his father—papers which have now disappeared, probably forever. The most amusing letters in my bundles were those Lord Conway exchanged with that extraordinary character Sir Kenelm Digby, scientist, philosopher, man of letters, great lover, and Exhibitionist-in-Chief of the seventeenth century, who, married to the most beautiful woman of the time, sought to preserve her beauty by strange brews until—rumor said—he killed what he loved, inadvertently poisoning his wife. Dozens—even hundreds—of personal letters with their human stories of past ages lie in the Public Record Office, unpublished and often unread since their authors penned them and their correspondents received them two or three centuries ago.

From London my pursuit of lost letters led me to many parts of England. Sometimes I stopped in small towns or villages to read parish registers, in small libraries in churches—in some of which I found the old "locked" books (often Bibles) fastened with chains so they could be read but not taken from the library.

More than once I was fortunate enough to find one of those antiquarians—often a local rector—who knew the local history of the parish, inheriting much of it from oral tradition that had come down for generations. Small libraries as well as great ones: in nearly all I had the same experience of being received with courtesy and kindness. Once in a while, to be sure, I found a dour old curmudgeon who objected to taking books from the shelves—largely, I gathered, because he thought that books belonged on shelves and not in the hands of itinerant scholars— but that was rare indeed. More and more I came to realize the goodly fellowship of scholars; that I was an unknown young person from a foreign country (and of the wrong sex) mattered not at all to most of them. I was a "scholar," and they—scholars in their way—did everything they could to further my pursuit. And always along the way came adventures and amusement.

I like to remember a day at Christ's College, Cambridge, after I had found my letters and had settled in and finally broken down the prejudices of the old librarian, so that he no longer objected to my youth or sex or nationality, but even shared his fire with me. I was waited upon by the college architect with a request that I visit one of the halls which had been built before the Civil War, all the records of which had been lost at the time the soldiers were quartered there in the 1640's. Because I had been reading so many letters of the period, he thought it possible that I might be able to identify some of the initials which students then as now had cut into the woodwork, or give him other clues as to who had lived in which room in the seventeenth century. All the fellows and dons were there to greet me; in twenty-three different rooms I was regaled with twenty-three cups of tea and twenty-three slices of what seemed the same tea-cakes. I know of Samuel Johnson's capacity for tea, which was greater than mine. I know too that since that day I have never drunk a cup of tea if I could possibly avoid it.

So the year went on and gradually my story took on form and

shape. From a chaos of crumbling letters, petitions, bills, and order books, from torn and faded journals and diaries, from wills, from commonplace books and college records, scattered throughout England, one character after another emerged in clear outline against a background of stirring events. It was a tale told against the background of one of the greatest periods in history, when the cannon thundered and England beheaded a king, when plague and pestilence and the Great Fire threatened to put an end to the London of the past, when that gallant city rose like a Phoenix from the ashes, as she was to rise from more terrible devastation in the twentieth century. It was an age when men everywhere, emerging from a narrower, more circumscribed, safer world, were questioning their beliefs; when the boundaries of the universe were enlarging as never before as the "new astronomy" destroyed those *flammantia moenia mundi* of the past; when a man, looking through a telescope, discovered universes of which men had never dreamed; when new philosophy called all in doubt and men, finding their old values challenged, strove to build new values. Repercussions of all the many revolutions in that Century of Revolutions I found in my papers and letters. But all these things I had known before. What was new to me was the human side of a great century. As time went on, these men and women of the past became as real to me as any friends of the present—more real perhaps because I knew them more intimately than one knows most friends. I had known that Lady Conway was a philosopher; I discovered her now as a woman—a woman who proudly made new curtains for her bedroom, only to find them too short so that she had to piece them; a woman who was as pleased as any woman of any age with her new "muffe and cambrick." I knew all the medical treatments that were used for those excruciating headaches of hers, and followed with sympathy the gradual change in her handwriting as "fitt" after "fitt" of devastating illness laid her low. I knew when her only child was born and when it died in infancy. I knew that each coach her husband ordered that she might take the air had to be specially made, each one "softlier" than the one before, until the time came when she could no longer leave her house. I was with her when she became a Quaker —a shocking matter for a lady of quality in her day, and when she surrounded herself with Quaker handmaids, because, as she poignantly said, they were a "suffering" people, and they were a "quiet" people. I seemed to be at her great home in Ragley when death came gradually, and a steward who loved her—as everyone who knew her loved her—set down day by day, then hour by hour, the account of her last illness. I knew how the great Van Helmont preserved her body in "spirits of alcohol" in a glass coffin so that her husband—abroad in Ireland—might see her again, and how she was finally laid to rest in the little village cemetery in a plain leaden casket on which someone scratched her only epitaph: "Quaker Lady."

And so at last I came to the end of my year—the end of my search. I had left until the last the great hall at Ragley which was her home, and which I seemed to have seen built, as she watched its building. It was a Sunday afternoon when a member of the family that now owns Ragley (the Conway line was extinct in the seventeenth century) took me into the house. I went into the bedroom where once had hung those curtains, pieced because they were too short. I went into the library and took down one after another books that I knew would be there. I stopped particularly over the volumes of his works which Henry More had sent her, each in its special binding ("volumes something handsomelyer bound up for your Ladiship"). I recognized some pieces of furniture she had bought, saw some familiar pictures on the walls and missed others that had once been there. I had come home to a great hall which long was home to Anne Conway, which was the home-from-home of Henry More, who spent all his vacations there, which was a home too to such Quakers as William Penn and George Keith and George Fox. The shadow of the Scholar Gypsy—who had ceased his roving life for many years to minister to the comfort of a sick woman—was always around me.

Perhaps my guide became weary of my reminiscences which he could not share. At all events, at the end of the afternoon, he took me to a room I did not know—a room built in modern times, where no shadow of philosopher or lady or Scholar Gypsy could fall. It was a room in which they would not have been interested—a modern gun-room, filled with trophies of hunting and fishing. In the center of the room on a table was a glass case containing the skeleton of a tiny animal. "Here," said my guide, "is one mystery I wish you could solve." A few years before, he said, one of the greatest oaks at Ragley had been struck by lightning, and had been cut down. In the bole of that tree, preserved for many years, they found the skeleton of this little animal, which the curators of a great museum had told the family was that of a small dog, not native to England, a skeleton they estimated as being more than two hundred years old. Standing there in a modern gun-room of a great English estate, a young scholar from a foreign land experienced to the full the poignance, the mystery, the enchantment of scholarship which makes past and present one. My memory went back across dead centuries, as I realized that only I—and men and women dead for more than two hundred years—could know that that was Anne Conway's pet dog, which her brother had sent her from Italy, which had wandered away and been lost. I did not know whether it was recognition or remembrance, as I said: "That? Why, that is Julietto."

WALTER LIPPMANN

Education vs.
Western Civilization

IT was once the custom in the great universities to propound a series of theses which, as Cotton Mather put it, the student had to "defend manfully." I should like to revive this custom by propounding a thesis about the state of education in this troubled age.

The thesis which I venture to submit to you is as follows:

That during the past forty or fifty years those who are responsible for education have progressively removed from the curriculum of studies the Western culture which produced the modern democratic state;

That the schools and colleges have, therefore, been sending out into the world men who no longer understand the creative principle of the society in which they must live;

That, deprived of their cultural tradition, the newly educated Western men no longer possess in the form and substance of their own minds and spirits, the ideas, the premises, the rationale, the logic, the method, the values or the deposited wisdom which are the genius of the development of Western civilization;

Phi Beta Kappa address delivered before the American Association for the Advancement of Science, December 29, 1940. Published in *The American Scholar*, Spring, 1941.

132

That the prevailing education is destined, if it continues, to destroy Western civilization and is in fact destroying it;

That our civilization cannot effectively be maintained where it still flourishes, or be restored where it has been crushed, without the revival of the central, continuous, and perennial culture of the Western world;

And that, therefore, what is now required in the modern educational system is not the expansion of its facilities or the specific reform of its curriculum and administration but a thorough reconsideration of its underlying assumptions and of its purposes.

I realize quite well that this thesis constitutes a sweeping indictment of modern education. But I believe that the indictment is justified and that there is a *prima facie* case for entertaining this indictment.

Universal and compulsory modern education was established by the emancipated democracies during the nineteenth century. "No other sure foundation can be devised," said Thomas Jefferson, "for the preservation of freedom and happiness." Yet as a matter of fact during the twentieth century the generations trained in these schools have either abandoned their liberties or they have not known, until the last desperate moment, how to defend them. The schools were to make men free. They have been in operation for some sixty or seventy years and what was expected of them they have not done. The plain fact is that the graduates of the modern schools are the actors in the catastrophe which has befallen our civilization. Those who are responsible for modern education—for its controlling philosophy—are answerable for the results.

They have determined the formation of the mind and education of modern men. As the tragic events unfold, they cannot evade their responsibility by talking about the crimes and follies of politicians, business men, labor leaders, lawyers, editors and generals. They have conducted the schools and colleges and they have educated the politicians, business men, labor leaders, lawyers, editors and generals. What is more they have educated the educators.

They have had money, lots of it, fine buildings, big appropriations, great endowments and the implicit faith of the people that the school was the foundation of democracy. If the results are bad, and indubitably they are, on what ground can any of us who are in any way responsible for education disclaim our responsibility or decline to undertake a profound searching of our own consciences and a deep re-examination of our philosophy?

The institutions of the Western world were formed by men who learned to regard themselves as inviolable persons because they were rational and free. They meant by rational that they were capable of comprehending the moral order of the universe and their place in this moral order. They meant, when they regarded themselves as free, that within that order they had a personal moral responsibility to perform their duties and to exercise their corresponding rights. From this conception of the unity of mankind in a rational order the Western world has derived its conception of law—which is that all men and all communities of men and all authority among men are subject to law, and that the character of all particular laws is to be judged by whether they conform to or violate, approach or depart from, the rational order of the universe and of man's nature. From this conception of law was derived the idea of constitutional government and of the consent of the governed and of civil liberty. Upon this conception of law our own institutions were founded.

This, in barest outline, is the specific outlook of Western men. This, we may say, is the structure of the Western spirit. This is the formation which distinguishes it. The studies and the disciplines which support and form this spiritual outlook and habit are the creative cultural tradition of Europe and the Americas. In this tradition our world was made. By this tradition it must live. Without this tradition our world, like a tree cut off from its roots in the soil, must die and be replaced by alien and barbarous things.

It is necessary today in a discussion of this sort to define and identify what we mean when we speak of Western culture. This is in itself ominous evidence of what the official historian of Harvard University has called "the greatest educational crime of the century against American youth,—depriving him of his classical heritage." For there will be many, the victims of this educational crime, who will deny that there is such a thing as Western culture.

Yet the historic fact is that the institutions we cherish—and now know we must defend against the most determined and efficient attack ever organized against them—are the products of a culture which, as Gilson put it,

is essentially the culture of Greece, inherited from the Greeks by the Romans, transfused by the Fathers of the Church with the religious teachings of Christianity, and progressively enlarged by countless numbers of artists, writers, scientists and philosophers from the beginning of the Middle Ages up to the first third of the nineteenth century.

The men who wrote the American Constitution and the Bill of Rights were educated in schools and colleges in which the classic works of this culture were the substance of the curriculum. In these schools the transmission of this culture was held to be the end and aim of education.

Modern education, however, is based on a denial that it is necessary or useful or desirable for the schools and colleges to continue to transmit from generation to generation the religious and classical culture of the Western world. It is, therefore, much easier to say what modern education rejects than to find out what modern education teaches. Modern education rejects and excludes from the curriculum of necessary studies the whole religious tradition of the West. It abandons and neglects as no longer necessary the study of the whole classical heritage of the great works of great men.

Thus there is an enormous vacuum where until a few decades ago there was the substance of education. And with what is that vacuum filled? It is filled with the elective, eclectic, the specialized, the accidental and incidental improvisations and spontaneous curiosities of teachers and students. There is no common faith, no common body of principle, no common body of knowledge, no common moral and intellectual discipline. Yet the graduates of these modern schools are expected to form a civilized community. They are expected to govern themselves. They are expected to have a social conscience. They are expected to arrive by discussion at common purposes. When one realizes that they have no common culture, is it astounding that they have no common purpose? That they worship false gods? That only in war do they unite? That in the fierce struggle for existence they are tearing Western society to pieces? They are the graduates of an educational system in which, though attendance is compulsory, the choice of the subject matter of education is left to the imagination of college presidents, trustees and professors, or even to the whims of the pupils themselves. We have established a system of education in which we insist that while everyone must be educated, yet there is nothing in particular that an educated man must know.

For it is said that since the invention of the steam engine we live in a new era, an era so radically different from all preceding ages that the cultural tradition is no longer relevant, is in fact misleading. I submit to you that this is a rationalization, that this is a pretended reason for the educational void which we now call education. The real reason, I venture to suggest, is that we reject the religious and classical heritage, first, because to master it requires more effort than we are willing to compel ourselves to make, and, second, because it creates issues that are too deep and too contentious to be faced with equanimity. We have abolished the old curriculum because we are afraid of it, afraid to face any longer in a modern democratic society the severe discipline and the deep, disconcerting issues of the nature of the universe, and of man's place in it and of his destiny.

I recognize the practical difficulties and the political danger of raising these questions and I shall not offer you a quick and easy remedy. For the present discussion all I am concerned with is that we should begin to recognize the situation as it really is and that we should begin to search our hearts and consciences.

We must confess, I submit, that modern education has renounced the idea that the pupil must learn to understand himself, his fellow men and the world in which he is to live as bound together in an order which transcends his immediate needs and his present desires. As a result the modern school has become bound to conceive the world as a place where the child, when he grows up, must compete with other individuals in a struggle for existence. And so the education of his reason and of his will must be designed primarily to facilitate his career.

By separating education from the classical religious tradition the school cannot train the pupil to look upon himself as an inviolable person because he is made in the image of God. These very words, though they are the noblest words in our language, now sound archaic. The school cannot look upon society as a brotherhood arising out of a conviction that men are made in a common image. The teacher has no subject matter that even pretends to deal with the elementary and universal issues of human destiny. The graduate of the modern school knows only by accident and by hearsay whatever wisdom mankind has come to in regard to the nature of men and their destiny.

For the vital core of the civilized tradition of the West is by definition excluded from the curriculum of the modern, secular, democratic school. The school must sink, therefore, into being a mere training ground for personal careers. Its object must then be to equip individual careerists and not to form fully civilized men. The utility of the schools must then be measured by their success in equipping specialists for successful rivalry in the pursuit of their separate vocations. Their cultural ideal must then be to equip the individual to deal practically with immediate and discrete difficulties, to find by trial and error immediately workable and temporarily satisfactory expedients.

For if more than this were attempted the democratic secular school would have to regard the pupil as having in him not merely an ambition but a transcendent relationship that must regulate his ambition. The schools would have to regard science as the progressive discovery of this order in the universe. They would have to cultivate Western tradition and transmit it to the young, proving to them that this tradition is no mere record of the obsolete fallacies of the dead but that it is a deposit of living wisdom.

But the emancipated democracies have renounced the idea that the purpose of education is to transmit the Western culture. Thus there is a cultural vacuum, and this cultural vacuum was bound to produce, in fact it has produced, progressive disorder. For the more men have become separated from the spiritual heritage which binds them together, the more has education become egoist, careerist, specialist and asocial.

In abandoning the classical religious culture of the West the schools have ceased to affirm the central principle of the Western philosophy of life—that man's reason is the ruler of his appetites. They have reduced reason to the role of servant to man's appetites. The working philosophy of the emancipated democracies is, as a celebrated modern psychologist has put it, that "the instinctive impulses determine the *end* of all activities . . . and the most highly developed mind *is but* the instrument by which those impulses seek their satisfaction."

The logic of this conception of the human reason must lead progressively to a system of education which sharpens the acquisitive and domineering and possessive instincts. And in so far as the instincts, rather than reason, determine the ends of our activity the end of all activity must become the accumulation of power over men in the pursuit of the possession of things. So when parents and taxpayers in a democracy ask whether education is useful for life they tend by and large to mean by useful that which equips the pupil for a career which will bring him money and place and power.

The reduction of reason to an instrument of each man's personal career must mean also that education is emptied of its content. For what the careerist has to be taught are the data that he may need in order to succeed. Thus all subjects of study are in principle of equal value. There are no subjects which all men belonging to the same civilization need to study. In the realms of knowledge the student elects those subjects which will presumably equip him for success in his career; for the student there is then no such thing as a general order of knowledge which he is to possess in order that it may regulate his specialty.

And just as the personal ambition of the student rather than social tradition determines what the student shall learn, so the inquiry and the research of the scholar becomes more and more disconnected from any general and regulating body of knowledge.

It is this specialized and fundamentally disordered development of knowledge which has turned so much of man's science into the means of his own destruction. For as reason is regarded as no more than the instrument of men's desires, applied science inflates enormously the power of men's desires. Since reason is not the ruler of these desires, the power which science places in men's hands is ungoverned.

Quickly it becomes ungovernable. Science is the product of intelligence. But if the function of the intelligence is to be the instrument of the acquisitive, the possessive and the domineering impulses, then these impulses, so strong by nature, must become infinitely stronger when they are equipped with all the resources of man's intelligence.

That is why men today are appalled by the discovery that

when modern man fights he is the most destructive animal ever known on this planet; that when he is acquisitive he is the most cunning and efficient; that when he dominates the weak he has engines of oppression and of calculated cruelty and deception no antique devil could have imagined.

And, at last, education founded on the secular image of man must destroy knowledge itself. For if its purpose is to train the intelligence of specialists in order that by trial and error they may find a satisfying solution of particular difficulties, then each situation and each problem has to be examined as a novelty. This is supposed to be "scientific." But in fact it is a denial of that very principle which has made possible the growth of science.

For what enables men to know more than their ancestors is that they start with a knowledge of what their ancestors have already learned. They are able to do advanced experiments which increase knowledge because they do not have to repeat the elementary experiments. It is tradition which brings them to the point where advanced experimentation is possible. This is the meaning of tradition. This is why a society can be progressive only if it conserves its tradition.

The notion that every problem can be studied as such with an open and empty mind, without preconception, without knowing what has already been learned about it, must condemn men to a chronic childishness. For no man, and no generation of men, is capable of inventing for itself the arts and sciences of a high civilization. No one, and no one generation, is capable of rediscovering all the truths men need, of developing sufficient knowledge by applying a mere intelligence, no matter how acute, to mere observation, no matter how accurate. The men of any generation, as Bernard of Chartres put it, are like dwarfs seated on the shoulders of giants. If we are to "see more things than the ancients and things more distant" it is "due neither to the sharpness of our sight nor the greatness of our stature" but "simply because they have lent us their own."

For individuals do not have the time, the opportunity or the energy to make all the experiments and to discern all the significance that have gone into the making of the whole heritage of civilization. In developing knowledge men must collaborate with their ancestors. Otherwise they must begin, not where their ancestors arrived but where their ancestors began. If they exclude the tradition of the past from the curricula of the schools they make it necessary for each generation to repeat the errors rather than to benefit by the successes of its predecessors.

Having cut him off from the tradition of the past, modern secular education has isolated the individual. It has made him a careerist—without social connection—who must make his way—without benefit of man's wisdom—through a struggle in which there is no principle of order. This is the uprooted and incoherent modern "free man" that Mr. Bertrand Russell has so poignantly described, the man who sees

surrounding the narrow raft illumined by the flickering light of human comradeship, the dark ocean on whose rolling waves we toss for a brief hour; from the great night without, a chill blast breaks in upon our refuge; all the loneliness of humanity amid hostile forces is concentrated upon the individual soul, which must struggle alone, with what of courage it can command, against the whole weight of the universe that cares nothing for its hopes and fears.

This is what the free man, in reality merely the freed and uprooted and dispossessed man, has become. But he is not the stoic that Mr. Russell would have him be. To "struggle alone" is more than the freed man can bear to do. And so he gives up his freedom and surrenders his priceless heritage, unable as he is constituted to overcome his insoluble personal difficulties and to endure his awful isolation.

THEODORE M. GREENE

In Praise of Reflective Commitment

HOW, in an age of unreflective commitment on the one hand and of non-committal reflection on the other, can we achieve a faith which is both ardent and informed, a loyalty at once dynamic and enlightened? How can we escape the paralysis of disillusionment and cynicism and at the same time the dangerous blindness of barbaric loyalties and prejudice? How can we combine reason and belief, reflection and commitment? How, indeed, can we convince ourselves that reflective commitment is the great need of the hour, the test of sanity, the hall mark of human dignity, the criterion of culture, the only road to ultimate salvation?

This, I believe, is the crucial problem of our times. It is of course a perennial problem, as old as human reflection and dedication to ideal objectives. It has been comparatively unnoticed in some periods of our Western culture and has become acute in other periods. It is a problem frequently sensed today but seldom clearly formulated. If we can grasp its import and if we can somehow think our way to its solution, we need have

Delivered before the Delta of New York, Columbia University, June 2, 1941. Published in *The American Scholar*, Winter, 1941–1942.

no tragic misgivings even in the face of social upheaval and military disaster. If we fail to do so, the most successful marshalling of all our physical and social resources will have been in vain.

This problem vitally concerns the younger generation—a generation distrustful of traditional standards, honest, bewildered, willing to sacrifice and suffer if, but only if, they can be convinced that the ends in view are worthy of their allegiance and that the means proposed are adequate to the attainment of these ends. Their youth and vitality naturally incline them to loyalties, enthusiasms and commitments, but they have been exposed since early adolescence to the virus of disillusionment and doubt; and many of them now find themselves, to their own chagrin and to our dismay, in the seat not, perhaps, of the scornful but of the suspicious and the skeptical.

But the younger generation is not alone in its bafflement and frustration. We older men and women are faced with the same predicament. We too are victimized by our sophistications, bedeviled by our lack of reasonable assurance and, as a consequence, compelled to act, when act we must, in relatively blind allegiance; to reflect, when we do reflect, without much hope that our reflection will discover and illumine ends worthy of our wholehearted dedication.

This cultural malady manifests itself in every walk of life and at every level of human experience. It shows itself in the political sphere. The present war is being waged by two rival camps clearly exemplifying the poles of our dilemma. The totalitarian regime in Germany is organized to facilitate quick effective decision and corporate action. Hence the amazing efficiency of its military machine. But this efficiency has been gained at the sacrifice of cultural reflection and social responsibility. The democracies, in contrast, have for the most part exhibited a tragic inability to decide and act with promptitude and unanimity. They have cherished what Germany has forsworn—freedom of speech and assembly, objective inquiry, individual liberties and corporate responsibility. But the result has been a chronicle of vacillation and procrastination. Unable to formulate a long-range policy and to act in anticipation of events, the democracies have again and again permitted events to drive them to belated action. Reflection and debate have dangerously, and often fatally, postponed decision and commitment.

Thus, reflective commitment, both prompt and informed, both reasonable and assured, has seldom been achieved in either warring camp. Both sides have been confronted with the disastrous either/or of freedom plus inefficiency or tyranny plus governmental competence, of education plus political procrastination or propaganda plus social unanimity.

Our malady manifests itself as virulently at the spiritual level. Consider the current tendency in religious belief. Is it not for the most part a dual tendency, on the one hand toward blind credulity and on the other toward sophisticated disbelief? How often is religious belief today vitalized by firsthand religious experience, or disciplined and informed by candid inquiry? And how often do knowledge and reflection issue in assured religious commitment? Witness the comparative failure of religious institutions seriously to affect our individual lives or our corporate behavior. Witness the comparative failure of our educational institutions, dedicated as they are to the dispassionate search for truth, to provide our society with significant leadership in the present crisis or the individual student with a philosophy of life that he can really live by. The exhortations from our pulpits bear little relation to the learned disquisitions from our lecture platforms. Many of our clergy are uninformed and unreflective, when information and serious reflection are at a premium. Many of our scholars and teachers are skeptical and irresolute in times which demand assurance and resolute commitment. Where, in such a society and culture, shall we turn for wisdom on ultimate ends and effective means to the achievement of these ends?

The first and perhaps the most fundamental cause of our

malady is the scientific naturalism of our age. This naturalism rests on the dogma that science is the only road to truth. The amazing progress of man's scientific exploration of nature since the Renaissance has demonstrated beyond all reasonable doubt the appropriateness of this approach to the end in view—to wit, an understanding of natural process and of nature's skeletal structure. But it has become equally clear that science, so conceived, is by its very nature incapable of validating any human values, esthetic, moral or religious. When scientific inquiry is directed to human experience and social behavior, it can indeed explore the phenomenal setting of individual evaluations and social norms. But such inquiry can do nothing whatever to evaluate these evaluations or to validate these norms.

The naturalism which is one of the causes of our spiritual frustration originates in the denial or neglect of this inescapable limitation upon scientific inquiry. Insisting that science is the only source of genuine insight, the only method of reasonable inquiry, the only technique of verification and validation, the naturalist is *ipso facto* compelled to deny that values, whether moral, esthetic or religious, permit of rational analysis and interpretation. He is accordingly compelled to embrace in the realm of value a highly romantic irrationalism that reduces all value-judgments to subjective or societal preferences.

This naturalism is, I submit, one of the most corrosive acids in our modern culture. It is corrosive because it denies with dogmatic finality the very possibility of reflective commitment to ultimate objectives since all values are declared to be, in the last analysis, equally subjective or socially conditioned. Religious belief becomes by definition mere wishful thinking, cowardly escape, the last resource of a feeble intellect. Social morality becomes no more than a function of this or that specific culture, individual belief no more than the reflection of social norms or idiosyncratic taste. There are not, it is true, many consistent and articulate naturalists in our society. But that the naturalistic temper has pervaded our life is evidenced by the initial prejudice of so many thoughtful men and women against religious belief and by the widespread skepticism regarding the ultimate dignity of man as a being of intrinsic value.

Naturalism in turn has fostered historical relativism. Historical studies have been undertaken increasingly in the spirit of scientific inquiry; every effort has been made to reconstruct the past without prejudice. Most historians will, of course, admit that history can only be written on some selective principle and from some interpretative point of view. But many would insist that such principles and points of view should not be normative or evaluative. This same spirit of scientific objectivity has characterized anthropological and sociological research. So studied, earlier epochs and contemporary cultures and societies have been found to exhibit the greatest variety of customs, the greatest diversity of beliefs and patterns of human behavior.

The value of these studies, like those of the natural scientist, is not in question, nor is the validity of factual conclusions. It is merely the relativistic interpretation of these facts which here concerns us—the view that because all norms and standards are socially conditioned, they are therefore merely a function of this or that culture, society and epoch. The corroding effect of this doctrine of cultural relativity is not far to seek. If all ideals and values are merely the product of historical forces and social patterns, all normative preferences, esthetics, moral or religious, are equally defensible or indefensible. The very search for more objective standards is vain, since no such standards exist and since all principles of evaluation are mere articulations of socially-conditioned prejudices. It follows that reasonable allegiance to any individual or social ends is a contradiction in terms and that moral, esthetic or religious "knowledge" is a sheer impossibility.

Another factor contributing to our cultural confusion is the tendency to utopian thinking. Utopianism is in essence a great oversimplification of a complex problem; it is the misguided belief that this or that reform will suffice to cure man of all his ills. This tendency to utopian simplism can also be described as a kind of infantilism. The psychoanalysts have demonstrated what, in a sense, we already knew, that physical maturity is not necessarily accompanied by spiritual maturity; man continues to crave, even in manhood, the safety of the womb and of the parental home. He longs desperately for absolute security, complete certainty, the luxury of unquestioned reliance on a beneficent power able and eager to satisfy his every want. He conceives of this power in terms of his temperamental bias and of the current ideology: now rationalistically, as the power of reason to achieve intellectual certainty; now biologically, as the inevitability of human progress through the survival of the fittest; now politically, as the power of the dictatorial state to guarantee human happiness; now theologically, as a divine initiative indifferent to human response.

Spiritual maturity can be defined in many ways but perhaps best as the ability to face the fact that nothing is absolutely certain in an uncertain world, that no absolute and final knowledge is possible in any universe of discourse, and that an element of faith, with all its attendant risks, is the inevitable corollary of human finitude. Man achieves maturity only as he is willing to face the fact that any belief may be mistaken, that all beliefs are partial and inadequate, but that some beliefs are better grounded and more reasonable than others. Yet our natural tendency is to fly to extremes—*aut omni, aut nullo*. Hence the attraction of fundamentalism, rugged individualism, communism and fascism—of all the isms which claim finality and absolute certitude and which, by that claim, repudiate human finitude and commit the sin of intellectual and spiritual pride. We are indeed bedeviled, as were our forefathers, by the Demon of the Absolute.

But what constructive insight can possibly emerge from the most careful scrutiny of so complex a scene? Will not such a scrutiny result in utter confusion, despair and paralysis of the will? In urging reflection upon these facts, am I not advocating a policy that must preclude commitment to any course of action, preclude decision, preclude the very possibility of vital dedication to concrete ends?

If these questions are interpreted as a demand for still another panacea the questioner must be told that his hope is vain. There is no easy and certain escape from our predicament, no course of action which is not precarious, and the policy of "safety first" is the most precarious course of all. To reflect is to postpone decision; and decision may be fatally postponed. But not to reflect is to court certain disaster. Belief may take the form of blind credulity; but to believe in nothing is to commit spiritual suicide. The only honest answer that I know is itself an act of faith, but of a faith made reasonable by the course of history, by empirical evidence and by interpretation in a wide philosophical perspective.

Let us first combat with all our power whatever destructive tendencies we discover in ourselves and in our social environment—the tendency to utopianism in all its forms, the craving for simplisms and absolutisms, the childish demand for absolute certainty and complete security. Let us then actively cooperate in free association and within the framework of whatever institutions give promise of aiding us most effectively to achieve our common goal. And above all let us strive as individuals for a maturity which, having surveyed the evidence, counted the costs and acknowledged the hazards, ventures all in an act of supreme belief.

The first prerequisite to progress in overcoming our cultural malady is honest diagnosis and courageous therapy. We must first know ourselves for what we are—a race given to blind enthusiasms and irrational vacillations, easily befuddled, endowed with reason but beset with the perversities of finitude, knowing only a little and seldom able to act in the light of such knowledge as we have, prone to childish hope and adolescent despair. Let us also mark with care those modes of thought and behavior that have contributed both to our facile optimisms and to our cowardly fears. Let us subject these movements, philosophies and slogans to a ruthless critique, acknowledging the element of truth in each, exposing the element of falsity, and purging spiritual and cultural poisons out of our system as best we may.

The institutions which experience has demonstrated to be most efficacious in curing a sick soul include the family and the state, the school and the church. All these, not excluding religious institutions in their temporal and visible aspect, are finite and fallible, no better than the individuals of whom they are composed. But with all their weaknesses they alone can provide us with the spiritual nourishment we so sorely need.

The family at its worst is a disaster; at its best it provides the ideal immediate social environment for human beings, old and young. One of the causes and one of the symptoms of our cultural malady is the instability of the family today and its frequent failure to provide children with the early training which it alone can provide. Yet, granting all the weaknesses of the family system, the course of wisdom is surely to attempt to correct these weaknesses in the light of a clearly envisaged ideal and, with patience and imagination, to strengthen the companionship and love of the family unit to which each of us belongs.

Like the family the political state has its essential functions and, like all human institutions, it varies in the effectiveness with which it performs them. Certain advantages derive from every form of government, even from the most anarchistic and the most despotic, and every known form of government has its grave weaknesses. Governmental perfection is no more attainable than individual human perfection. But for the attainment of certain ends some forms of government are demonstrably superior to others. Desirable ends in turn can be determined only in the light of a teleology of human nature. Only on the basis of a philosophy of human life and human destiny is a reflective choice of the ideal objectives of political organization possible, and only in terms of such ideal social objectives can the comparative merits and demerits of any specific type of governmental organization be appraised.

The school and the church are the two institutions which more than any others have preserved and transmitted to us our cultural and spiritual heritage, and it is they and they alone which, I believe, can save us from a return to barbarism. Whatever our individual beliefs, we must all grant our profound indebtedness to our Western heritage, Hellenic and Roman on the one hand, Hebraic and Christian on the other. We must also admit that positive beliefs in the realm of the spirit do not arise in a cultural vacuum and cannot be evoked in solipsistic solitude. All cultural and spiritual achievement is a cumulative product, the result of patient cooperation through many generations. Our cultural tradition is what it is because of the insights, duly transmitted and interpreted, of countless individuals in many lands and epochs, and these insights, as well as their transmissions and interpretations, would have been impossible without the aid of educational and religious institutions. It is essential, then, that we make every effort to support these institutions, whatever their deficiencies; to abandon them because of their admitted weaknesses would be to prefer a greater to a lesser evil.

It is also important to distinguish the complementary functions of these two institutions. The school is, or should be, dedicated primarily to the pursuit and dissemination of truth; it is the training ground for informed reflection. Religious institutions are the training ground for ultimate commitment, for they are, or should be, dedicated to worship and all that religious worship implies. Indeed, the difference between school and church, and their mutual dependence, perfectly exemplify at the institutional level the meaning of reflective commitment. Mere reflection is noncommittal; so is the purely academic pursuit of truth. Mere commitment is unreflective; so is religious worship when it is un-tutored and uninformed. Man cannot live by intellect alone and he is less than human if his commitments remain wholly blind. He can achieve the full status of a human being only by com-bining reflection and belief, and he is unlikely to achieve this status without the continued aid of those great institutions whose function it is to promote these essential ingredients of his hu-manity.

The final step toward a recovery of our spiritual health must be taken by the individual on his own initiative. The potential and actual contributions to human life of such institutions as the family and the state, the church and the school, can hardly be exaggerated; yet in the last analysis each individual *must* as-sume the ultimate responsibility for his own destiny. This is the teaching of all religions save those which embrace a completely fatalistic position; all the great religions, including Judaism and Christianity, insist, in one way or another, on human freedom and man's responsibility to respond to the divine initiative. The need for individual initiative and response is present in every state, for even a despotism can survive only with the coopera-tion of some of its people, and a democracy can flourish only with the active support of a vast majority of its citizens. No school can educate the persistently recalcitrant pupil; no family life is possible without individual good will and effort.

Nor is any one of these institutions able to relieve the indi-viduals associated with them of the responsibility for individual decision at the individual's own risk. On whose responsibility save our own can we accept the authority of the most authori-tarian church or religious tradition? Onto whose shoulders can we slough off our responsibility for acquiring an education or for accepting as true the conclusions of intellectual inquiry? We are, it is true, born into a family and a state; we are sent to school and we may be subjected to early religious indoctrination. We can, if we like, accept these social commitments passively, without reflection or explicit decision. But even this passive acquiescence is our own; this is the bed on which, even without taking thought, we choose to lie. We can continue to be infantile or adolescent in our beliefs and our behavior. But we can also, if we have the wit and energy to do so, achieve some measure of spiritual maturity. We can make a resolute attempt at independent reflection and appraisal and we can strive to indulge in commitments as forthright, prompt and enlightened as possible.

Thus, and only thus, can we, I believe, hope to realize our humanity and save our souls in a time of crisis. Our ultimate salvation depends not on allegiance to slogans, though these have their uses; not merely on institutions, though without institutions and some measure of paternalism we can do little; but on the effort which each individual must make to attain his spiritual majority through reflective and reasonable belief. The more successfully we undertake this difficult task, the brighter is our hope for the future, however discouraging the past and bleak the present outlook.

ANDRÉ MORIZE

Foreign Cultures
and the World Crisis

EXCEPT for his deficiencies in the use of the English language, I beg you to forget that your present speaker is a Frenchman. I want to forget it myself, at least for a few moments. Although France is closer to my heart than anything else in the world, it is not the proper time and place to remember it, except in the measure that it can give me a better understanding of a problem much broader than any national question.

Please consider me only as a teacher who, for twenty-five years, has tried to interpret for young Americans a culture which for them is naturally a "foreign culture"—and who, today, wishes simply to outline a few views which center around three principal questions:

First, what is the meaning of the so-called "crisis" in the teaching of foreign cultures in America?

Second, what is, in the general landscape of human culture, the responsibility of America?

Finally, is not the question of foreign cultures in the United States linked to another question—infinitely more important—

Delivered before the Delta of Virginia, Randolph-Macon Woman's College, April 22, 1942. Published in *Alumnae Bulletin*, June, 1942.

153

namely, the problem of the responsibility of individual man in the reconstruction of the world?

Yes, we are told that there is a "crisis" in the teaching of foreign cultures: "French and Italian are on the decline," "German enjoys no favor in a country at war with the Third Reich," and "Spanish gains some ground only thanks to a half-political, half-pedagogical propaganda"—and so on; or, as a Western politician put it bluntly: "We are Americans, are we not? So let's get rid of all that foreign stuff."

There is no doubt that many of these objections are based on a sort of intellectual isolationism more or less acknowledged and recognized as such; based also on a rather narrow conception of Americanism and an intolerant ideal of Americanization. The formula "To be first an American" has been, in various forms, the theme song of those who prefer to believe that, for the young American, this teaching is a luxury, not an essential. They proclaim that there are more urgent and vital obligations than to initiate him in the language and literature of countries which he will never visit and never know; that if, perchance, some capital foreign works deserve not to be totally ignored, we have good translations, perfectly sufficient; and that it is infinitely more important to orientate the student's efforts either toward things purely national, or toward a more immediately productive utilitarianism.

This is why the apostles of this doctrine have tried to limit the zone allotted to modern languages in our curricula, and to oppose—as if we had to deal with two enemy armies and with contradictory notions—modern humanities on the one hand and on the other those sciences which are more or less arbitrarily grouped under the common heading of Social Sciences. With all this you are thoroughly familiar. It is needless to reopen a discussion in which every possible argument has been exhausted.

In fact, it appears to me as nothing but a particular—and an

American—aspect of the gigantic battle which is being fought today between two forms of civilization, between two fundamental concepts of the very notion of culture.

On one side, we find a concept of culture founded on the desire to broaden man's horizon to the point where he will really grasp the true idea of humanity; the desire to make him understand and feel that the language he speaks, as well as the country he belongs to, are part of a large family to which he is bound by thousands of necessary ties, and that all thoughts expressed by the literature of his own country are linked to a tradition which is neither an enslavement nor a limitation, but an inspiration and a source of strength. Such a conception of culture tends to restore within the individual all universal and human values, at the very moment when all the forces at work in our modern world are tending to destroy in man everything human, to substitute automatism and machinism, standardization and the pursuit of utilitarian ends. This is the kind of culture in which most of us have placed our faith and our hopes. It is also the essential creed of Phi Beta Kappa.

On the other side, we see a concept of culture founded on a narrow definition of what is considered specifically useful for the development of a nationalistic spirit and for the integration of the individual in the frame of collective utilitarianism. "Such tactics," Professor S. A. Freeman wrote recently, "we should never let ourselves be persuaded to adopt. It would be worse than being defeated by Hitler's armies, if America should decide to climb on the band wagon of Hitler's mechanized system." Now there are reasons to feel worried. I read a few weeks ago a circular of the Navy Department inviting men's colleges to organize a curriculum of technical, scientific, and practical studies indispensable to a future naval officer, which is in every respect desirable and admirable. But the same circular intimated also that such a curriculum would be a step forward in the direction of a better adaptation of our education to the needs of a machinist and mechanistic civilization—which I consider as extremely dangerous. Doubtless very few, if any, American educators would wholly subscribe to it. Common sense as well as the sense of higher values will always act as antidotes in democratic America. Nevertheless, such is the ideal towards which such principles are bound to tend; what is taking place today in totalitarian countries is a sufficient proof.

Moreover, nothing, in the great intellectual tragedy of today, seems to me more artificial than the so-called "opposition" and contradiction between "foreign cultures" and "social sciences." I feel much distressed at the idea that many of our colleagues, in our own field, have considered it their duty to raise their banners and organize a sort of counter-offensive. If they believe that by so doing they are helping the cause of foreign languages, I am afraid they have an erroneous or warped idea of the nature and range of their own teaching. Personally, I resolutely count the teaching of foreign cultures in America as one of the social sciences—and among these sciences, as one of the most practical as well as most humanistic. If a language or a literature is taught as it should be (which is not always the case), if it is taught by competent, cultured, inspiring teachers (which, unfortunately, is too often not the case), it becomes a discipline in which both the element "science" and the element "social" play a part of paramount importance. If it is true that in the present crisis a country which wants to preserve its own civilization needs minds both trained in the use of scientific methods and made aware of their social responsibilities, then we find here an excellent reason to found our hopes not on the opposition but on the alliance of foreign cultures and social sciences. This alliance is today a part of the cultural responsibility of America.

In fact, I see several good reasons for launching at the present moment a very active movement in favor of the teaching of foreign cultures in this country, and to consider it one of the measures and activities demanded by the great national emergency.

Against all the shortsighted ones who have used the argument of the practical uselessness of foreign cultures, we must assert once more, in new terms, and in the light of the present crisis, their practical necessity, both for national defense and for the future of the nation and of the world.

We must persuade our American youth, not in terms of pedagogic doctrine, but in terms of national and individual utility, of the necessity of knowing those languages which are instruments of international exchange and the voice of world humanism.

They must know the zone of action of English, its extent but also its limits.

They must know the necessity of Spanish and also of this Portuguese, which it seems has just been suddenly discovered, as the means of contact with their immediate neighbors.

They must understand the necessity of knowing French, not only because it is the language of an essential culture, but because French always plays an important diplomatic role (see the inter-Balkan treaties), and because French, much more than English, will be for the Americans, who, after the victory, will want to collaborate actively in the reconstruction of Europe, the language in which they will communicate with the Belgians, the Poles, the Czechs, and others as well.

A South American educator recently wrote that "as Chinese from distant provinces can best understand one another by speaking English, cultured Brazilians and other South Americans find in French a common language."

They must, if they can, learn Russian, in order to come to understand a country about which we are so poorly informed; Italian, in order to see clearly into the development of Occidental culture; and finally German, not only as a scientific language, but to permit them to read directly in the original all those tragic texts in which the chiefs of Naziism cynically set forth their doctrine of enslavement and domination.

The American must learn these languages to be in a position

to combat in all countries the frightful action of the enemy agents whom we call "fifth column" without realizing yet the mortal danger of these preliminary invasions. Never would an Otto Abetz or a Sieburg have been able to do Paris the harm that they accomplished there if they had not spoken French admirably. We must be able to send everywhere other columns to do as much good as the enemy does evil—and we must furnish them with the same weapons.

It is only at this price that we shall have an efficient and fruitful information service. I have the profound conviction that one of the essential factors of the success of Hitler is the linguistic superiority of his information service. We are often beaten by people who know more about us than we know about them, and they succeed in their efforts because they are masters of the language of their adversaries.

They are beginning to realize that in Washington. At the request of the government they are setting up everywhere "intensive courses" in Japanese, German, Portuguese, and even Dutch. All of which is cause for rejoicing to the few Cassandras like me who for a quarter of a century have been talking of the national and practical value of the study of languages.

And all that is still another aspect of the responsibility of America toward foreign cultures in the midst of a world crisis.

But one must look higher and farther. This responsibility goes beyond practical problems and immediate necessities. It extends to the very destiny of human culture.

We are here face to face with a problem, or rather, with a duty, which goes far beyond our professional discussions or our specialists' worries. In fact, it amounts to a grave and far-reaching mission, with which, in a sudden and almost dramatic manner, America finds herself confronted.

In all earnestness, I beg you not to consider this part of my remarks as a sort of romantic view, or as an emotional outburst. Nothing is farther removed from my thoughts. I believe, on the contrary, that we have to deal here with one of the most con-crete, practical, and urgent tasks this country has ever had to cope with.

Do not expect from me a sensational picture of what is going on in Europe at the very moment of this speaking. Facts talk for themselves, as well as the pages of *Mein Kampf* and other writ-ings. Some time ago you heard what the President of the United States had to say about the systematic will on the part of the Third Reich to destroy, to annihilate, all religion in Germany, and elsewhere; to replace it with the worship of the Reich, to substitute for the Bible, *Mein Kampf,* and for the cross on the altar, the swastika and the naked sword. All this is no legend, but intolerable truth. The official Nazi documents which Mr. Roo-sevelt referred to I have known of for some time and publicly quoted on several occasions. But it is only a fraction of the truth and a chapter of the Nazis' diabolical plan. "Total war," as Hitler wants it, includes death of the spirit and assassination of the soul. Wherever his hordes have trod, everything that has to do with intelligence sinks into darkness and silence. Thought is gagged; real humanistic teaching is suppressed or domesticated. Masters of great renown, inventors, creators, are expelled or killed. Books are burned, libraries looted. In Paris, Brussels, Warsaw, Lwow, Louvain, Vienna, Prague, Amsterdam, Oslo, Helsinki, wherever there existed centers of culture, of art and beauty, there is noth-ing left except a tragic silence. The greatest authors are sup-pressed. It is *verboten* to teach history, or to write it. Corneille's *Horace* and Schiller's *Wilhelm Tell* are condemned as if they were plain criminals, for they speak of freedom and praise the dig-nity of man. A sorrowful and sterile winter sets in over lands which for centuries and centuries have fed the whole world with thought and humanism. No longer is it "the decline of the Occi-dent"; what we witness today is literally the methodical murder of the Christian and humanistic civilization of the Occident.

Now when the storm and disaster fell upon those countries, the "overrun nations," people managed to save all they could of their art treasures. In France, to speak only of what I could see, safe shelters were organized for paintings from the museums, for the stained glass and rose windows from the great cathedrals. In hundreds of places, in obscure villages, humble families have become, day and night, the unknown curators or guardians of the statue of an angel, of a famous portrait, or of one of those windows which used to filter into the nave of a church the rays of the sun of France.

For the intellectual treasures of civilized Europe, for all the cultures—the so-called "foreign cultures"—of the Occidental world, America is today entrusted with the divine mission of becoming this responsible guardian, who preserves and who saves. America is being given a solemn task, which no other country can fulfill. Because we share in the great gift of human culture, each of us is personally responsible for one or several items of this treasure. Figuratively speaking, Europe has been and is being compelled to "evacuate" the treasures and the very life of its mind and spirit, and to each of us she has given a share of it to safeguard. And so, viewed from this angle, these "foreign cultures" are no longer a discipline to be taught, a "subject matter," whose place in our curricula is a matter for professional discussion—they are a sacred trust. It is given to us because we are supposed to be understanding and faithful, and because we have all the possible means, physical as well as intellectual, to discharge such a stewardship and insure that safeguard.

When that many-centuries-old civilization of Europe "delegates" to us in such a way the responsibility of continuing its own life, however, the methods of achieving the task can no longer be those of the people who hide and bury the art treasures in the darkness of vaults and cellars. These things of the spirit need the light of day, the warmth of life, the continuity of human fellowship. And Europe, who created them, asks us to make them live; and to make them live, we must teach them and learn them.

We must teach what cannot be taught any longer in Poland or in France, or in Spain and Italy, which are overrun and subjugated as badly as the other victims. America must be the land of refuge for Dante and Molière, for Cervantes and Voltaire, for Baudelaire or Leopardi, for Dostoievsky or Victor Hugo. More than this, even: we must teach that true and real Germany which has disappeared under the same dark shroud. We must keep alive Schiller and Goethe and Heinrich Heine and all those who are banished today from the knowledge of the Nazi adolescent. A day will come when Germany—real Germany—will find herself again; and on that day, it will also be America's mission to bring back to her what she has destroyed today, and to help her to rebuild the human soul which she has lost.

More and more these ideas are becoming the rule and inspiration of my own teaching. It seems to me—an illusion, perhaps —that it helps me to give it more freshness and vitality. I feel sometimes that to present a beautiful French poem to a young American amounts to saving an object of art from oblivion or decay. To reveal to him the intellectual and moral value, the beneficial content of the capital works of various periods, gives me the joy of thinking that the France of the spirit, and the spirit of France, cannot disappear, since, no matter how modest my share may be in this achievement, eager hands offer themselves to take up the torch and keep it alive.

And so, the teaching of foreign cultures in America today assumes an importance and value never known before. It is no longer an educational problem, but a direct and fecund participation in the general effort of the world to save itself. It is a new battle fought on a line of defense in which all, men and women, old and young, as in the suburbs of heroic Moscow, are given a chance to work for victory. Beyond national defense, it is the very Defense of Man.

Every page, every work, every idea, every line which we entrust in this way to a young American takes on that unique value of a painting, a bust or a medal which the Louvre or Cluny or the Amsterdam Museum would have left in our hands, with the personal responsibility of saving it from the disaster.

Let the masters and students who, by the thousands, are interested in the teaching of foreign cultures encompass the grandeur and beauty of this new task. Let them realize the urgent necessity of their mission, and they will be rewarded by the gratifying certainty that, thanks to them, something of the intellectual and spiritual capital of mankind is actually rescued.

Such is the role of the teaching of foreign cultures in the present world crisis.

In fact, it goes further. We have another responsibility; for every educator and every educated American who realizes the importance of this task immediately becomes an active element in the reconstruction of the world. Before closing my remarks, I should like to define this duty.

Is it not an obvious truth that tomorrow the world will need workers; and another truth, not less obvious, that there is no good worker, no efficient artisan, without the proper apprenticeship? This is why, in that apprenticeship which will form the architects and masons of a new world, we must clearly perceive our personal responsibility.

Now who are they going to be, these workers and collaborators of the great reconstruction?

Of course, all those who will have kept faith in Man and Mankind in a general way, faith also in the higher notions of liberty and democracy for which every citizen of a civilized country is willing to fight.

But it will also be that great army of men and women who will be able and ready to restore, to transmit, to the world the indispensable values, the human values, expressed and handed over to us through centuries of effort and creation; men and women who will have made themselves, through voluntary choice and untiring study, the conservators and apostles of these values. Apostles, even more than conservators—men and women who will consider culture not as a pleasant and distinctive luxury, not as a means to adorn our leisure or add to our lives a tone of fineness and aristocratic achievement, but as a dynamic and beneficial and productive force. This is why it will be necessary for the soldiers of that spiritual army to know—to know from intelligent, clearsighted, and sympathetic knowledge—this vast world of ours in which they will be able to live on only if they first give it its proper shape. It will be necessary to orientate their education in such a way that the thought, history, tradition, and culture of every one of the great human families will be for them neither a "foreign" subject nor a closed book nor a dead letter.

I see the salvation and liberation of the world in the hands of America—of the America of today and the America of tomorrow.

I beg you to consider and fully understand the universal horror. One after the other, all the lands where man was allowed to live free among free men—all the lands where man used to see his ideal of life, not in the domination and enslavement of other men but in life itself, not in war but in peace, not in terror but in work, joy, and beauty—one after the other, all these lands have been submerged by the somber tide which has no other gift to bring to the world than despair, slavery, and hunger. Nowhere will this tide fertilize the lands it has flooded; nowhere will it restore life to the people it has invaded. These people will never be born again, never live again, until the evil forces of catastrophe and destruction are conquered, paralyzed, annihilated.

Today America, side by side with those who are still able to fight, has surged into action—to stop and suppress this universal curse. "Hitler," said your President, "must be stopped; and he will be stopped." When? How? After what immense and mysterious events? I don't know. But we all have the absolute certainty that it will happen.

Now for that day which is to come, have we given proper thought to the nature and range of our common task?

When the day comes, gaunt and pale faces will rise all over the liberated countrysides, beings who will have known the depths of distress and suffering, faces which will be nothing but eyes, ghastly because of the things they have seen, beautiful because of the fever of energy and resistance which helps them to hold. And on that day, we shall understand that their problems are our problems; understand that, above all the individual super-human tasks which each and every country will have to accomplish, there will be the great human task, the immense collective effort; and on that day, America will be the hope of the world.

But then, those only will be efficacious who will participate in the communion of the world. Those only will be useful who will have built up, within themselves, the knowledge of the world that will qualify them to share in the common work; those only will be in a position to collaborate in the work destined to heal a sick world who, in the construction of their own culture and of their personal efficiency, will have provided a place for foreign cultures.

May I quote here a few lines from an address of Walter Lippmann printed in last Spring's number of *The American Scholar*:

Modern education, however, is [too often] based on a denial that it is necessary or useful or desirable for the schools and colleges to continue to transmit from generation to generation the religious and classical culture of the Western world. . . .

There is no common faith, no common body of principle, no common body of knowledge, no common moral and intellectual discipline. Yet the graduates of these modern schools are expected to form a civilized community. . . . They are expected to arrive by discussion at common purposes. When one realizes that they have no common culture, is it astounding that they have no common purpose? [1]

[1] For the entire Lippmann address, see above, pp. 132–141.

The life of every country will depend upon the general order established in the world, and we do not want this order to be what Hitler calls "my order." It will be an order in which America will play the part of a protagonist, the part of a guide and of an architect. It will be an order in which every man will work not only as a citizen of his own nation, but, in the noblest sense of the word, as the citizen of a convalescent world which wants to live again. And the only ones who will be able to discharge such an obligation will be the English who will know more than England, the French who will know more than France, the Americans who will know more than America.

The preservation, the development, the teaching, of foreign cultures is precisely what will give to every man that "something more" which he will add to himself.

There are men, I know, who do not believe in the necessity of such an addition. Some go so far as to imagine that they help and serve their own country by refusing it. They try to justify their position with reasons that do not convince me. They like to consider that it is enough to be what they are, and to limit themselves to what their own country represents and includes. I do not dispute their right to entertain such an ideal. I have the conviction that they are mistaken, but I do not feel free to dispense them blame or irony. One thing to me is beyond doubt: an hour will come when destiny will require every man to give a full account and measure of himself.

Then, we who believe that the task of the educator and of the educated human being has something to do with the future of the world, we who have the conviction that there is no real and complete man except the man who, on one hand, is bound to his own country by indestructible ties, and who, on the other hand, shares by his own culture in all the cultures which have built up the very civilization we want to save, we shall persevere in that great task of human understanding and spiritual communion with all the forces of the spirit as they have manifested and expressed themselves in all the great countries of the world. And it will be our pride and our gratification, when the day of the great accounting comes, to have added or helped to add to the minds and souls of thousands of young people in this country something that will enable them to offer to destiny a measure of themselves that will be higher and broader.

MORRIS BISHOP

Faith in Literature

SOMETIMES the teacher of literature is granted one of those moments of mystical understanding wherein his soul journeys as far as the ceiling of his classroom, and thence contemplates his body *sub specie aeternitatis*, with the camera-angle of eternity. He watches himself writing on the blackboard names which are hard to spell. He listens to his own thin voice proclaiming: "A poetic achievement of the utmost importance was . . ."—whatever it was. He observes the forward quarter of the class eagerly noting what sounds like an examination question of the utmost importance, while the rear three quarters fix upon him that bright stare, reflections from a glassy eyeball, behind which their minds are happily busy with their own concerns. The teacher is assailed, for a grievous moment, by the conviction that he is lying. The poetic achievement, whatever it was, is of no importance. The students' deep instinct, bidding them erect defenses against the teacher's campaign, must have its psychological justifications. The literary experience about which the teacher prates at such length is a rare occurrence, evidently of no meaning for those who have never had such an experience.

Delivered, substantially as here printed, before the Eta of New York, Colgate University, in 1947. A revised form of the address was published in *The French Review*, October, 1955.

In the mood induced by such a revelation, the teacher of literature may well flagellate his spirit by putting together certain facts, or sets of facts.

There is this set of facts: With our college population of two and a half million, or one in four of those of college age, we have given higher instruction in literature to at least fifteen million living Americans. At no other place, in no other time, has there been such an experiment in mass higher education, and noteworthily such a mass introduction to the purposes and rewards of literature. We have had fifteen million students or more captive in our classes, and we have told them that in literature is all beauty, all wisdom, the means of spiritual delight, and solace for our woes and despairings. But let one of us write a book about literature, its beauty, wisdom, delight, and solace, and not one of our fifteen million former students will buy a copy.

"Not one," did I say? I did. Perhaps that is not scrupulously exact. Let me be scrupulously exact. Not nine of our fifteen million former students will buy a copy. If you will permit me to intrude a personal experience—and I don't know how you can stop me—I myself once wrote a book on Ronsard. I cozened myself with the thought that among perhaps two hundred thousand students who had made the acquaintance of Ronsard in French classes, there would be a fair number who would welcome a book on this sweetest of poets and his glorious song. I sent the book first to Little, Brown and Co. And Little, Brown replied to me: "Your book is wonderful; your book is great. We are crazy about it. But we shall not publish it, for two reasons: first, it is about a person whose name the American public does not already know; and second, what is far worse, it is about a poet."

So this is the result of our introduction of fifteen million Americans to the beauties of poetry! It has become an axiom in the book trade that the American public will not buy a book about a poet! It will indeed buy a book about Byron, because of his mistresses, or about Poe, because he died drunk in a gutter. It will not buy a book about a poet who was merely a poet.

Oh but my Ronsard. I eventually got it published by a famous press. In three years it hurtled on to a sale of 595 copies, and then the remainders were pulped. And all of these 595 copies, except for three I have been unable to trace, went to professors of French, who knew all about it already, or to college libraries, which are not very responsive to popular demand.

Then there is this set of facts. In our courses we reveal to our students the inestimable treasures of literature. Apropos of Pascal, or Goethe, or Wordsworth, we exclaim: "These are some of the most profound and beautiful lines ever written by man." The students conscientiously note in the margin of their required texts: "Most profound beautiful lines written man." They then pass our examinations, quoting the lines more or less correctly. Then they sell the required texts to the second-hand bookseller for twenty-five cents a volume.

And there is this fact: America is a country of magazine readers. Specialized magazines exist to deal with every trade, sport, recreation, and hobby. How many magazines are devoted specifically to literature, aside from the booksellers' trade journals, and the professors' own trade journals? I could list ten admirable high-minded quarterlies. But all of them are, I believe, kept by an institution or by individuals; to call their circulation infinitesimal would be a gross exaggeration. I do not include the *Saturday Review*, for that worthy magazine found the words "of Literature" in its former title too much of a handicap, and it has twisted them off. Like Dr. Kane of Kane, Pa., it has cut out its own morbid appendix.

Then there is this fact, or set of facts. We have informed millions of students that the highest form of literature is poetry, in which the boldest efforts of the imagination are expressed in the precise forms of beauty. If our students actually believed what we tell them, they would insist on a regular ration of poetry in their magazines and newspapers. But in fact, the magazines of general circulation publish about 300 poems a year. Almost none of these poems are over 30 lines in length, and most of them are sixteen lines or under. If you should write a new "Adonais," or "To a Nightingale," or "Scholar Gipsy," you could not publish it in any American magazine of general circulation today.

Well, here are facts enough. I grant you there are other facts, encouraging to us but unfavorable to my thesis; and of these facts I would write large the success of the paper-backed collections of new writing. However, in order to get on, I must ask you to accept my premise, that faith in literature as a preparation for life and as a revelation of significant truth has dwindled. Literature, the best that man has ever thought and dreamed, has always been the basis of education, in the Western world, in Moslem lands, in the Far East. But this, as you well know, is hardly the case in the United States today.

Is there something wrong with the faith we profess? Or something wrong with our students? Or something wrong with us?

Is there something wrong with the faith?

Well, what is our faith? I can state my own credo, and I suspect that most of you could recite it with me. I believe that literature tells all the past of our race and of other races; it reveals the mysteries of universes seen and unseen. Literature is the repository of the world's wisdom, garnered in every age, in every corner of the earth. Men of old have written their joys for our delight, their woes to save us from their sins and errors. In literature we find strength against the world's assaults, healing for our grief, rescue for our despair. In her, beauty lies captured, ready for release by the desirous spirit. Literature preserves the truth that men have pursued and found, and all the wonder and amazement which assuredly bear the mark of the divine. In literature is joy, the pure joy of the soul, freed from time and circumstance to dwell in the realm of the everlasting universals. This I believe; amen.

Is there anything wrong with this faith? Try as I will, I find no fallacy in my statement. True, I think we have made our errors in interpretation. We have sometimes made this happy thing unduly grim and solemn. And I think we have unwisely restricted our definition of literature. Greek literature includes philosophy, history, and geography. Rousseau's *Social Contract* belongs to literature as it does to Government; his *Émile* belongs to *belles lettres* as well as to the Department of Education. We have given away too much of our wealth. However, our mistaken generosity does not affect the truth of our faith.

But they don't believe us. You know perfectly well that they don't believe us. Either they do not find in literature the wisdom and joy we promised them, or they don't want wisdom and spiritual joy.

Is there then something wrong with our students?

That is a question which each teacher must answer for himself, according to his experience. In my experience, all too many of my students reveal that they come from social settings in which disinterested intellectual curiosity is not a reality, and too many give evidence that they have read almost nothing beyond the exiguous requirements of the schools. But they are quick, eager, and intelligent; they will work hard and well; many of them seek with delight the literary experience.

I have little complaint to make of our students, but I have much to make of the social complexes from which they come, to which they will return. Modern reverence for sports and diversion distracts the young at an age when, traditionally, they were learning about life and the spirit in the pages of great authors. Now most of them learn about life and the spirit by watching the gray ghosts of television, and I hope they will profit by them as much as we did from the poems and tales we read in quiet, accompanied only by our entranced imaginations.

One of the saddest experiences of the teacher is to meet, after a passage of years, one of his good students, especially one of his good women students. The teacher remembers her as passionately eager for the revelations of literature, for the joys of the intellectual life. He finds her sunk in some gross suburb, tending irreproachably a husband, children, house, and garden, and filling her brief leisure with women's magazines, television, and canasta, or whatever may have taken the place of canasta. Literature, intellectual curiosity, the life of the mind, have been abandoned. I suppose we can hardly blame her. The enormous white hams of Society have rippled over her and pinned her down. For a time, no doubt, she fought with her little fists; but Society, unstirring, smiled sleepily on, barely conscious of the minutest itch.

Some time ago I met a former student. "Professor," she said, "do you remember when I took French with you?" As a matter of fact, I didn't remember ever seeing her before. "Well," she said with an air of triumph, "your French has never been any good to me in helping my husband sell automobiles!" It was evident that she, like innumerable others, passed through our College of Arts and Sciences, and presumably was awarded the degree of Bachelor of Arts, with no suspicion that a liberal arts college has any other purpose than to help its graduates to sell automobiles.

I might have replied to this triumphant lady: "But you mistake our purpose! The aim of the professional schools is to teach you to make money; that of the Arts College is to teach you to spend money. You will no doubt recall the great phrase of Confucius: 'The superior man understands what is right; the inferior man understands what will sell.' We propose to beautify your leisure hours. Surely, from time to time, you take down your beloved Montaigne, and meditate for an hour on the human soul and its destiny! Surely you open again your well-thumbed Musset, and, as you read, weep tears of delicious woe! Or at least, surely you keep up with contemporary French literature, and find pleasure in the profundities of André Gide and the Existentialists!"

I might, in more disconsolate mood, have gone farther, and told the worst about books and reading. I might have said: "To tell you the truth, my dear young lady, the study of literature will never make you a dollar. It may even leave you minus the dollars you will spend for it. If you take literature really seriously, you may well learn from it your insignificance in the great drama of space and time, and you may even conclude that your own part in that drama is so small that it is hardly worth while making any great effort to play the part well. You may learn to regard the world under the species of eternity, and the man of action must regard the world under the species of the moment. A glance at the *Congressional Record* will persuade you that we are ruled largely by illiterates, whose strength lies in their ignorance of past error, whose public meditations are seldom impeded by concern for English syntax. And the great business men are typically men of deeds, impelled by obscure instinct, not guided by Aristotelian rules of logic. If you accept seriously the maxim of the Phi Beta Kappa Society, that philosophy is the guide of life, you may well find that Diogenes and Epictetus unfit you for the conflicts of the market-place. You will apply the values of the philosophers to the values of the business world, and your mental turmoil will soon attract the unfavorable attention of the boss. Thought may paralyze the motor controls. When you are pursuing success, you must not murmur: 'What is Success?' Whatever your means of livelihood, it is fatal to ask 'Why?' In the circumstances, it would be fatal for you to say: 'Why, in the shadow of universal doom, should the professor buy an automobile? And why should I sell him one?' No, thought prepares for the life of thought, and action for the life of action. Take my advice and don't mix the two. And incidentally, now that I have asked myself the question 'Why?', I shall not buy one of your automobiles."

That is what I would have said to my interlocutor, if I had thought it worth the trouble, and if she had been willing to pause for an hour or two while I prepared my answer. The defense of

173

literature lies not in its utility for the routine of our gainful concerns, except insofar as it is useful and practical to possess the common intellectual background of educated men and women, and hence to gain entry to the socially dominant class. The defense of literature consists in the fact that it brings us wisdom and understanding, and in the fact that it brings us pleasure.

And if, as seems to me the case, literature is now losing in popular esteem, it is because more people than in the past do not want wisdom, or because they do not find wisdom in literature. And it is because more people than in the past do not want the kind of pleasure that literature gives, or because they do not find in literature the pleasure they seek.

You know the public's pitiable excuses for not reading books. "We are so busy, so tired, so sleepy. After a hard day at the office or taking care of the children, we don't feel in the mood to settle down with a really good book. We would rather go out and putter in the garden for a while. And then come in and turn on the radio, and let our minds be submerged in a soft wave of perfumed glue. Or we might go to the movies, and see one of these books you talk about on the screen, or at least see the plot of it, with all the undertones of meaning and the overtones of beauty removed. Or we might play a little bridge, or get in the car and drive twenty miles for a coca-cola, and then drive back."

"But these are not ways of gaining wisdom."

"We don't know much about wisdom. It is probably very exhausting. We amuse ourselves, because we just want to kill time."

"The chief end of man, said Anatole France, is to kill time."

"Anatole France? Oh, a book."

The public's excuses are not valid. The public refuses to read books, not because it is tired, but because it does not want to. And it does not want to because it is not much interested in the past of mankind, in the dreams of poets, in speculations on the ultimate nature of reality, in the reconciliation of faith with the evidences of the seen and the unseen world. What the average person wants to learn from the accumulated fund of human knowledge is just what is going to affect him personally. And mostly he wants what will help him to kill time. He does not know what time is, and he does not want to know, but he wants to kill it. Thoreau said: "As if you could kill time without injuring eternity!"

The trouble lies, then, not with the students, many of whom accept our faith—and especially if they are Phi Beta Kappas. The trouble lies with the public, which imposes its values even on the valiant isolated Phi Beta Kappas in its midst. And why has the public failed to heed us, its teachers? Have we been remiss in our great task of revealing literature to the young?

We are used to public accusations. How often do people write, or say: "I hated Shakespeare because I had to study him in school!" And how often: "I studied Latin, and never found out that Caesar is exciting and Vergil beautiful!" We are not usually moved by such strictures. We know that there are dull teachers, incompetent teachers, pedantic teachers. We know also that the people who complain the loudest about their teachers' failure to teach them are the very ones who fought like panthers to avoid learning the things they complain of not knowing.

We should, perhaps, give some heed to these censures. In the secondary schools particularly the teacher's little flame of inspiration may be blown out by the hurricane of education. In the dull routine of the classroom the teacher of literature may forget his or her vows before the altar. And yet I think we need make no general confession of our sins. We all remember teachers of our own who kept their faith in literature, and who inspired us with their enthusiasm, and who fed our hunger with their wise counsel. And in the colleges we know that students come to us who have had their imaginations fired at every level of the educational system.

Within my experience, I should absolve the teachers, as teachers. I think that we have kept our faith in literature, and that we propagate it with zeal and understanding.

But if we absolve ourselves as teachers, a further question remains. Can we absolve ourselves as human beings?

We have made for literature a bold, an arrogant claim. We have said that the study of literature brings wisdom, intellectual joy, and beauty of spirit. Have we proved our case by such tests as science would demand? We have been made by literature. Are we wise? Are we joyful? Are we beautiful? At least, are we wiser, happier, and lovelier than those who have not had our training in literary appreciation?

If we are not, we must either abdicate our claim or become deliberately wiser, happier, and lovelier than other men. Those of us who have been formed by literature must demonstrate to the world that literature has made us something that the world will respect. We must allege, and we must prove, that literature has brought us wisdom. We must prove that our wisdom is useful, that it can serve in finding true answers to problems of life and conduct. We must show forth in our lives the virtue that we have learned from books. We must lead courageously the intellectual life. We must man the defenses against folly, malice, stupidity, prejudice, anger, and all unreason. We must continue to be, as men of enlightenment have always been, bulwarks against the barbarian.

The barbarian is at our gates, and within our gates. The barbarian hates our mysteries. His impulse is to destroy what he cannot understand, to destroy the idols of the mind. He may succeed; in so doing, he may succeed in destroying civilization, and in breaking it down to a universal barbarism, wherein he may rule without the reproach of civilized memory.

Sixty years ago Paul Bourget wrote, in an essay on Baudelaire, some words which sound strangely new today. He said:

The present indications reveal a spirit of the negation of life which day by day is further obscuring Western civilization. No doubt we are far from the suicide of our planet, which is the supreme desire of the theoreticians of misfortune. But slowly and surely, a belief in the bankruptcy of nature is being elaborated, which runs the risk of becoming the sinister faith of the twentieth century, unless a renewal, which can only be an outburst of a religious renaissance, saves a too morbid humanity from the lassitude of its own thought.

It is the duty of men schooled in humane letters to oppose this belief in the bankruptcy of nature, which may well lead to the actual bankruptcy of nature. In Literature we may find our weapons and our armor. For Literature, in its broadest sense, is wisdom. It represents the long effort of man to understand himself and his world and his relation to the world. It is the record of man's aspirations and dreams, and of his struggle to make his dreams come true and to find a truth beyond reality. It is the wisdom of fifty centuries of toiling humanity, reduced to the compass of a single room. Most of the world's wise men are dead, but their wisdom is the substance of our courses. They look over our shoulders as we expound their texts; they nudge our elbows.

And what do they tell us? Why, that men have always been sitting down to complain of the iniquity of their times and of the fast-approaching doom of the world. And that one just man has always been found in time to save the city or to carry culture onward. And that the race is worth running, and the game worth playing to the end, and life worth living, and faith in man justified. This is really about the same thing as faith in literature.

JULIAN P. BOYD

Thomas Jefferson Survives

JAMES PARTON'S description of Jefferson as "a young man of thirty-two who could calculate an eclipse, survey an estate, tie an artery, plan an edifice, try a cause, break a horse, dance a minuet, and play the violin" is, for all its incongruity, only a partial analysis of his enormous versatility. To catalogue the areas of his explorations is to list most of the principal categories of knowledge: law, government, history, mathematics, architecture, medicine, agriculture, languages and literature, education, music, philosophy, religion, and almost every branch of the natural sciences from astronomy through meteorology to zoology. This exploration of science and culture, much of which Jefferson enriched and all of which he gathered within the orbit of his lofty purpose, is apt to be misunderstood in a day when the vast accumulation of knowledge has made universal inquiry impossible and specialization inevitable. Yet his insatiable thirst for knowledge was neither dilettantism nor pedantry. Its most salient characteristic was its purposefulness.

"Jefferson aspired beyond the ambition of a nationality," wrote Henry Adams, "and embraced in his view the whole future of man." Nevertheless this grand object could be achieved only

Delivered before the Alpha of North Carolina, Woman's College Section, April 21, 1950. Published in *The American Scholar*, Spring, 1951.

through proof that government by consent as inaugurated in the American republic was practicable, that the ancient philosophical concept was able to survive its test before the eyes of the world. Jefferson wrote to John Dickinson a few days after his inauguration as president:

A just and solid republican government maintained here will be a standing monument and example for the aim and imitation of the people of other countries; and I join with you in the hope and belief that they will see from our example that a free government is of all others the most energetic; that the enquiry which has been excited among the mass of mankind by our revolution and its consequences, will ameliorate the condition of man over a great portion of the globe. What a satisfaction have we in the contemplation of the benevolent effects of our efforts, compared with those of the leaders on the other side, who have discountenanced all advances in science as dangerous innovations, have endeavored to render philosophy and republicanism terms of reproach, to persuade us that man cannot be governed but by the rod, &c. I shall have the happiness of living and dying in the contrary hope.

What for us is a proof was for him still an untried hope. Its realization depended upon the character of the citizens of the Republic. Hope and satisfaction alike would disappear if the standing monument fell. Its strength and virtue lay in its quality as an example to be emulated. Its force among the nations of the earth would, therefore, be a moral force, and its empire would not be one held together by armies, fleets or commerce, but bound by the strong ties of an idea holding sway through the ever-increasing Empire of Liberty. This being so, every citizen faced a responsibility to sustain the example and keep it from failing.

None realized this more clearly or met the responsibility more heroically than Jefferson. The urgency that permeated all of his versatile explorations of the fields of knowledge, the unremitting effort to improve himself and his countrymen, betrayed, perhaps, a fear that the great experiment might fail; that the mass of the people here might not be, as he knew they were not in some parts of the world, ready for the trial. If he exhibited a missionary zeal in what he called the "holy republican gospel," it was no doubt because he felt it necessary to set an example for his fellow citizens, as they in turn were obligated to set it before the world. This idea, that the successful establishment of a republic governed by the consent of the people would " ameliorate the condition of man over a great portion of the globe," was one to which, for all his versatile and ramifying inquiry, Jefferson gave a single-minded devotion.

If this was the central core of his purpose, there were other beliefs and propositions that necessarily and logically followed. The citizens of a republic, to meet their exacting responsibilities, would need to know their rights and duties. Therefore, the establishment of a system of universal public education was necessary—not a system leveling all to a drab and uniform mediocrity, but a system so organized as to bring forth the best minds and elevate them to that position in which their talents would be best employed for the general welfare. If self-government was to succeed, the voice of the people must determine their affairs. Therefore, all barriers to free inquiry must be removed, freedom of access to information protected, freedom of speech and of assembly safeguarded. Since ecclesiastical systems had historically marched hand in hand with governments of varying kinds, had often asserted a power transcending that of the state, and had frequently opposed the spread of science and learning, the individual right of conscience must be protected by separating church and state. Since science and the progress of society daily brought about changes in the economic, social, and spiritual status of mankind, it was necessary to establish fundamental constitutions which could not be altered by any power other than the people—though these should never be regarded as sacred and unalterable, but adjustable to inevitably changing conditions.

These necessary consequences of Jefferson's central purpose were not, of course, his beliefs alone. Their lineage was already ancient when he appeared on the scene. Yet, although he and his compatriots merely inherited the legacy of the sixteenth century at one of those pivotal moments of history when concept and opportunity are joined, Jefferson was the pre-eminent spokesman for the idea that became, under his felicitous pen, both the fundamental act of union and an exalted expression of the national purpose.

In the face of the capital fact that the nation which began such a great experiment under such high ideals has become the oldest, the largest, and by all standards the wealthiest and most powerful republic on earth, it seems needless thus to restate the principles which moved its founders and its chief spokesman. Are we not already sufficiently aware of our deep-rooted beliefs and principles: have we not glorified the Declaration of Independence, sanctified the Bill of Rights, proclaimed our allegiance to their principles in coast-to-coast broadcasts, speeches, loyalty parades, prizes, Freedom Trains, pledges, and many other ways —so much so that our ears and eyes are benumbed by the very din? Surely. But when we escape at last the noise and the public spectacles and the fervid orators, we are assailed by skepticism. And we conclude that there are at least two compelling reasons for re-examining and restating the Jefferson philosophy.

First, the voices that echo his words are often discordant, contradictory voices, lacking conviction and creating the uneasy suspicion that the true purpose is not so much to understand and apply his principles as to clothe hidden motives and attitudes with a semblance of justification through the employment of his name and his words. The voices do not ring true. Second, though actuality and ideal seldom if ever coincide, there is such a wide discrepancy between what the voices proclaim and what the proclaimers perform as to raise grave suspicions about their understanding of Jeffersonian ideals, or their intent, or both. The voices echo the word, but the action does not so much embody a constructive attitude toward mankind as special pleading for a group of men or for a restricted and unstated group of special interests. The principles are emblazoned on the billboards, in the subways, in children's comics, in the housewife's opiate taken in the form of true-to-life drama synthesized in the radio booths, repeated endlessly and (we suspect) on the cynical conviction that anything reiterated enough will at last be believed. But the principles, in large part, are not the touchstones of action and policy. The voices and the actions do not square.

Let us listen first to the contradictory voices that today re-echo the words of Thomas Jefferson. On the far Left, which of course becomes at full circle the far Right, we find Jefferson's stalwart championship of individual freedom voiced by those who, when in power, destroy all liberty which the individual may claim as of natural right. Their particular darling among historical American figures is, of course, Thomas Paine, but Jefferson's words are soothing and useful to them on occasion. Jefferson, who preferred chaos to government if government could be had only at the price of individual liberty, is quoted, but the one the quoters have in mind is Robespierre, progenitor of the modern totalitarian, who would sacrifice all personal liberty for the sake of order in society. Far off to the Right are those who, calling themselves Jeffersonians, embrace the doctrines of States' Rights not, as Jefferson did, for the purpose of advancing and strengthening the Empire of Liberty, but for the purpose of buttressing the *status quo*. Nearer the center, but still on the Right, are those who find solace not only in Jefferson's defense of States' Rights, but also in his assertion that the best government is that which governs least. They use—or more particularly in the past fifteen years they have used—Jefferson's words, but their allegiance really goes back to Hamilton and Marshall. They speak, for the most part, from honest conviction; they regard themselves as the true protectors of society and its institutions; they believe fervently in what they consider the American concept of government. But in actuality they cannot accept Jefferson's fundamental premise: that the people may be trusted to govern themselves. Near the Center and extending slightly to the Left are Fair Deals and New Deals, claiming not only legitimate descent from Jefferson but also an authority to wear his mantle and to employ his precepts. Here there is a measure of justification. Certainly, insofar as general policy and attitudes are concerned, there is some identity of statement and intent. But all too often there is a wide and, at this moment, an apparently increasing discrepancy between preachment and practice. The voices *ought* to ring true, but they rarely do.

Somewhere in this wide spectrum of opinion and belief somebody is bound to be wrong. Jefferson might on occasion have agreed with any of these groups on a given proposition, but on the fundamental principles of government and the inalienable rights of the individual he could only have agreed with those who have confidence in the people and who support individual rights as against any arbitrary and irresponsible power existing anywhere.

The thoughtful citizen may well ask himself which of the self-styled spokesmen for the Jeffersonian point of view is entitled to the claim. Which merely employs his words to fit a preconceived purpose? Which endeavors honestly to understand Jefferson's meaning, to discover what in his philosophy is living and valid today, and to strive toward the application of those principles that are not obsolete? The question is not an idle one. In many respects it is the gravest question that a citizen can ask himself today. For if, as I believe, Woodrow Wilson was correct in saying that the immortality of Jefferson lay not in any of his achievements but in his attitude toward mankind; and if, as I also believe, though many thoughtful men do not, his philosophy of government and of the individual's rights and responsibilities have not been rendered obsolete, though the natural law upon which these were based no longer seems worthy of historical or philosophical support, then it is a matter of grave concern to the American people and to the world that the conflicting echoes of his voice should be judged. For we are in serious danger of having, if we are honest, to give a new answer to Crèvecoeur's famous question, "Who is this new man, this American?" In his day the answer would have been Jefferson's: He is a man self-confident and self-reliant; he believes himself capable of governing himself; he is weak in physical resources and national power, but his inner convictions are indomitable and will prevail. Today, we should have to say: He is a citizen of the most powerful nation on earth, but he is frightened—or at least his leaders in government, in the press, in the church, and even in the universities tell him that he *ought* to be frightened—by the specter of communism. And fright has caused him to do violence to the things which he once prized most dearly.

As Tocqueville said with prophetic insight more than a century ago, "No form or combination or social policy has yet been devised to make an energetic people of a community of pusillanimous and enfeebled citizens." The weakness we have to fear is not one of material resources, but of the moral fiber of our nationhood and its principles. I do not mean to imply that the Jeffersonian precepts, however applicable they may have been to the society in which he lived, should be respected today merely because he entertained them or because they were once applicable to our national welfare. "The earth belongs in usufruct to the living; and . . . the dead have neither powers nor rights over it," he once declared, and his entire career reflects a magnet-like steadiness of aim in supporting this revolutionary and radical proposition. He not only recognized the absolute necessity of change if his dream of substituting reason and justice for authority and superstition were ever to be realized, but his ceaseless, versatile activity throughout life was, for all its diverse ramifications, a single, purposeful, dedicated effort to bring change about (though not "for light and transient causes") by peaceful means if possible, by revolution if necessary.

Though a revolutionary in deed and in thought, and one who calmly accepted the inevitability of turbulence and conflict in a republic, he was, in a true sense, the greatest of conservatives. For that which he sought to conserve was, by comparison with the objects of all other forms of conservatism, such as to make them seem almost trivial and irrelevant. All other forms of conservatism sought, in the end, to protect custom or property or established order; he sought to conserve the rights of men, over which neither the customs of society nor the property of individuals nor the order of established institutions nor any other earthly power should take precedence, since all found their ultimate justification in man, who had formed society and created these things for the better protection of his rights. On all other matters his moral philosophy was relativistic; on *this* he was inflexible. "Nothing, then," he declared, "is unchangeable but the inherent and inalienable rights of man." Each generation should face its new problems in its own way, unfettered by the dead hand of the past. But none could justly or with impunity violate the basic assumption on which the state rested.

We may at once, then, dismiss the clamors of the extreme Right and the extreme Left, however much they may quote Jefferson in justification of their purposes. For by no stretch of reason or of the imagination could his lofty purpose be made commensurate with the kind of authoritarianism exhibited in these quarters. Indeed, we may dismiss all of those groups who appeal to the name of Jefferson either for the purpose of maintaining the *status quo* or for the purpose of returning to the past, so long as these purposes do not aim at the preservation of the "inherent and inalienable rights of man." They may quote Jefferson's words about the folly of directing agriculture from Washington; about the danger of a national debt and of high taxes; about the perfection of that government which governs least. There are many bold and quotable words on these subjects which, superficially, seem to lend the weight of Jefferson's authority to such a position. The words are the same, but the discordant voices quoting them are as out of key with the world of today as the pony express would be. Clearly, the government that governs least would in this twentieth century of corporate power be the worst possible form of government. I feel sure that Jefferson could detect the corporate abuse of the right to life, liberty, and the pursuit of happiness, and would oppose it quite as readily as he did similar abuses by government in the eighteenth century.

James Bryce, half a century ago, observed that in Jefferson's day the restraining hand of authority was laid upon the individual by government, and that Jefferson and his contemporaries made the mistake of considering "the pernicious channels in which selfish propensities had been flowing for those propensities themselves, which were sure to find new channels when the old had been destroyed." Yet Bryce himself erred in thinking, with many today, that Jefferson feared only the power of government; that he set form above substance, channel above propensity. As for his attitude toward the abuses of power outside government, we need only recall his impassioned indictment of ecclesiastical authority, and of the power of manufacturing and commercial interests. As for government, it was what he called the "desolating pestilence" of power and its corrupting and abusive quality that he attacked, not its form. Proof of this is to be found in the Declaration of Independence itself: one of the self-evident truths there proclaimed was that "whenever *any form* of government becomes destructive of" the inalienable rights of man, the people could "institute new government, laying its foundation on such principles, and organizing its powers *in such form*, as to them shall seem most likely to effect their safety and happiness."

The voices on the Left and the Right are apt, like most of us, to read these exalted words in the context of 1776 and in reference to the single aim of justifying independence as against the supposed tyranny of George III. But they are for us now, as they were for Jefferson throughout life, not words to be remembered from the past as applicable to an obsolete purpose, but rather as a perpetual, living affirmation of an unalterable right, accessible at any time, in our day or in the distant future, to a people who will "suffer, while evils are sufferable," but who will not endure the intolerable. They are, of course, dangerous and inflammable words, useful to the subversive as well as to the reactionary, but their danger is a calculated risk and not regarded as a danger at all by those who, like Jefferson, regard the people as the safest, though not always the wisest, repository of power. They are also words of warning. They warn those who stand at the head of government—as well as those who represent economic, ecclesiastical, military, racial, or other groups of society and who endeavor to bend government to their wishes—that the limits of sufferable evils must not be transcended.

These limits are being approached. The warning flags have been run up, but they have been disregarded. In 1948, despite the fearsome predictions of those whose preoccupation it is to instill a sense of fear, the people gave an overwhelming demonstration of the fact that they are not and have no intention of following after the false gods of communism. On top of this came the result of the loyalty investigation in government. Of the more than two million persons employed by government and investigated, less than one one-hundredth of 1 per cent were found to be suspected of disloyalty. In the face of these irrefutable demonstrations of the sense and loyalty of the people of this nation, men may still be accused of disloyalty, may be denied the right to be confronted by the accuser, and may thereby stand in jeopardy of loss of reputation or livelihood. The highest legal officer of the government still possesses the power to say what organizations may be regarded as subversive, and citizens belonging to them may be placed under suspicion, investigated secretly, and made the object of humiliation and calumny. Elected representatives may still, though servants of the people, assume to themselves the supreme arrogance of defining for the American people what constitutes good American behavior, compounding insult, injury, and denial of the principles they profess. State after state has required oaths of loyalty to America—oaths the real object of which is the illusory hope of exposing loyalty to Russia. Textbooks are being banned, writers boycotted, libraries told what can be safely placed before readers, teachers investigated, not for the competence of their teaching, but for the danger of their ideas. As the supreme evidence of confused thinking, an honored liberal journal has been struck from the list of school libraries in our greatest city, not because what it published was asserted to be untrue or libelous, but because three articles were said to be offensive to a particular church. These things, and more, are done often in the name of Thomas Jefferson, though by no tenet in the entire canon of his faith can any suppression of access to information, any denial of freedom of opinion, or any compulsory affirmation of belief be justified.

Despite the doctrine of fear on which moral, political, economic, and other issues are being resolved, a few courageous voices re-echo the faith that Jefferson expressed when we experienced a similar wave of hysteria in the years 1798-1800. They believe, with him, that government by the people is the most energetic, though not necessarily the most orderly form; that the people may be trusted when left free to decide; and that those who offer false and seditious counsels should be allowed to "stand as monuments of the freedom with which error of opinion can be tolerated where reason is left free to combat it."

If I know anything about Thomas Jefferson and his principles, I believe these voices to be authentic echoes of his voice. They are honest, courageous, influential voices. They will not be silenced by the demand for conformity or for articulate hatred. They will grow in eloquence and influence. But they will influence only the spirit of the nation; they cannot yet determine policy.

For our policy as a nation is determined in the contest for power. This global struggle has brought forth two immense dangers, each of which threatens a betrayal of the principles for which Jefferson spoke. Internally, we profess that tolerance that is a necessary and essential element of society under a republic, but at the same time we are doing our utmost to compel uniformity, to level dissent, to suppress unorthodox ideas, and to organize an hysterical and potentially tyrannical public sentiment around the false proposition that the thing we hate can be eliminated if only we are unanimous in our hatred. Externally, we are in danger of forgetting, in our effort to win the peaceful nations of the earth to our side, that the world at this particular juncture may be more critically in need of moral leadership than of vast supplies of machines, arms, material goods, and extensions of dollar credits. Either course, long continued, could destroy forever the kind of free republic composed of free men that Jefferson envisaged.

The compulsory uniformity now demanded of men in public life is the very antithesis of what Jefferson contemplated. For, as was observed by a wise philosopher a century before Jefferson, where there is uniformity, there also is tyranny. The temptation to adopt a new kind of imperialism which the mere possession of power brings with it may prove in the long run to be the undoing of ourselves as well as those who seem to stand in our path. At any rate, in pursuing either course, let us not malign the name of Jefferson by attempting to identify his ideals with our actions. Let those who would compel uniformity at home, who would deny the right of dissent to some, who would control our thinking and channel it in one single direction, who would decide our national issues by reference to the acts of another nation rather than by the principles we affirm, who would use our vast strength to mold and direct the governments of other nations to our desires, attempting to impose an international conformity similar to that now threatening the life of individuals and their freedom of choice—let all these reflect upon Jefferson's final affirmation of the meaning of American independence and of the establishment of a new nation:

May it be to the world what I believe it will be (to some parts sooner, to others later, but finally to all) the signal of arousing men to burst the chains under which Monkish ignorance and superstition had persuaded them to bind themselves and to assume the blessings and security of self-government. The form which we have substituted restores the right to the unbounded exercise of reason and freedom of opinion. All eyes are opened or opening to the rights of man.

We have had proof enough, in our lifetime, that all eyes are *not* opened to the rights of man. We have had proof enough that the right to the "unbounded exercise of reason and freedom of opinion" has indeed been bounded, and has in many respects been suspended. But, dismaying though this is, the greatest of tragedies in this conflict would be for this nation, which first erected a monument to stand as an example of man's capacity to protect his rights by a government of his own ordering, to deny its own birthright. The evidence that we are in danger of doing so, at home and abroad, is all too obvious. The final irony is that, in committing violence upon our professed principles, we should endeavor to justify our shameful default by appealing to the name of the man who was the author of that statement of our national ideal whose words we parrot while our acts desecrate its spirit.

190

CHARLES GROSVENOR OSGOOD

The Proper Study

"THE proper study of mankind is man." The meaning has pretty well faded out of this line from long overuse. If I am not mistaken, Pope was saying in effect that the best education is a humanistic education in the liberal arts. But in these days even that idea is showing signs of wear.

This year Phi Beta Kappa attains the venerable age of one hundred and seventy-five. Out of the thousand and more orations and poems that have been composed in her honor, two have emerged as classic: Emerson's speech to the Harvard chapter in 1837, known as "The American Scholar," and Woodrow Wilson's address to the same chapter in 1909, entitled "The Spirit of Learning." Though differing with the differences of time and author, they are alike in that they both express discontent with the education of their day—a discontent with its tendency to withdraw from life.

This is an old story. Throughout its history education has always leaned to this deviation. It is forever slipping out of the swift-flowing main streams of life into safe little eddies and quiet academic backwaters and shallows of peaceful sloth, from which it has periodically and forcefully to be reclaimed by the Wilsons

Delivered before the Beta of New Jersey, Princeton University, March 27, 1951. Published by the University.

and the Emersons to its main business. "School," as ancient writers do report, once meant "leisure," and the life of learning is necessarily a life of peace and detachment; but it cannot justify itself, nor survive, if it drifts away from the intellectual and spiritual realities of man alive.

Emerson proposed to restore education by renewing its proper alliance with Nature, with the Past, and with what he calls Action, that is, taking part in life itself. Wilson proposed to restore it by reviving the daily association between older men, learned and experienced, and younger men, alert, inquiring, and absorbent.

What has happened? Well, the alliance of education with Nature has been partly strengthened by the advance and prestige of the physical sciences. Still there is much in Nature and the meaning of Nature to men that will forever lie beyond the ken of physical science. As for Action, our present undergraduate life offers enough to satisfy, or even astonish the Sage of Concord; though he might press an embarrassing question as to the difference between Action and mere activity or play.

As for the Past, it is fast fading out of our academic field of vision, as history foreshortens into "Social Studies," the Classics in all literatures into what is modern and contemporary, and the subjects of study more and more justify themselves by their immediate practical usefulness, not by their value in the long run of a lifetime—or of an eternity.

And now here comes one of the staff of a well-known university proclaiming that "physical education will lead to a well-rounded life for more Americans than straight liberal arts training"; and that such training in this modern day "fulfills the best aims of education." If we had him in a preceptorial corner, he would not escape before he had given his idea of a well-rounded life and an educated man, and taken the consequences.

Wilson's demand for closer intimacy between teacher and

taught has found result in our "preceptorial system," and in the residential colleges, both of which have put forth their influence far beyond the institutions of their origin. We are proudly and justly devoted to the preceptorial system. But those of us who have had to do with Princeton during the forty-six years of its history know only too painfully what unremitting vigilance has been the price of its survival, threatened as it constantly is with the interruption of war, with economic pressures, and with the inability of many, both preceptor and student, to appreciate its high privilege and opportunity.

With two precedents as eminent as Emerson and Wilson, I am emboldened to rehearse certain present discontents with our education; and these too bear upon the same old propensity of organized learning to lapse from its proper source of life and energy in life itself.

When you give an emeritus a chance to talk, he is likely to begin: "Now in *my* time. . . ." Well, in my time the liberal arts in school and college consisted of little more than Latin, Greek, mathematics, and a modern language, with a few limited upper-class electives. To the undergraduate of today it looks like a lean diet; but we thought it was very liberal. And so it was compared with the prescription of a generation or two before. But I had altogether a dozen or so very good teachers, as good as any then or now; and I have no regrets, for good teachers are more important than anything they teach.

The Classics are now well-nigh gone, in spite of gallant last-ditch action. It was partly their own fault too. And the modern classics also have declined. Yet consider the dazzling variety of our present academic display. I confess to moments of wistfulness when I survey such features as the Department of Music, the School of Art and Architecture, the Woodrow Wilson School of Public and International Affairs, the Industrial Relations Section, the Special Program in the Humanities, the Department of Religion, the great new laboratories, the preceptorial privilege, and the long-considered and carefully built plans of study, designed to fit every aptitude and bent.

And yet we are not satisfied. For out of the clamor of present discontents I hear oft repeated four particular criticisms of our education.

First, that it has gone hopelessly vocational. We have not found the remedy, though we know the answer. President Dodds has uttered it when he said: "It is clear that our vexed world will not be saved by the purely vocational mind." Vocational training we must have, but as Wilson said, it does not "beget the generous comradeships or any ardor of altruistic feeling such as the college begets." The popular mind persists in the idea that training in a special technique is education. But what shall it profit a man if he learn a trade but lose the full realization of himself?

Secondly, critics observe that Science is driving the Humanities to the wall—perhaps beyond it. For three hundred years the process has slowly been going on. In uncertain times, when inherited articles of faith have faded and grown weak and dim, men have turned to Science for security of mind, because Science at least offered certainty and firmness of ground. Science, it seemed, had the facts. But as it has turned out, the more Science, the less certainty.

I would not disparage Science, being mindful of its immense benefits as applied to the needs of mankind and of its unique values as an element in our liberal culture. But while the age is prone to deify Science, let us realize that after all it is only an unmoral instrument. As Sir Richard Livingstone has reminded us within a year, there are vast paramount regions of vital concern to us that transcend the inquiry of physical science—regions of love and hate, of life and death, of right and wrong, of beauty and ugliness, liberty and bondage, prophetic insight and religion. If human life *is* measurable by three score and ten, then these matters concern us little. But the human spirit will not have it so.

Not only has the mind of our day become preoccupied with

the study of Science, but the scientific method has invaded the Humanities until our scholarly attention has almost gone blind to human values in our zeal for scientific studies of sources, influences, history of ideas, minute details of biography and bibliography, the microscopic scrutiny and jargon of the so-called "new criticism." It has little room left for the human sympathy and understanding needful for the true and just appreciation of the creative genius or his creations. So we teachers are lazily prone to shrink our truly humanistic and more difficult task of releasing to our students the springs of humanity within our subjects, and to content ourselves with the easier process of merely dispensing the facts as scientifically discovered.

But it is no more just to blame Science and the scientists for this warp in our culture than to blame the law of gravitation for the crash of an airplane. Some of the deepest and most sincere regrets for the present decline of the Humanities are uttered by the men of science themselves, especially as they shrink in horror from some of their more recent discoveries and cry out for at least the human moral control over the terrible energies they have released.

We are memorializing the late James V. Forrestal with a magnificent provision for scientific study. As we do so, let us recall his own words during the last war, when he returned to receive honor from his Alma Mater. Out of his experience in the Navy at war he expressed his conviction that, beyond all specialized and technical training, the liberal arts college is indispensable to the support of democracy and the breeding of that character upon which leadership must rest. Said he: "Its curriculum must return, if our Navy is any index, to certain basic compulsory courses rather than allow complete freedom of selection to its students. It must recover its ability to turn out men soundly trained in mathematics and sciences, as well as in the broadening humanities. There may be some argument on this, but I would like to see Greek and Latin restored to their ancient glory."

Thirdly, our education, some say, is specializing itself out of all conception of a *Studium Generale* or university; it has lost its philosophic and encyclopedic control and import. In the old days at Princeton, and no doubt elsewhere, one man often taught two or three subjects. President Maclean taught mathematics and classics; Albert Dod taught mathematics, architecture, and political economy and was well exercised in literature and theology; President Stanhope Smith taught belles lettres, ethics, and theology, and made highly original studies in anthropology.

From the proud but narrow height of our expert specialization we may smile at what must have been the limits of their knowledge. But by all accounts they taught; that is, they superinduced in young men the power of safe judgment and prompted them to wise and generous action as well as we do it now. It would seem that specialization, desirable and inevitable as it is, is not indispensable to sound education. Indeed, unless appraised at its true and proper value, it may even corrupt our liberal training. For these men of old, with less specialization, could better command an overreach of the field of knowledge, a more philosophic mastery of their smaller world. And such overreach, such mastery, is, I believe, a prime measure and condition of the teacher's power.

I recall a very bright undergraduate, with a few crumbs of his sophomoric shell still clinging to him, who stoutly proclaimed: "All I ask of my teacher is that he know his subject. I don't care what he thinks!" We can only hope that he did eventually encounter a teacher who thinks, and who gave him at least some elementary exercise in the gentle art of thinking.

And fourthly, men complain that, with the vast expanse of our knowledge, the body of learning, once so well ordered and compact, has swollen until it has burst into ten thousand fragments, and no turn of the academic kaleidoscope can bring these fragments into a consistent or lasting design. It is like the proverbial man who gave up reading the encyclopedia because he couldn't follow the story.

In the face of this situation we are doing our best to put things to rights by grouping and planning and replanning our course of study. But somehow matters seem never to get settled. We are forever ripping up the curriculum and rearranging it so that the House of Knowledge is never in order for enough time to let its teaching occupants settle down to the devoted practice of their art in the peace that the practice of a high art demands.

Why this restlessness? Is there no criterion, no clear, fixed, common conviction by which to arrive at a settled order, settled at least for a generation?

These four obvious defects of our education—Vocationalism, the domination of Science, Specialization, Disintegration—are they remediable, or are they hopeless? So inevitable do they seem that most academic administrators wearily accept them as demands of the time and make shift to keep house as best they can in helpless conformity.

But in reality they are only superficial symptoms of a deeper disorder.

In the long course of history men have repeatedly been making up their communal mind and then unmaking it, only in slow course of time to make it up anew. Fortunate indeed the young men born into an age of communal security of mind and spirit and faith—times like the Fifth and the Fourth Century before Christ in Greece, the Twelfth and Thirteenth Centuries in the Western world, the Sixteenth Century in Europe. But such secure times do not remain secure; their communal security at length dissolves into a flux. In such a flux, such a rapid or "riffle," we now find ourselves, making on, we hope, to a new calm reach, but for the present tossed and whirled about in confusion and noise. Our minds are uncertain, our opinions tentative, our expression meticulous. Current words are chips adrift that show the direction of their time. These very words, "tentative," "meticulous" (which really means "full of little fears"), words not met in earlier writers but now in everybody's mouth and on everybody's pen—such words as "attitude," "approach," "point of view," "angle," "feeling," and "impression" (instead of "belief" or "conviction")—they are all words expressive of a timid, shifting, weltering state of mind.

It is each man for himself, intellectually and spiritually. We are all, as Thoreau says, living lives of quiet despair. We have often been warned to read the philosophies of a time for reliable signs of its tendency. Creeping slowly but relentlessly upon us from every side, like a ring of poison gas, are philosophies (if one may dignify them with that name) of materialism, and determinism, and decadent existentialism, whose sum is pessimism, atheism, lawlessness, paralysis, and insulting humiliation of the individual man—the very process that ripens, softens, and rots the world into communism or fascism, ready for the tyranny that can thrive only on such corruption. The scale of values is leveled and all standards extinguished.

Of course, this is probably only a fashion. The world follows fashion and fashions change. In the present shrinkage of the world by lightning intercommunication the changes are much more rapid than ever before. But in mere fashion there can be little hope or security or anchorage.

What hope, then, of stability? What security of foothold? What effective remedy for our discontents with our education? What therapy for the cause of our disordered symptoms?

Through all time there has been, and still is, one constant, the spirit of a man, the man who teaches and the man who learns. For teaching is far more than an academic profession. These two men are almost one, for they are both enlisted in the same enterprise, and distinguishable less by function than by degree of maturity. Our restoration can proceed only out of such a constant. It can spring only from a true and sympathetic appraisal of the makeup of an individual human being and a paramount concern for his intellectual and spiritual destiny.

We need, therefore, teachers who care most of all for other men as individuals, wherever they find them, on the campus, in the world, men of all sorts and conditions. We need teachers who, however learned and expert, transcend their specialty with a constant sense of its final value in human terms; so that whatever they teach, whether science or humanities, their teaching is authenticated, not only by their expert knowledge, but by this transcendent sense of its real values—in short, the teacher who is humanly greater than his subject.

There are at least three ways of teaching. The first, and commonest, and easiest, and too often the only way, is the imparting of information. But as Wilson used to say, "The mind does not live by information. It is no prolix gut to be stuffed." And yet, how large a portion of our time is spent in administering and testing just this process and no more. How limited to this conception is the common notion of education.

But a higher process of training—the soul of the preceptorial method—is the superinducing of action and reaction in the student's mind by the interplay of question and answer after the manner called Socratic. Long ago it was demonstrated in the dialogues of Plato. Indeed I can think of no better induction into the privilege of preceptorial teaching than reading and re-reading the *Phaedrus,* or the *Lysis,* or the *Phaedo,* or the *Gorgias,* or the *Republic,* especially their dialogic parts.

For in essence this way of teaching is not mere storage of information, but the exercise of the student's whole mind and spirit toward a right sense of values and in the direction of truth. He is taught to see and think and judge and act safely for himself. But a third way of teaching is more subtle and unconscious. We might call it infection. The teacher's whole personality engages that of the student, reinforcing, enlarging, elevating the younger men within its reach who are susceptible to its power. It works quietly, unconsciously; it is incapable of manipulation, test, or measurement. It is especially characteristic of the greatest teachers, such as Witherspoon, Henry, McCosh, Wilson. Their students testify not much to the facts they learned from these men, nor usually to the correction of thought and feeling and observation wrought by the training these men gave them. Both of these benefits they doubtless received. But what they somewhat incoherently express is the expansion and revelation they caught from immediate contact with the very genius and greatness of these men.

Now this power, I believe, is not confined to such eminent instances as I have mentioned. In some measure it lives in every man worthy to profess the art of teaching. And though it may not touch every young person assigned to him for instruction, there will surely be some to whom he belongs in this intimate and edifying relation. But, as we say, it is an unconscious matter, and the more unconscious the better.

By these three ways the genuine teacher will teach, transcending all the so-called pedagogy and doctrine of schools of education, or what the regulars call "teacher-training."

The true teacher will be a sophisticate. In the true sense, I mean. For true sophistication is not a matter of usage, or the little proprieties, or knowing one's way about at court or in the high world, or being a shriner in the mysteries of Emily Post. A remote tiller of the soil may be more sophisticated by far than a seasoned and blasé man-about-town. Sophistication is measured by knowledge of men, and by the scale of values in human nature. The city business man may have a range in such values of but two octaves or less. The intelligent countryman may compass a range of eight octaves or more. And the range of human values within the teacher's reach should be as wide as he can make it. He, of all men, should be the sophisticated man.

It is time, according to honored custom, to fetch out and dust off our ancient motto, "Philosophy the Helmsman of Life."

Plutarch in one of his essays remarks: "We ought to make Philosophy the chief of all our learning. . . . For by the advice and assistance thereof it is that we come to understand what is honest and what is dishonest, what is just and what is unjust; in a word, what we are to seek, and what to avoid." In short, true education, true sophistication, implies standards of value, discrimination, discernment, intelligent self-protection, and insurance against imposition however specious. And it implies more —the enlistment of one's energies in the quest to save oneself and others from spiritual wreck.

All of which is well enough in a safe, secluded, comfortable moment like this. But I know full well how disturbed all of us, especially you younger men, are at this very instant by the shifty and uncertain state of things, the world's insecurity, the muddle of men's minds, the distant alarms, the confused clamor of many voices.

Have you never noticed in a crowd of men, on the street, in a train, at a game or party or the theatre, now and then a man with a pair of eyes that are different—the eyes perhaps of a sailor, a mountaineer, a plainsman? Have you not seen in them a kind of contracted keenness from their long habit of looking with distant focus to far horizons and beyond them? Such eyes, you will notice, are brighter, steadier, more expressive, and far more interesting than the dull and common eyes of an office clerk, or even of a scholar subdued all his days to a range of two feet or less. Such should be the eyes in the mind and spirit of the teacher, looking far beyond these temporal disorders we have rehearsed to the eternal values, and training the focus of younger men to the same range. For these values lie latent everywhere in our liberal studies—in science, in literature, in art and history and philosophy, in social studies, above all in religion.

But they come true only as they become incarnate in living men. Therefore, it is first of all the man, the teacher, we must make sure of. "Is he alive?" McCosh would ask about every candidate for the Faculty. So don't choose courses, choose men. And you will be lucky to have discovered, through your years in school and college, a dozen such men—men who incarnate their subject and by all three processes of teaching transmit to you some of its long-run power and significance, because their paramount interest is in you even more than in their subject, in your intellectual and spiritual fulfillment as a man.

The times are treacherous and uncertain. Men are losing their interest in the individual human being. They are forfeiting it to the fashionable unbelief of an evil day. They will realize their loss and turn again to the light and fresh air, and will clear the poison from their brains.

The tide will turn again to flood. Meanwhile it is ours not to yield to the ebbing pull, but to hold our course against it—even desperately—until it turns, and men do their work and rethink their thoughts to new agreement on a scale not shortened to the squint focus of this little life, but adjusted to the infinite reaches apprehended by the faith that transcends knowledge.

LEWIS WEBSTER JONES

The Spirit of '76 and
the Barbarian Culture

I AM honored to be asked to address the members of this distinguished Society, on the occasion of its one hundred and
seventy-fifth birthday. Any anniversary which is a multiple of
twenty-five is always regarded as especially important, justifying
reminiscences and comparison; and rightly so today, when
twenty-five years, or a quarter of a century, has brought changes
more drastic than any of our forefathers of 1776 saw in a long
lifetime.

Indeed, the most striking contrast between then and now is that
of tempo. Few of us nowadays have time for contemplation,
time to cultivate the "friendship, morality and literature" which
were the guiding principles of the original Society of Phi Beta
Kappa. Especially is this true of university presidents. I ought
to be sufficiently experienced to know that it is devastatingly
true of presidents in transition from one university to another;
but my pleasure at being invited to meet this learned group made

Delivered before the Alpha of New Jersey, Rutgers University, the
Beta of New Jersey, Princeton University, and a group of Phi Beta
Kappa alumni, December 5, 1951. Published by Rutgers University.

me forget, when I accepted the invitation, how scarce time for reading, thinking, and writing was likely to be.

Though the original Phi Beta Kappa Society, organized at the College of William and Mary on December fifth in 1776, was as much social as intellectual in its purposes, it has come to embody and symbolize the highest ideals of American scholarship. And I think we may fairly take that early group at William and Mary, and the chapters which were soon organized at Harvard and Yale, as symbolizing the ideals which inspired all the little group of Colonial colleges, among them Rutgers and Princeton, during the latter half of the eighteenth century.

I should like to recall to your minds the intellectual climate of those days, and then to ask what are the tasks for American scholarship today, when the climate is far less favorable, the weather often quite deplorable, and most of the predictions are of storms or hurricanes ahead.

It is hard to suppress a feeling of nostalgia for the Spirit of '76. It was an age in which the greatest and most generous aspirations of men were coming to flower. Those were the days when men believed in reason, in human perfectability, in natural rights and a natural law guided by Divine Providence. The conception of a man as a person of moral choice, capable of personal responsibility and therefore of self-government, came from the Greeks and from the Renaissance; but in the eighteenth century the ideal was active and immediate; people looked forward confidently to a state of society where the dignity of all men would be recognized and realized. They believed in the possibility of sweeping away bad governments and setting up a government which would embody the Rights of Man, laying a foundation for a civilization on this great new continent immeasurably superior to anything which had gone before.

True, there were terrible conflicts ahead: the War of Independence was just beginning; the French Revolution loomed ominously in the future. But the objectives for which men were willing to fight were clear and inspiring, the fruits of victory foreseen as definite and of lasting value. It was an age of fervor and conviction. Speculation about human society was exciting. People believed in rational solutions; in liberty, under the guidance of God. Such a faith is at a low ebb today.

Typical of the spirit of the age was Adam Smith's *Wealth of Nations*, first published in 1776. Smith's book had two essential ingredients for arousing enthusiasm: a definite object of attack, and a promise of boundless benefits when the offending object should be successfully removed. He attacked the obsolete hodge-podge of laws and restrictions on trade which had accumulated over the centuries; and he pointed to a natural law which would ensure that individuals, free to follow their enlightened self-interest, would, under the guidance of the Hidden Hand of Providence, make their maximum contribution to the common welfare. Smith offered also a new hope of peace; he showed that trade between nations was mutually beneficial. Adam Smith's doctrines achieved immediate success because they fitted the experience and expressed the needs of the growing and powerful class of manufacturers and business men. But they also had some of the general appeal of all the reforms not yet accomplished. We can always see more clearly what is wrong with the present system than we can imagine the ills which may accompany our proposed remedies, once they are put into practice. Dicey expressed this melancholy truth when he wrote about the growing appeal of socialist and collectivist movements; the attractiveness of socialism, he said, was due to lack of testing. "It has not yet achieved in practice that self-success which, to ardent believers in plans for the improvement of mankind, is equivalent to something more disappointing than failure." In '76, no one could foresee the full effects of the industrial revolution or imagine the international tensions we face today, so different from the peaceful, productive, mutually beneficial international co-operation envisaged by Adam Smith. In '51, we cannot expect a new

Wealth of Nations, which will promise to solve all the infinitely complex economic problems of the contemporary world by means of a few simple legislative changes.

The latter half of the eighteenth century was an age of political giants. The founders of this republic were truly great men. No amount of debunking or the economic or psychological interpretation of everything can detract from the stature of Washington, Jefferson, Hamilton, Adams, and Monroe as political philosophers and statesmen.

These men debated their differences with all the fervor which belonged with a conviction that the future welfare of the country, indeed of mankind, hung on their decisions. Today, threatened with atomic warfare, we feel a comparable sense of urgency. But if we compare the speeches and writings of the founding fathers with the so-called Great Debate recently raging about the conduct of our foreign policy, we can only blush for our contemporaries. Instead of reasoned arguments, we hear charges and counter-charges of "smear" and "whitewash." Instead of *positive* conviction about the rights of man, a *positive* faith in American destiny, we have competition in expressions of anti-communism.

It is true that the great statesmen of '76, and of the early formative years of this republic, were drawn from a relatively small class. They were educated men, men of position and substance. But they were fired by an ideal of an American society in which all men could be given the opportunity to lift themselves to their own high level. Science, education, and the republican form of government were to achieve this leveling upward, which was the essence of the American dream of '76.

Brooks Adams has commented sourly on this democratic hope in his essays on *The Degradation of the Democratic Dogma.* He marks the beginning of its decline at the death of Washington; its decisive defeat at the election of Jackson over John Quincy Adams in 1828. Adams, who was, I think, a member of Phi Beta Kappa, had believed firmly in science and education and had been convinced that God supported him in his high ideals for America. The introduction of the spoils system and the exploitation of the public lands broke his heart and almost persuaded him that God had deserted both him and the American people.

Writing in 1919, Brooks Adams had seen nothing to correct his grandfather's despairing impression. He was convinced that democracy, coupled with competition, meant a leveling down, not up. He quoted his brother Henry Adams in likening democratic mediocrity to the ocean: the inflowing waters are engulfed and have fallen to a common level, where they can no longer do useful work; and the whole mass is blown upon and stirred into tempests by random winds.

Brooks Adams is undoubtedly biased in equating the defeat of his grandfather in a presidential election with the downfall of democracy. But most of us would agree that the statesmen of '76 make those of 1951 look less than giants. This is surely not because of any lack of talent. There must be thousands of men whose abilities match those of the founding fathers. It is rather because of the changed political climate, in which great qualities no longer flourish. Politics, which should be the foremost interest of civilized men and the noblest calling, has acquired a meaning which Washington did not foresee. The word has become a term of opprobrium. To say that a thing is "political" is to imply that it is devious, dishonest, designed for personal or party advantage, never for the public good.

The founding fathers relied on public education to uplift and enlighten society by providing an intelligent electorate as the basis for a sound republic. A project dear to Washington's heart was the founding of a great national university; and Jefferson founded the University of Virginia. In drafting the report of the Visitors of the University, in 1821, he said:

We fondly hope that the instruction which may flow from this institution, kindly cherished, by advancing the minds of our youth with the growing science of the time, and elevating the views of our citizens generally to the practice of the social duties and the functions of self-government, may ensure to our country the reputation, the safety, the prosperity, and all the other blessings which experience proves to result from the cultivation and improvement of the general mind.

Faith in education has been a continuing theme throughout our history. It inspired the Morrell Act, establishing the Land-Grant Colleges in 1862. In these new, democratic institutions, the benefits of learning were to be brought to bear on the ordinary pursuits of men, through research and instruction in the agricultural and mechanical arts as well as in the liberal studies.

Today, we are educating an unprecedentedly large number of our young people. In 1951, 75 per cent of all boys and girls of high-school age are attending school; and about 14 per cent of young people of college age are receiving higher education. What can be said of the results?

From the point of view of citizenship, a recent report by Dr. George Gallup is discouraging. Most of you probably saw it. The usual cross section of the population was asked six very simple questions relating to foreign affairs: Where is Manchuria? Where is Formosa? What is the 38th Parallel? What is meant by the Atlantic Pact? Who is Chiang Kai-shek? and Who is Marshal Tito? Only 12 per cent of the adults who were questioned could answer all six questions correctly; and 19 per cent could not answer a single one. It was further discovered that one-third did not know that Dean Acheson was Secretary of State, and one-third had never even heard of Senator McCarthy. Dr. Gallup also explored the prevailing ignorance about the effects of the atomic bomb, which were in general greatly exaggerated; and about the probable effects of a future war on the United States, which were in general alarmingly underestimated.

There has never been a generation so continuously bombarded with information—in the press, on the air, on movie newsreels or television—as this one. Ignorance must reflect in part a lack of interest; and some of this may possibly be explained by the fact that foreign affairs no longer make sense to the average man. He might as well not worry about them, as he feels himself powerless to influence them.

In '76, foreign affairs did make sense, readily intelligible to any American. Anyone could see that we ought to get rid of the British, court the assistance of the French, then concentrate on building up our own country and beware of further entangling alliances. Then, and indeed until very recently, some rational behavior could be counted on, even from our potential enemies. The language of diplomacy was a synonym for excessive politeness, certainly not for the crude brand of mutual vilification which has recently replaced it in international conferences. Discussions between diplomats assumed at least some measure of good will and a willingness to arrive at a reasonable compromise of differences. Today, discussion has become fantastically devious. Neither side considers any proposal emanating from the other side on its merits, but each looks for some hidden propaganda purpose. The terms "waging peace" and "peace offensive" are typical of the degeneration of international conversations. The possibility of reasonable compromise and ultimate agreement on any point seems to be excluded. I don't know what Jefferson, or the founders of Phi Beta Kappa, would have made of a televised interchange between Gromyko and Austin.

In short, the general leveling-down process, of which Brooks Adams wrote, seems to have gone on at an accelerating rate, as science and universal literacy have increased the media of mass communication.

The Spirit of '51 is on the whole sadly confused and pessimistic. In the last ten years I suppose more has been said about our respect for the dignity of the individual human being than was ever said in the whole of the eighteenth century. But much of the contemporary protestation sounds like a pious utterance rather than a true statement of conviction. Our conviction has been sapped by Darwin, Marx, and Freud, as well as by our contemporary experience. Darwin reduced the human spirit to the chance result of millennia of accidents; the environment was the determinant, not human will or reason. Marx substituted the impersonal forces of economic history for man's moral purposes. Freud substituted rationalism for reason. All these trends of thought, in conjunction with our experience of individual helplessness to affect mass political, cultural, and social movements, have weakened our faith in individual rationality, responsibility, and dignity, in spite of our increasing verbal allegiance to these things.

Yet civilization, as we understand it, surely means the fullest development of whole men, of individuals who are morally responsible for their actions. The subordination of the individual to the mass is the essence of barbarism.

Ortega y Gasset, writing some thirty years ago, warned that Western civilization was threatened, not as Rome was by the barbarians from without, but by the barbarians from within. Ortega defines the barbarian as the mass man, the self-satisfied man. Just as the primitive barbarian takes the trees of his forests for granted, so the modern barbarian accepts as given all the wonders of his own civilization, and feels no personal responsibility for them. He enters his heated apartment, switches on the light, sits down to amuse himself by staring at the television screen. His wife meanwhile defrosts a precooked meal, keeping one eye on the children, who are now rapidly recovering from an extended illness with the help of streptomycin. He expects to take the family on an automobile trip this summer, riding thousands of miles on concrete roads, finding gasoline, restaurants, and sleeping accommodations wherever and whenever he needs them, reasonably safe all the time from robbery, oppression, or arbitrary violence. He has little understanding of the scientific discoveries which make his physical comforts possible, less of the complexities of the economic system which brought them within his purchasing power. He seldom thinks of the centuries of struggle and sacrifice, the great political accomplishments, which have given him his freedom and relative security. The modern barbarian merely expects to exploit all these things for his own advantage. He holds up no high standards of behavior for himself, he strives for nothing beyond his everyday satisfactions. He is the average man, who takes pride in this mediocrity. If he admires anything outside himself, it is success. He admires the smart operator, the getter-by, the fixer, the man who can beat the game.

In contrast to this modern barbarian, Ortega puts the aristocrat. He does not mean the man of wealth and social standing, the aristocrat of birth. He means the aristocrat of the spirit, the man who holds up a standard for himself. He is the man of effort, striving for excellence and admiring it in others. He is guided by a sense of duty and obligation which he puts above his own comforts and security.

I think that the Spirit of '76, from which our democracy was born, was essentially aristocratic. It believed that all men, given political liberty, equality before the law, and the great economic opportunities of this vast new continent, would be ennobled. They would acquire and practice the aristocratic virtues. These virtues seemed at that time no more than could be expected of free, educated men; and all men were to be free and educated. Democracy was to be a process of leveling upward, not downward; a progress toward the standards of honor and duty characteristic of the gentleman, not the barbarian.

It may be objected that I am attributing to the men of '76 beliefs which few of them would have expressed. If so, I apologize to all the historians present. My sweeping generalizations must be excused because of the lack of time I have already deplored and in any case they are useful in order to make this point: that we must in this democracy slant our educational policies in the direction of more conscious inculcation of the political virtues I have called "aristocratic."

It may be further objected that the aristocratic virtues have always depended on privilege and status. Can we expect "noblesse oblige" if we eliminate the "noblesse"? Churchill represents the aristocratic tradition in England, and he has made a striking gesture in reducing his own and his ministers' salaries on his return to office. As we admire, we cannot help reflecting that most Conservatives can afford such generosity, while labor politicians typically have no outside source of income. It has often been pointed out that lack of interest in personal gain is easier if one has a comfortable bank balance.

I am ready to admit that history affords more examples of "noblesse" without the "oblige" than of "oblige" without the "noblesse." Yet I am convinced that the health of our civilization depends on a much more widespread and thorough inculcation of what Ortega has called the "aristocratic virtues" than has so far been achieved here, or indeed anywhere. If you insist that the aristocratic virtues are associated with privilege, I would reply that the privilege now belongs to all of us; it is the inestimable privilege of membership in a democratic society; we can only justify this privilege, and preserve it, if we understand and assume the corresponding obligations.

During the nineteenth century we could perhaps afford what Brooks Adams has called "the degradation of the democratic dogma." It was a century of expansion, of new physical frontiers, of a rapidly growing population which still found plenty of room. Our civilization could advance and flourish in spite of bad government, bad because we were too busy to pay much attention to it. We thought we could afford to concentrate most of our educational efforts on training people to achieve individual success, with the excuse that in building their own fortunes they are also building up the country. We thought we could afford to give students the technical, vocational education they demanded, at the expense of the liberal education which used to produce the "scholar and the gentlemen."

In the mid-twentieth century, it is clear that we can afford these luxuries no longer. We must give our most serious attention, not a cynical or amused side glance, to politics. And we must make a dogged and concerted effort to teach, in schools, colleges, and adult classes, the political virtues which are the only possible foundation for a sound democracy.

In saying this, I am aware that I am echoing the cry of all social reformers, from the founding fathers on down, who have put their hopes in an improved standard of public morality. John Quincy Adams thought it would come as a result of the application of science to human affairs and the spread of universal literacy. Lenin belived that the abolition of capitalism would result in the appearance of men "unlike the present man-in-the-street" who would no longer "calculate with the shrewdness of a Shylock whether he has not worked half an hour more than another, whether he is getting less pay than another." A new morality would automatically emerge after the revolution, when men were freed from the evil effects of the economic system which Lenin thought responsible for most existing forms of human misbehavior. Today more sober and realistic views prevail. Soviet Russia, with its ruthless materialism and its denial of the rights of individuals, is not the outcome of an evolution towards a higher social order. It is black reaction and the triumph of barbarism. No glorious new morality will follow automatically from any revolution, whether socialist or fascist or of any other kind. Nor can we expect any sudden change in morality to *precede* and usher in any hoped-for Utopia. Our hopes must be more modest, but our needs are more urgent. It is very clear that we must do our best to revive and re-energize the ideals of individual responsibility and political integrity which animated our forefathers of '76, because we need them *now*, in order to preserve ourselves from barbarism *now*, not in some remote future.

If I thought we could only be saved by a radical transformation of human nature, I should give up hope, or at least quit my present profession. But I find myself in 1951 still obstinately imbued with some of the Spirit of '76. I believe, as our forefathers did, in the great and inspiring potentialities of American civilization. I believe that the American Revolution is a continuing thing, and that its purposes offer us a continuing guide to action. And I share the faith of Jefferson and Adams in the promise of education. Mere universal literacy is now obviously inadequate, if not positively dangerous. Man is not as rational as all that. But an education which deliberately sets out to teach students that civilization is their responsibility still seems to me to be well worth our most devoted efforts.

In spite of Darwin, Marx, and Freud I don't really believe in the mass man, shaped by the all-powerful and nonmoral environment. I don't believe the Russian people will permanently lose their human individuality, or remain forever docile. If I have drawn a dreary picture of our more obvious barbarian characteristics, I know from my own experience, as you do, that these are not the whole story. Unfortunately, we put our worst foot forward. Our more public and conspicuous expressions often reveal, not the best nor even the average, but the least common denominator. Clowns and blackguards make the headlines, while the solid work of countless good citizens in thousands of communities goes unnoticed.

Nevertheless the menace of barbarism is real and urgent, and unless we make a deliberate effort to reshape our own environment, we shall become its victims. W. H. Auden fixes the responsibility squarely on us when he says:

> But the new barbarian is no uncouth
> Desert-dweller; he does not emerge
> From fir-forests: factories bred him;
> Corporate companies, college towns
> Mothered his mind, and many journals
> Backed his beliefs. He was born here.[1]

[1] *The Age of Anxiety* (New York: Random House, [1947]), p. 19.

214

In other words, he is a product of the education we have given him. It is the task of American scholarship to reshape education, so as to produce civilized men, and thus to reshape the environment in the direction of civilization.

In order to do this, scholarship must leave the ivory tower. It must become less withdrawn, less anemic, than it has sometimes been in the recent past. Scholarship cannot be a refuge from the distressing problems of contemporary life. The scholar must face them, and do his best to exemplify active virtue, rather than mere piety. If he is merely pious, holding right beliefs but not acting on them, he is a pedant, not a scholar.

Above all, it is the duty of the scholar today to teach, with real dedication and conviction. We are all now keenly aware of the misdirection of American higher education which has concentrated too heavily on techniques and neglected the civilizing influences of the humanities. Most of us are trying to correct this by reorganizing the curriculum. But it is neither necessary, nor desirable, to eliminate specialization. We cannot give all our attention to teaching the humanities, or to training our students in economics and political science. But we can surely teach all subjects, no matter how specialized or technical, with a clear and explicit recognition of their human relevance and their humane purposes.

If we don't do this, we face the nightmare prospect of George Orwell's *1984*, a world in which the tools and techniques which were a product of human reason are used to suppress, distort, or deny all human values.

To combat this threatened barbarism, American scholarship must get rid of selfishness, stuffiness, and pedantry, and take up its task with a missionary fervor comparable to the Spirit of '76. True scholarship, I repeat, is an exercise of virtue, not of piety, relating the scholar in a responsible way to the practical problems and the great moral issues of his times. If our times are more difficult than those of the founders of this Society of Phi Beta Kappa, our task is certainly not hopeless. The most powerful force in the world is still the creative imagination. We should not allow ourselves to be cowed by its inert results, the mechanical forces which threaten to overwhelm us. Instead, we should attack with courage and conviction the task of controlling the human environment in such a way as to use our marvelous scientific achievements for humane ends—a prospect even more inspiring today than in '76. We must reaffirm our faith in truth as the only weapon against propaganda, and in the active intellectual virtues, the individual excellence and integrity for which Phi Beta Kappa stands, as the proper weapons of civilization against barbarism.

Above all, we must fiercely defend the positive principle of liberty and the freedom of the human mind and spirit against those barbarians, both from the outside and from within, who in the name of freedom seek to enslave mankind. Our universities must proclaim, if I may again be permitted to quote the authentic spokesman of 1776, Thomas Jefferson, concerning his plans for the University of Virginia: "This institution will be based on the illimitable freedom of the human mind. For here we are not afraid to follow truth wherever it may lead, nor to tolerate any error so long as reason is left free to combat it."

WILMARTH S. LEWIS

The Trustees of the Privately Endowed University

THE subject of this oration is one that I have been warned against choosing. Everyone agrees that it has never been more important than it is today, "but," as one expert on it said to me, "no one knows enough to talk about it." Another friend said, "You will not please anybody with your Oration and you will exhaust yourself and your wife writing it." During the past three months both of these statements have been confirmed.

Why is this subject so difficult? Considering how much time is given to talking about trustees, it is remarkable that people should be so muddled about them. They are regarded with esteem, envy, and suspicion; they are honored and caricatured. Why is there this confusion? Are not the functions of trustees of a privately endowed university perfectly clear? As a matter of fact, they are not. The four sets of people who are most concerned—the president and his officers in administration, the faculty, the graduates,

Delivered before the Alpha of Massachusetts, Harvard University, June 16, 1952. Published in *The American Scholar*, Winter, 1952–1953.

and the trustees themselves—agree pretty much within their own groups about what the trustees should do and not do, but there agreement ends. And now, with utter recklessness, I shall try to say what each of the four groups thinks the functions of trustees are.

Most presidents believe that the functions of trustees are few and formal; the presidents who think otherwise are likely to be men who but for the grace of God might themselves have been trustees. A familiar attitude is that of the administrator who said at the inaugural of a young president, "Don't let the trustees push you around." This advice suggests a certain tension that is also discernible in an article called "Why Presidents Wear Out." There the author lists at the head of the forces in league against the president "the board of trustees (by whatever name)" and states that an active trustee is "a domineering" trustee. These remarks are more outspoken than the summary of an eminent president: "The proper work of the board," he said, "is to choose a president. Having done so, the internal affairs of the institution must be left to the president and his faculty." Thus even a temperate observer of trustees recommends their effacement, except when the need for a new president gives them their rare season of flowering, and he believes this so strongly that he suspends them in a hanging participle.

So far as the faculty is concerned, trustees are all but mythical. The average scholar knows little about what they do: he may never meet one. To the scholar the trustee's chief significance is his reputed power of making faculty appointments. The scholar is well aware of the protracted exploration that his academic superiors make into the records of candidates, but he is told that the ultimate decision rests with the alien governing body. If the scholar's subject is Sanskrit, he is bound to question the trustee's capacity to pass upon his professional merits; if his subject is economics, he may fear that the trustee's personal views will lead him to doubt the scholar's fitness for promotion. In any event, it is easy to see why the scholar may also view the trustee with a somewhat cold eye and why he writes papers to say that there should be "legal representation of the faculty on the governing board of every college and university in the country."

In the minds of graduates, to become a trustee of one's university is to receive one of the most coveted honors in the country. Graduates believe that the trustees' power is absolute, and they frequently think that too little use is made of it. If you walk into any university club at the end of an afternoon, you will find groups of graduates gravely talking about some aspect of university affairs that they would like to see altered. The subject of these colloquies may be the university's lack of a cosmotron or a Gutenberg Bible; the subject could be the desirability of hiring a football coach who would win games instead of losing them; the subject is sure to be, somewhere in the building, the presence of certain men on the faculty who are alleged to hold views that differ from those held by the graduates discussing them. At length someone will ask, whatever the subject may be, "Why don't the trustees do something?" Heads shake sadly; the last glass is put down; the group goes silently home to dinner: it is all too clear that the trustees will do nothing whatever.

And how do the trustees view themselves? Far more modestly than is sometimes supposed. A graduate is justly proud of his trusteeship; he is ready to spend a great deal of time and thought on it. Yet on taking his place on the board, he becomes aware of how little he knows about the university, no matter how faithfully he has read the alumni magazine and gone to alumni dinners and talked to his undergraduate sons. Can this be the place that was a part of him years ago? These new schools and institutes and centers, what are they, anyway? What has happened to the things that meant most to him at college—the friendships he made there, the furious undergraduate activity, the teacher whose wisdom or eccentricity lingers in his mind? He sits through his first meetings in a haze of bewilderment, painfully aware of his ignorance. In this trying period he may well ask himself, "What are the functions of a university trustee?"

Some weeks ago, when dining in a certain company of gentlemen, I put this question to them. Although nearly all of those present were university trustees, my question was not answered with the fullness and clarity I had hoped for. Trustees elect the president, it was agreed; they oversee the university's investments; they may also, as individuals, give advice in technical matters of which they have extensive knowledge. They may further, it developed, serve a function of considerable usefulness: since the consent of the trustees is necessary for university legislation, the president and his lieutenants must prepare their proposals for it with care, bearing in mind the dread possibility that the trustees may exercise their right to ask questions and raise objections. Here we have, it was recognized, an incentive to sober planning, a function that might be called Being a Cloud no Bigger than a Man's Hand. There it is, the Cloud, always in the sky, "A sight to dream of, not to tell." Yet the president may be glad to point to it on occasion. To illustrate: When Professor A goes to the president with a request that the president does not wish to refuse in his own person, it is helpful to him to be able to say, "I'll take your request up with the trustees, if you insist, but I am certain that they will turn you down and that this inopportune request may jeopardize a timely one later." Professor A withdraws his request, and the trustees, all unknowing, have eased the burdens of administration. Apart from these functions, little was certain to the group at the dinner table; in fact, the discussion was concluded with the question, "Why do there have to be trustees, anyway?" The full duty of trustees is not evident even to trustees.

Why, indeed, do we have them? The obvious answer is found in the original charter of the university, an example of which is furnished by the Act to Erect a Collegiate School in Connecticut in 1701. The Act named ten clergymen of the Colony as "Trustees, Partners, or Undertakers" for the School, "who should imploy the moneys or any other estate" contributed for the benefit of the School and who should "have henceforward the oversight full and compleat Right Liberty and Priviledge to furnish direct manage order improve and encourage" the School "in such ways orders and manner and by such Persons Rector Master and Officers appointed by them as shall according to their best discretion be most conducible to attaine" the desired ends of the School. These ten clergymen represented the orthodoxy and authority of the time as well as its learning. During the past seventy-five years the clergymen have largely given way on the governing boards to financiers and lawyers, the modern representatives of orthodoxy and authority. They exercise two of their predecessors' powers without challenge: the right to appoint the president and the right to hold title to and control the university's property. Much of the difficulty in trying to define the trustees' role today arises from the fact that the third characteristic of the original trustees, learning, has passed to the faculty. And learning is the primary concern of the university.

Let us now try to answer the far more difficult question: What should the trustees do today in addition to choosing the president and "imploying" the moneys of the university? Trustees, we have seen, are a jury whose favorable verdict must be secured by the president; as individuals they may be able to give expert advice upon a particular university problem; the board as a whole, through its collective wisdom, its inherited sense of continuity and its objectivity, may serve as a temperate balance and guide through the years. This is much, but today trustees have a still further duty, and that is to bridge the gulf of ignorance that divides the professionals (the scholars) and the laity (the graduates and friends of the institution whose continuing gifts are necessary to its welfare). This may not be a new duty, but it is an urgent one. The view, which was prevalent in university administration at one time, that the graduates are a nuisance to be tolerated only because the university needs their money, has yielded to the more sensible course of seeking, and taking, the advice of outstanding graduates upon matters in which their advice is valuable. This has been pure gain for all concerned; yet there remains the problem of the graduates whose connection with the university is second-hand. Among them—who are necessarily the majority— are found those who really do believe that scholars are allied, in a greater or less degree, with the enemies of our society. These graduates say that scholars are just the people the enemy would suborn, because scholars are gullible idealists, because they are underpaid, and because they speak directly into the ears of the picked youth of the land. Anyone who travels about this country will hear them make all of these statements and will be able to say with the Bastard in *King John:*

> . . . as I travell'd hither through the land,
> I find the people strangely fantasied,
> Possess'd with rumours, full of idle dreams,
> Not knowing what they fear, but full of fear.

A few graduates go so far as to claim that their contributions to the university entitle them to dictate what the university shall teach and how it shall teach it. To them the trustee can speak better than anyone else because he is a surrogate for the graduates in the administration of the university, whether he is elected by them or not. When a classmate says to him, "I know you must have academic freedom and all that, but why can't you see to it that the right ideas are put in the students' heads before they graduate?" he will be wise not to ask his classmate what he means by "right ideas," but content himself with pointing out that if the trustees attempted to do anything of the kind, the entire faculty, including its most conservative members, would resign as soon as they could. The trustee may add that he is a conservative and that he is opposed to his classmate's radicalism, which would tear the place up by the roots. To the more hysterical he can say that by undermining confidence in the patriotism of the American scholar they may be serving the Soviets just as much as any card-carrying Communist. Finally, in response to the argument that he who pays the piper calls the tune, he can say what trustees have said before him—and none more eloquently than a recent trustee of Harvard—that the university is not for sale. The trustee can, in short, cease being the whipping-boy of American scholars and become their champion.

Trustees are the ideal spokesmen for graduates. Yet before they can say what they should say, they must usually undergo a course of instruction. The modern American university is so complex that only a few administrative officers have detailed knowledge of all of it. Tours arranged for the benefit of the trustee, gallops through the library or physics laboratory, show him how little he knows. Of the immensely important personal relationships that exist in every corner of the university and that make every situation unique, he has probably no knowledge whatever. The sensible trustee gradually realizes that he must leave the running of the university to the president and his colleagues, that he must be content to consider the problems they bring to him and be ready to carry out any specific tasks the president may ask him to perform.

The president is required by law to bring to the trustees many matters on which their approval is routine. The absurdity of their passing on the merits of a Sanskrit professor is plain; it is equally absurd to think that they can make a thorough, or even a superficial, study of the budget. Once a year the budget is solemnly presented to the trustees in a summarized form. Their eyes travel over the figures and schedules that have been prepared by dozens of people during the past months, all of them experts in their subjects. The merits of scores of items, from the new claims of the Law School to the amount to be spent on floor wax, have been weighed and debated. Why should a trustee question the judgment of the informed men who have arrived at the decisions

223

represented by these figures before him? His eye lingers longest on the projected deficit, that hardy perennial, but he has learned that it is not so alarming as it appears to be, for three reasons: first, the congenital pessimism of treasurers that makes them take a gloomy view of the future; second, the reserve funds that have been prudently stored away for seasons of drought; and, third, the manna that mercifully falls upon the university the year around. The veteran trustee turns the pages of the budget silently and murmurs "Aye" when the question of its adoption is finally reached: he has "put on the napless vestment of humility."

For some trustees this self-abnegation is as difficult as it was for Coriolanus. It is easier for those who are members of a learned profession, since they have had the first-hand experience of a graduate school and understand the difference between a college and a university. Furthermore, if they have known teachers as fellow-professionals, the awe and resentment of teachers that non-professionals tend to carry into adult life and that make them uneasy in the presence of teachers will be lessened: trustees who are members of learned professions are cousins of the scholars on the opposite side of the academic world.

To be as useful as he can be, the trustee must be helped by the president, who is the main bridge between the two sides of the academic world: its professionals, the faculty; and its laity, the trustees and graduates. Although the university cannot be fully known by anyone who does not live in it, it is not so large nor the trustee so busy that he cannot become an expert upon one important aspect of it. His experience and predilections will suggest to the president and himself which aspect of the university this shall be. For one, it may be "the portfolio"; for another, the medical school; for a third, the art gallery. If the trustee's energies are focused in this way, he will lose his sense of frustration and impotence and become an informed ally. The presidents who treat their trustees as friends and not as potential enemies are not the presidents who are worn out by them. The model trustee will, of course, not meddle in the conduct of "his" segment of the university; whatever he does will be done "through channels," through the president, as he would wish a trustee to do if he were himself the president, but he will probably be able to give excellent advice about his segment. Being a model trustee, he will not become so concerned with it that he loses sight of his larger obligation to the entire university. In short, our model— this not impossible trustee—works for the good of the whole in sympathy with the rules of American academic societies.

To study his segment of the university may be an easier and pleasanter task for the trustee than to learn these rules. They have been made for the most part by the scholars, who are now a guild that presents a united front on questions it considers to be of primary concern to its profession, however much it may differ within itself on scholarly matters. When the new trustee is catapulted into academic society, no one tells him the rules that govern it. His plight is almost as bad as it would be if he were sent into a cricket match knowing nothing of the game except that tea is served in the middle of it. If the trustee is fortunate, he will discover five of the rules that will be of particular help to him:

Rule One is that the scholar is a citizen of the Republic with the same rights as other citizens.

Rule Two is that the trustee must not think of the scholar as an employee.

Rule Three is that once a scholar is wrapped about in the magic mantle of "tenure," he is invulnerable to attack unless it is proved that he is immoral, incompetent, or a traitor.

Rule Four is that the scholars recommend the appointment of new colleagues to the president; if he approves them, the trustees should appoint the candidates unless they have proof that the candidates are immoral, incompetent, or working for the overthrow of our government.

Rule Five is that scholars teach what they please in their own way, but that they should not use their classrooms to in-

225

doctrinate students with pet "ism's," their own or those of the trustee.

There are many other rules for the faculty and president, but these five are perhaps the most important ones for the trustee to learn, because they are the rules that he will have to explain most frequently when performing his function of liaison between the scholars and the graduates. If he is to be a successful liaison officer, it is essential that he rid his mind of lingering doubts about the honesty and decency of the American scholar. To be a convincing liaison officer he must get himself to the point where he believes in the right of scholars to hold views that he may hate. To be an enthusiastic liaison officer he must have the co-operation of the faculty. They can reassure him by being as mindful of their obligations to the university as they are of the university's obligations to them. They should realize that they wear the label of their institution, and that they should be careful not to allow their personal prejudices and activities to embarrass it. There will always be a few who flout this principle, and it is part of the trustee's education to recognize that he must not attempt to punish them for their inconsiderateness, but leave them to their long-suffering colleagues, who have their time-honored methods of dealing with them.

The trustee will perhaps be helped in his understanding of his duties by going back to the Oration that Emerson delivered on this occasion 115 years ago. There he will find the celebrated definition of the scholar as "the delegated intellect" of mankind, whose spiritual welfare is essential to the health of society. He will also find described certain characteristics of the American scholar that disturbed Emerson, and, if he knows anything at all of modern American scholarship, he will know that these characteristics have been modified. For one thing, our scholars are no longer "fed on the sere remains of foreign harvests," as Emerson accused them of being; they have, along with the rest of the country, come of age. Thanks to the exertions and generosity of other Americans, they have been given in our libraries, museums, and laboratories the tools that they must have to maintain that independence. The trustee will readily believe that the American scholar of 1952 is a better technician than was his great-grandfather, but he may dare to ask: Is his mind as richly stocked? Is the scholar "an university of knowledge," as Emerson said he should be? In rejecting the labors and enchantments of a classical education, has he found a more invigorating substitute? If the trustee happens to have a literary turn of mind, he will believe that the American scholar of today falls short of his 1837 ancestor in one essential particular, his use of our difficult and beautiful language. In the American scholar may still "slumber the whole of reason," but many of his number speak and write a jargon that is incomprehensible, misleading, and graceless. Yet our model trustee will realize that it is not for him to suggest to scholars how they shall write, any more than how they shall vote. Nor should he try to do anything about the other enemies of thought that beset the scholar today: the narrowness of inquiry, for example, that buries itself deeper and deeper in a tiny pocket in the mine of learning. The philologist who knows no history, the historian who knows no science, the scientist who knows no poetry—such men do small credit to their profession; but their shortcomings, the trustee learns, must be corrected by the scholars themselves.

But of course the greatest good that the trustees can do is to exercise the function named in the charter I read a few minutes ago, the "full and compleat Right . . . to improve and encourage." This is a right that many trustees ignore because encouragement can be expensive, and expense is just what they believe must be avoided. Far from exercising this unquestioned right of encouragement, many trustees instead exercise their right to discourage. But the trustee who feels that he has done his "compleat" duty when he has said "No!" is not the man we have been talking about. On the contrary, our trustee gives all possible encouragement to the president to raise the standards of the university ever higher and higher. He contends that the university cannot afford to be anything but first-class in whatever it does, and that he and his colleagues should resist the timid and the second-rate, the tired compromise, with the scorn of fanatics. As the nominal custodians of universities, trustees should do everything in their power to press for an impossible perfection, because nothing less than perfection is worth struggling for. That is the goal in this fabulous country where anything can happen, with all its skepticism and idealism, ruthlessness, generosity, shrewdness, and naïveté. In our society, education has a venerated place. All Americans believe in it as much as they believe in any-thing; even our demagogues make sacrifices to get it. The trustees are, somehow, the lords of this mystery; and theirs, it is believed, is the ultimate responsibility for it.

To be healthy, a university must be in ferment; it will never be just one big happy family. Still, the longer a trustee's experi-ence, the stronger, I think, grows his awareness of the university's essential unity and the dependence, one with another, of its dis-parate elements. All concerned in the conduct of its affairs may say, "Consider that I labored not for myself only, but for all them that seek learning." And this can be said not only of the university that one serves, but of those other universities with which it is linked in spirit. Certainly, no trustee of Yale can stand in this place without a sense of fraternity with Harvard. For 250 years we have jointly upheld the same cause in friendly rivalry and mutual esteem. Our common aim is to teach the best, chosen from the many, and to give to their teachers all possible aid in the pursuit of their calling. Harvard and Yale today are not cloistered seminaries whispering from their towers the last enchantments of the Middle Ages; they are fortresses of the civilization that is under attack at home as well as abroad. Majestically they stand in the strength of their years and service, honored wherever learn-ing is honored, and served with devotion by their presidents, scholars, graduates, and trustees.

DOUGLAS BUSH

On Being One's Self

I VALUE the honor of being invited to this Phi Beta Kappa dinner, and I am grateful for the cordial welcome I have received. It is very pleasant to be here. At least it has been very pleasant up to this point.

Candor, if not diplomacy, suggests that I should begin with two apologies. One is for such a lamentable breach of decorum as producing a manuscript at the dinner table. The truth is that, although for many years I was able to conceal mental decay, I can't any longer. As for the second apologetic note, according to all tradition a Phi Beta Kappa discourse ought to be a steady stream of urbane wit. I used to be capable of sparkling, if I had sufficient notice, but years of living in our world seem to have dried up the springs of humor in me as in many other people. So I fear that what I have to say is more of a sermon than it should be. At any rate it is addressed to the young, and it may be hoped that young people elected to Phi Beta Kappa are in a state of exalted beatitude that can sustain anything. Their elders are hardened by long experience.

I cannot help recalling that the first time I talked at a Phi Beta Kappa dinner the world was at peace, while now no one can

Delivered before the Alpha of Rhode Island, Brown University, March 5, 1953.

think of anything but war. You may have heard of the ocean passenger whose stateroom was so far down in the ship that the directions on his door said, "In case of emergency don't do anything." Many of us, observing the course of events, the helplessness of any private citizen, and the actions and utterances of some of our politicians, may have developed that kind of hopeless fatalism. The older generation, however, have known periods of peace and normality. The young have lived their whole life in an age of war and anxiety, and, except through hearing and reading, have no knowledge of any other sort of world. Young men in particular have on the one hand the normal zest for life and the normal ambitions of youth, and on the other hand the melancholy sense of living on borrowed time, with only one thing to look forward to. It would be natural enough to say "What's the use?" and give up the effort to fulfill one's dreams and make something of life.

But even if war is now far worse than it has ever been before, it has always been a scourge, and yet man and civilization have survived, as in Thornton Wilder's play, by the skin of their teeth. One of the great things in the *Iliad*, to take a long jump backward, is the way in which, through the confusion and slaughter of war, the brief similes give rich and refreshing glimpses of the normal life of peace, the traditional and fruitful activities of nature and man. The same kind of assurance is the theme of Thomas Hardy's massive little poem, "In Time of 'the Breaking of Nations.'"

I should like to urge that, difficult as it is, you should fight against the desperation we all feel and try as best you can to live for the things you believe in—for, in spite of the many diagnoses of the younger generation, I think most of its members have ideals they believe in or would like to believe in. I heard a tale of a young man, now a colleague of mine, who, while in an army camp, read as assiduously as his duties allowed. Some less literate companions indulged in a good many gibes, and finally words led to blows. They did not know that the studious sissy was an intercollegiate boxing champion. After that he read in peace. You may not find yourselves in that particular situation, and I am not suggesting boxing as a solution for the problems of life; but you will find on all sides, you have probably found already, the temptation to give in and go along with the main stream, to acquiesce in the loss of one's own identity and become just one of the crowd.

In recent years, of course, one kind of pressure toward unthinking conformity has come from some of those who are elected to rule over us, the politicians who, whether hysterical themselves or taking advantage of the hysteria they promote, have more and more insisted on obedience to the party line. I remember hearing, many years ago, a well-known writer—who has since moved from the left to the right—complain that you could hardly collect your thoughts without the fear of being arrested for illegal assembly. We seem now to have come pretty close to that point. One way in which that ugly change of temper, and of principle, has been borne in upon me has been through the teaching of that notoriously subversive author, John Milton. When I began, twenty-five years ago, one would have said that *Areopagitica* was a treasured historical document, the most eloquent of pleas for free inquiry and discussion, but that the issue itself was happily no longer alive and never could be again, at least in the English-speaking world. But now it is formidably alive all around us. Some of our governors have the will, and the power, to suppress or intimidate all nonconformity, all freedom of discussion, and they are carrying the inquisition into the very citadels of free inquiry, the universities. However, I do not intend to dwell on a sinister phenomenon that everyone is aware of. And perhaps a citizen of Massachusetts has no occasion to dwell on such a theme in the state founded by Roger Williams.

While recognizing the active presence of that spectre, I wish rather to speak of less conspicuous pressures that were at work long before so many people began to see Red and that continue to work. Even if there were no war going on now, and no bigger one to be dreaded, there would still be the problem of maintaining not merely civilization but the best in civilization, not merely gaining our livelihood but preserving and enriching the best in ourselves and others. If we can, by a strong effort of the imagination, conceive of the world as at peace, there is much in our civilization and in ourselves that is sufficiently disturbing, and the threat of war does not make it any less so. Some of these disturbing phenomena belong to the world at large; some are perhaps especially visible here at home.

For one thing, we have undertaken education on a far larger scale than any other country, and that of course is a grand enterprise. But in the process we have allowed much secondary and some higher education to be pushed down to an often appalling level. Professor Bestor, an historian, has lately been calling attention to the kind and degree of deliberate anti-intellectualism that animates a great deal of educationist theory and practice, a doctrine that reduces education to the lowest common denominator or even below that. Then if we think of the amount of imbecility poured out in print, on the radio, and in television, we cannot help wondering how long it will be before we are a nation, or a world, of subnormal and illiterate children. About the quality of the average popular mind any individual has of course only rough impressions, but the directors of many newspapers, magazines, movies, and radio programs have studied the public, and we must infer that these experts put its mental age at about fourteen.

For a random but concrete example of cultural leadership, I might quote a declaration of faith delivered a while ago by the chairman of the department of humanities in a well-known technical institution. We will call him Professor X. This is the condensed report of his speech to a meeting of the American Society of Mechanical Engineers:

Professor X . . . asserted last night that it would be "morally wrong" for him to advise the reading of the literary classics in this fast-moving age of television, radio and movies. . . .

One should read for the purpose of doing something with what one reads, he asserted: not of polishing one's mind like a jewel, but of improving the world around.

Take up a book because it will tell you something of the world . . . ; read what you want to read, not what you think you should read. "This is the frame of mind that makes reading worthwhile and often deeply rewarding."

"For example, it would be morally wrong of me to urge you to take up a classic like 'David Copperfield' and to settle yourselves in easy chairs for winter evenings' reading. If you tried 'David Copperfield' you would grow restive; you would think of all the other things you might be doing more consistent with your daily environment—looking at television, listening to the radio, going to the movies.

"Moreover, you would wonder why you should spend so much time laboriously reading 'David Copperfield' when you could see the book as a film, should it return some time to the neighborhood movie."

The days of the contemplative life, the long, uninterrupted winter evenings are gone for most of us.

"The single prescription for adult reading," he added, "should be to read something different, something that will change your mind. Herein lies compensation for the loss of the purely reflective life." [1]

This is not a satirical invention, it is honest-to-goodness counsel offered to mature men. The state of mind revealed here, if we can call it a state of mind, is not new, though modern "progress" has greatly nourished its growth, and it is not of course peculiarly American, though the spectacular course of American "progress" may have especially nourished its growth among us. As reminders that such barbarism is not purely modern or American, I should like to read two famous portraits from English literature—portraits that will also remind us of the immense store of rich humor in the great writers of the past.

Mr. Podsnap, in *Our Mutual Friend*, is a classic example of

[1] *New York Times*, November 28, 1950.

unenlightened absorption in business and routine as well as of childish patriotism:

Mr. Podsnap's world was not a very large world, morally; no, nor even geographically: seeing that although his business was sustained upon commerce with other countries, he considered other countries, with that important reservation, a mistake, and of their manners and customs would conclusively observe, "Not English!" when, Presto! with a flourish of the arm, and a flush of the face, they were swept away. Elsewise, the world got up at eight, shaved close at a quarter-past, breakfasted at nine, went to the City at ten, came home at half-past five, and dined at seven. Mr. Podsnap's notions of the Arts in their integrity might have been stated thus. Literature; large print, respectively descriptive of getting up at eight, shaving close at a quarter-past, breakfasting at nine, going to the City at ten, coming home at half-past five, and dining at seven. Painting and Sculpture; models and portraits representing Professors of getting up at eight, shaving close at a quarter-past, breakfasting at nine, going to the City at ten, coming home at half-past five, and dining at seven. Music; a respectable performance (without variations) on stringed and wind instruments, sedately expressive of getting up at eight, shaving close at a quarter-past, breakfasting at nine, going to the City at ten, coming home at half-past five, and dining at seven. Nothing else to be permitted to those same vagrants the Arts, on pain of excommunication. Nothing else To Be—anywhere!

As a so eminently respectable man, Mr. Podsnap was sensible of its being required of him to take Providence under his protection. Consequently he always knew exactly what Providence meant. Inferior and less respectable men might fall short of that mark, but Mr. Podsnap was always up to it. And it was very remarkable (and must have been very comfortable) that what Providence meant, was invariably what Mr. Podsnap meant.

In that urbane and pungent satire, *Friendship's Garland*, Matthew Arnold gives a picture of three typical county magistrates. Lord Lumpington and the Rev. Esau Hittall are unsatisfying products of traditional education.

"That will do for the land and the Church," said Arminius. "And now let us hear about commerce." "You mean how was Bottles educated?" answered I. "Here we get into another line altogether, but a very good line in its way, too. Mr. Bottles was brought up at the Lycurgus House Academy, Peckham. You are not to suppose from the name of Lycurgus that any Latin or Greek was taught in the establishment; the name only indicates the moral discipline, and the strenuous earnest character, imparted there. As to the instruction, the thoughtful educator who was principal of the Lycurgus House Academy,—Archimedes Silverpump, Ph.D., you must have heard of him in Germany?—had modern views. 'We must be men of our age,' he used to say. 'Useful knowledge, living languages, and the forming of the mind through observation and experiment, these are the fundamental articles of my educational creed.' Or, as I have heard his pupil Bottles put it in his expansive moments after dinner . . . : 'Original man, Silverpump! fine mind! fine system! None of your antiquated rubbish—all practical work—latest discoveries in science—mind constantly kept excited—lots of interesting experiments—lights of all colours—fizz! fizz! bang! bang! That's what I call forming a man.' "

"And pray," cried Arminius impatiently, "what sort of man do you suppose this infernal quack really formed in your previous friend Mr. Bottles?" "Well," I replied, "I hardly know how to answer that question. Bottles has certainly made an immense fortune; but as to Silverpump's effect on his mind, whether it was from any fault in the Lycurgus House system, whether it was that with a sturdy self-reliance thoroughly English, Bottles, ever since he quitted Silverpump, left his mind wholly to itself, his daily newspaper, and the Particular Baptist minister under whom he sate, or from whatever cause it was, certainly his mind, qua mind—" "You need not go on," interrupted Arminius, with a magnificent wave of his hand, "I know what that man's mind, qua mind, is, well enough."

To recall Mr. Bottles is to think of his creator's serious and constant theme in his poems and prose—the essential, and the difficult, effort man must make to possess his own soul, to keep his true self, his buried life, from being lost amid the distractions and business of the modern world, and the individual's need of seeking his own total perfection as the only sure way of promoting real social improvement; Arnold's poetry and prose are not less alive and important now than when he wrote.

However, to return to our own time and the advice given to the Society of Mechanical Engineers, if we can get that sort of thing from a professor of the humanities, what can be expected from the mass of people? So, even while barbarism threatens us from without, let us not forget the barbarism within; of that we have plenty. As we have invented more and more ways of wasting time and stultifying the human faculties, more and more people may be drawn away from the experience and insight distilled in great works of art. In the words of our humane oracle, why read *David Copperfield* when you can see it as a movie? Why read at all when you can turn a knob and exist in a state of lazy collapse? Or, according to the latest invention of pedagogy, let us read the classics in the form of comic books—if we can, that is, for some educationists are happily looking forward to the utopian time when children will not all be compelled to learn to read and write.

Similar attitudes appear on higher levels, and also derive their strength from our predominantly technological civilization. I remember a talk I once had with a positivist philosopher—the adjective is doubtless unnecessary, since almost any respectable philosopher nowadays is a positivist of some sort. He laid down this clear and cogent syllogism: the end of life is the contemplation of true propositions; Shakespeare contains no true propositions; therefore Shakespeare is not worth reading. While I remained dumb, the philosopher went on to say that nothing can be accepted as true unless it can be measured; to which I replied that nothing that really matters can be measured; and so, with a reproof valiant and a countercheck quarrelsome, we measured swords and parted.

In a civilization that is in a considerable degree represented by our professor of the humanities and our philosopher, the humanities, the great works of imagination and art, have a relatively small following. That situation, to be sure, has existed throughout the past; what is new in our time is the variety and strength of the pressures that work against the humanities. Of course most people pay lip service to them, since even those who are actually indifferent have to recognize that the humanities have been the flower of civilization, the standard by which a civilization is judged. But everyday practice is another matter. To mention one concrete example, the philanthropic foundations will pour out money lavishly for any project in the physical or social sciences, but when it comes to a bit for the humanities, the usual answer is No.[2] The common attitude might be summed up in a couplet once uttered by Will Rogers when he was speaking at an agricultural college:

> A million dollars for manure,
> But not a cent for literature.

For a more general indication of our dominant creed, I might quote a sentence from the social and scientific writer, Horace M. Kallen:

In terms of their consequences to the health, the comfort, the security, and the joy of life, the labors of men like Pasteur or Watt or Faraday or Edison or Ford have earned better at the hands of mankind than the labors of men like Jesus or Moses or Buddha or Mohammed.

I am not tilting against science and the social sciences, to which we owe so much, but it would seem very plain that the ideals and pressures of a technological and positivistic age have grievously distorted our scale of values. Moreover, it is in the nature of science and the social sciences to deal with things that are

[2] Since this was written, there has been a notable, if somewhat belated, change for the better.

tangible and, up to a point, readily comprehended; but the humanities come from and work upon the mind and character of the individual, and their effects, while immense, are not readily computed by the social statistician. It has been noted, especially by foreign visitors, that among our college students there is often a sense of irrelevance, even of moral guilt, attached to the idea of studying literature and the arts, of becoming a fully perceptive, sensitive, imaginative being. A good many people, young and old, seem to regard as a betrayal of one's social obligations what is really a central fulfillment of them. Our professor of the humanities said that we should not be polishing our minds like a jewel but improving the world around. What he meant by improvement was not clear; or perhaps it was only too clear. At any rate it has always been of the essence of the humanistic tradition that man should seek to improve the world around him; but, in that tradition, it has been no less essential that he should make himself worthy to do so. One of our perennial troubles is that improvement of the world is undertaken by so many people who have not waited to polish their minds. We have only to read our daily paper to see how little value is placed on knowledge, intellectual and aesthetic cultivation, and wisdom, and how much power is possessed by insensitive, dogmatic ignorance.

In addition to these things, there are more special obstacles in the way of the humane life. There is, in school and college and afterwards, a considerable worship of mediocrity, of commonness, a fear of seeming to have tastes and interests above the average level. Obviously members of Phi Beta Kappa do not share that worship or that fear; yet I imagine that few would deny the solid pressure of the herd mind.

Then there is the tendency, so common in this country, to regard great books as something quite divorced from life, as school and college assignments to be read only as ordered and dropped when examinations are over. Hence the painful saying that a liberal education ends on Commencement Day. Many young people, while in college, respond wholeheartedly to great literature, and then, somehow or other, they settle down into flabby middle-aged vacuity, content with the distractions of the passing moment. Starry-eyed undergraduates turn into alumni —into the Helen Hokinson woman and her husband. In no other country, so far as I know, do literary papers print weekly lists of the best-selling books. Such lists, and the much-publicized choices of the book clubs, exert their steady pressure toward the reading of only current popular successes and toward the neglect of the great books of the past. If the saving remnant of readers, readers who are concerned with more than the popular and ephemeral, is to be enlarged, surely the ranks of Phi Beta Kappa ought to furnish the highest proportion of recruits.

To mention only one more obstacle to full development of our faculties, there is the doctrine of vocational specialization. In spite of our tradition of the college of liberal arts, it is commonly assumed, for instance, that a scientist does not need to take very seriously anything but science. One result has been the rapid advancement of science. But another result is that the scientist may be an impoverished and stunted human being, an expert technician who may, outside the laboratory, be quite undeveloped and immature. It should be said at once, of course, that there are many scientists who represent not only science but the humanities at their best. Moreover, the so-called humanist may suffer from a parallel kind of narrowness—although in his case the result may be less fatal because the humanities, by their very nature, have to do with the meaning of life.

A scientist might break in here to say something like this: "What you say about the humanities is all very well, and all very commonplace, but I find scientific research wholly absorbing and satisfying, both in itself and in the possibilities of what it may contribute to human welfare. Also, it is a rigorous discipline which inculcates high respect for hard work and unpreju-

239

diced pursuit of truth; and it both demands and nourishes a high kind of imagination." No one would hesitate to grant such claims. Yet along with those claims and facts there does often go, in practice if not in theory, the belief that science is enough; and it is not enough, because science, however important, is an acquired and a secondary part of life. Man's primary interests and needs belong to man as man. Even a scientist does not love and marry on scientific principles. And we might remember Darwin's acknowledgement that exclusive devotion to science had atrophied his aesthetic sensibility.

Further, although science does have a stake in the realm of value, it is a very limited stake. Science has little to offer concerning the moral ideals, the admiration, hope, and love by which we live—unless of course we go along with the modern proponents of what is called "a scientific morality." On that problem I recall a saying of Julian Huxley, the eminent biologist, that we must now give up all intuitive theories of morality because we know that the conscience originates in the infant's conflicting love and hate for its mother. To come back to the general question of value, one might quote a less cocksure observer of life than Mr. Huxley; it was Lord Bryce, I think, who remarked that, in a time of moral crisis, it is no great help to be able to reflect that the angles at the base of an isosceles triangle are equal. But it is of infinite help to have absorbed the moral insights, the artistic power and beauty, that are alive in the great writers of the world. Without forgetting our immense debts to science, we might think, say, of the behavioristic principles of psychology, or of the wholly mechanistic assumptions and methods of the Kinsey report. I am reminded here of a favorite sentence from an essay [*The Liberal Imagination*] by Lionel Trilling:

A specter haunts our culture—it is that people will eventually be unable to say, "They fell in love and married," let alone understand the language of *Romeo and Juliet*, but will as a matter of course say, "Their libidinal impulses being reciprocal, they activated their individual erotic drives and integrated them within the same frame of reference."

This not overcheerful glance at some aspects of our world might be darkened still further by further evidence, but these bits are enough to recall much that may constrict or corrupt our daily living. It is not intended to deepen depression. We can, in our own small orbits, live in the spirit of that double anecdote of Benjamin Franklin and Tom Paine: when Franklin said, "Where freedom is, there is my country," Paine said, "Where freedom is not, there is mine." And surely the first obligation, the first natural impulse, of the humane spirit is to oppose surrender to the debased values of a mass-production era and the no less debased values of a narrowly positivistic view of life. The chief battleground may prove to be within our individual selves, and the struggle may be so prolonged and exacting that we shall not be able to do much toward improving the world around us; but we shall have really improved one bit of it. And we can best fortify ourselves against the dislocations and dangers and corruptions of the present and future by actively cherishing the humane and spiritual resources of the past. Along with the normal human affections, those resources are, we may remember, just about all that we possess. They are an inalienable, tax-exempt inheritance, and if we do not possess and use them, though we may be professionally successful, in ourselves we shall not amount to much.

I don't mean to suggest that the earnest soul should resolve to read the Hundred Best Books, at twenty pages a day. Nor do I mean that we should never read trash—we all do, and need to; but we should know that it is trash. And there are good movies and radio programs. But what I do mean, if in this intellectual company I may emphasize another cliché, is that, if we wish to be fully human, if we wish to attain some real individual strength and security and happiness, we cannot do without perpetual assimilation of the wisdom and beauty of the world's great writings. I would not of course forget music and the fine arts, which make their unique and essential contributions. But reading is our most common and obvious recreation and resource, and it is at the same time the area in which we are most likely to relax our discrimination and accept anything that comes along.

There are major writers of our own time, and it is our time that we are living in. But the great bulk of great literature belongs to the many centuries before us, all the way back to Homer and the Bible. Many people, both young and old, are given to saying that the past is dead, that they live in the present, and so on. But people wholly immersed in the present cannot understand the present—or anything else; they are like victims of amnesia. What psychologists would say of the individual holds for the race also: the present condition is unintelligible without knowledge of the past. As for those people who insist most vigorously on living in the present, you seldom find that they know much about the chief interpreters of the present; their oracles are likely to be the *Saturday Evening Post* and the *Reader's Digest*.

The notion that the great literature of the past is dead, that it does not speak to us, is based on the obvious fallacy that art, like science or machinery, goes out of date. But great literature is never out of date. Man and his problems, his joys and sufferings, his hopes and visions, remain essentially the same in all ages, and the greatest writers of all ages have had the finest insights and the finest power of expressing them. If we want recreation and refreshment, it is those great writers, tragic and comic, who can best give it to us. And they give us infinitely more at the same time. They enable us, confined as most of us are in our own small cages, to have the experience of living intensely, at our highest pitch; we get that sense of liberation and growth that is so profoundly exciting and satisfying.

I have touched only on imaginative literature, because that is likely to be most completely enjoyable, but of course there are many other areas that can be explored. One may be inclined in scientific or historical or philosophical directions. One may have had all sorts of impulses that undergraduate schedules did not permit to be gratified, and one may follow these up—unless one has fallen a victim to that curious American belief that one cannot look into a subject for one's self but must take a course in it. One may not be able to read a large amount, but the great thing is to have an inward life that is always being lived, an inward life for which one is willing to sacrifice less valuable things. The mind and character will not become a stagnant or a frozen pond so long as there is some movement in the water.

Since I have cited a number of disturbing elements in the cultural scene, I might put in here a little tale that reminds us of the individuals, sometimes very humble individuals, up and down the country who may have more wisdom than persons who get quoted in the newspapers. I heard this tale from Dr. Louis Wright, Director of the Folger Library. One day he summoned a taxi to go to a club and the driver, talkative like most of his kind in Washington, asked if he was going to give a lecture. Yes, said Dr. Wright, on American colonial history. "Oh," said the driver, "that is my line." He went on to say that, although the black sheep of his family, he was compiling a sort of family history, and spent many hours in the Library of Congress. What did Dr. Wright think the best book on the colonial period? Dr. Wright mentioned Andrews' big work. Yes, said the taximan, but he is weak on social history. Dr. Wright observed, by the way, that the man drove by a rather circuitous route, apparently in order to prolong so rewarding a conversation. It came out that he had once been a reporter for the *Chicago Tribune*, "but me and the Colonel had ideological differences." This is, I think, an inspiring anecdote.

I have said nothing of poetry, and I must say a final word about that, since great poetry embodies the very quintessence of man's experience and vision. I once sat next to an eminent economist at a dinner and he, as host, politely introducing a topic of interest to me, remarked, "I suppose nowadays poetry is on the way out." Since I am not quick-witted, my reply was doubtless an incoherent mumble. What I might have said is that poetry can no more be on the way out than breathing. To carry on the metaphor, possibly many readers might complain that modern poets have suffered from adenoids. Much modern poetry has been difficult, until one gets used to it, yet the greatest modern poets, Yeats and Mr. Eliot, are worth all the effort they require; and Mr. Frost is not so simple as he looks. It is of the nature of great poetry to make the most direct and powerful impact upon us; and the tragic vision of life, which all the great poets have had, is, by one of the paradoxes of the human spirit, a supreme aid to fortitude, to belief in man's unconquerable mind. From Homer and the Book of Job up to the present, the great poets have faced, and generally surmounted, despair, and their vision, their courage, their affirmation of life, can become ours. Through imaginative participation in man's greatest works we can really live ourselves, and feel that we are greater than we know. For the prime factor in being one's self is the full and active recognition that there are things above the self and its normal world that claim our loyalty and our reverence.

What I have said is, I know, a tissue of commonplaces, but there are some commonplaces that cannot be too often reaffirmed. For a final testimony to their reality, I should like to call an impressive contemporary witness. You have all heard or read more than once the speech delivered by William Faulkner when he received the Nobel prize, and I shall quote only a few sentences from that eloquent assertion of faith. Speaking as a writer to young writers, in a world half-paralyzed by force and fear, he urged young men and women to shake off base fear and leave no room in their minds for anything but

the old verities and truths of the heart, the old universal truths lacking which any story is ephemeral and doomed. . . .

I believe that man will not merely endure; he will prevail. He is immortal, not because he alone among creatures has an inexhaustible voice, but because he has a soul, a spirit capable of compassion and sacrifice and endurance. The poet's, the writer's, duty is to write about these things. It is his privilege to help man endure by lifting his heart, by reminding him of the courage and honor and hope and pride and compassion and pity and sacrifice which have been the glory of his past. The poet's voice need not merely be the record of man, it can be one of the props, the pillars, to help him endure and prevail.[3]

[3] From *The Faulkner Reader* (New York: Random House, 1954).

ELMER DAVIS

Are We Worth Saving?
And If So, Why?

A CENTURY or so ago a Harvard graduate wrote a hymn whose opening line, plausible enough when written, turned out to be one of the most inaccurate forecasts ever set down:

> The morning light is breaking, the darkness disappears.

The final couplet of that stanza, however, would—with the omission of a single word—be a fairly accurate picture of the world today:

> Each breeze that sweeps the ocean brings tidings from afar
> Of nations in commotion, prepared for Zion's war.

Commotion indeed; but it is not Zion's war for which they are preparing. Yet in his day the Reverend Samuel F. Smith seemed to have good reason for his confidence in the success of the missionary enterprises that were then spreading over the world; and not only in their direct success but in the derivative benefits that would flow from them. He had faith—not only faith in his religion; but back of that, like most men of his day, he had the

Delivered before the Alpha of Massachusetts, Harvard University, June 8, 1953.

general confidence of the Western world in that golden afternoon, the immensely successful nineteenth century; an assurance
that it had not only a religion but a culture which was so good in
itself that it was the Christian duty of all who possessed it to extend it to less favored races.

To its intended beneficiaries that assurance must often have
seemed arrogance. Especially as expressed in the most famous
missionary hymn of the time—

> By many an ancient river, from many a palmy plain,
> They call us to deliver their souls from error's chain.

The call was audible mostly to the inner ear, but there it rang
loudly.

> Shall we whose souls are lighted by wisdom from on high,
> Shall we to men benighted the lamp of life deny?

Responding to that appeal, many men and women went forth
into the foreign field, performed the most heroic, arduous, and
often hazardous labors, and sometimes laid down their lives. We
owe them the utmost respect; yet I am sure we all wish that the
appeal had been phrased more tactfully. The missionary techniques of Olaf Trygvasson no longer commend themselves; but
at least, when he gave his subjects the choice between accepting
the lamp of life and getting their throats cut, he didn't pretend
that they had asked for it.

But Bishop Heber and the Reverend Samuel Smith profoundly
believed what they wrote, as did most men of their time. The
principal group that disagreed with them, the Hard-Shell Bap-
tists, did so only in an even greater faith—that when God chose
to save the heathen He could do it by Himself, without the help
of contributors to foreign missions. Logically and theologically
they seem to have had the better of the argument; but they were
a feeble and dwindling group because the vast majority was inspired, for the most part unconsciously, by a faith which com-

prehended and transcended theology. The great Protestant missionary effort of the nineteenth century, like the great Catholic missionary effort of the sixteenth century, was the expression of a strong and vigorous culture—different phases only of the culture of what we call the Western world though a Polynesian or even a Japanese might reasonably ask, west of what? In the sixteenth century the West was just awakening, with a delighted surprise, to an awareness of its own strength, which had seemed gravely in question in the opening phases of the Turkish onslaught. By the nineteenth century the West had no doubt that it was the culmination of all human progress to date, with even more dazzling achievements lying beyond.

In the middle of the twentieth century the principal questions in dispute among Western intellectuals seem to be whether the West can be saved, and if it is worth saving. The two most popular of recent historical philosophers both think the Western world is going down hill, and one of them seems to feel that it won't be much loss. Spengler appreciated the loss more than Toynbee; if he felt that it was inevitable, that was perhaps because he was an artist rather than a philosopher. Yet, though it may be only a coincidence, it is certainly a disquieting one that he and Toynbee, starting from very different premises, come out to about the same conclusion as to the phase of development that our civilization has reached. It is a still more disquieting one that they have reached similar conclusions as to what lies ahead—what Spengler called Caesarism and Toynbee the universal state.

There are optimists of course who think that a really universal state—a worldwide state—could be created by some other means than military force; Spengler and Toynbee are not among them nor, to campare small things with great, am I. So long as Communists remain Communists, any world coalition government would be subject to the same dangers, and likely to meet the same fate, as the coalition governments of Poland and Czechoslovakia; and there is still wisdom enough in the West not to run that risk.

Others think that even if a universal state were created by military force, the result would not be Caesarism—provided of course that our side won. A couple of years ago Bertrand Russell was one of these; lately he seems to have become discouraged, and offers us the variant but not very cheerful prospect of a dual Caesarism, with Premier Malenkov and President McCarthy dividing the world between them and collaborating to suppress dissent in both their realms. I do not suppose that Russell was entirely serious in suggesting this; he may only have been reading Orwell's *1984,* or he may have been reading the *Congressional Record.* Such a future seems improbable; but in the world we live in, no one can be sure that it is impossible.

II

Spengler is dead and can write no more; he has said his say; within his artistic scheme, the progressive deterioration of any culture seemed inevitable. Any man who keeps on writing and talking is likely to contradict himself; Toynbee has written so much that he has involved himself in about as many contradictions as Dr. John H. Watson, when he set down the history of Sherlock Holmes. A few years ago Toynbee seemed to have some hope that the creative minority of our civilization had not yet lost its creativity, not yet become a merely dominant minority, for the inadequacy of whose rule the internal proletariat would have to compensate by creating or adopting a universal religion; now he seems to think we have passed the point of no return. We passed it, apparently—or at least so he thought when he delivered the Reith Lectures last year; he may since have changed his mind again—we passed it toward the end of the seventeenth century, when men became disgusted with the endless religious wars which neither side ever decisively won, and turned to secular interests—turned from preoccupation with preparation for the next world to consideration of what could be done with this one, and, increasingly, to what could be done with it through technology.

And for this apostasy, thinks Toynbee, God has punished us—punished the West by the loss of the East; not only our territorial possessions and our commerce there but our moral influence in an East which increasingly turns toward our Communist enemy. The East rejected our religion, and our technology with it, when they were parts of an indivisible way of life; it accepted our technology when it was divorced from our religion (and incidentally had become far more efficient, that is to say far more worth accepting) with consequences which became apparent at Pearl Harbor in 1941 and more recently in Korea. "The fortunes," he says, "of Western civilization in the mission field veered right around from conspicuous failures to conspicuous successes as soon as its attitude toward its own ancestral religion had veered around from a warm devotion to a cool skepticism." Which appears to mean, when the mission field had become the field of a new kind of missionary, offering no longer the lamp of life but oil for the lamps of China, and all that went with it.

History does not support this interpretation. It has lately been subjected to a number of searching criticisms—notably by Professor Karpovitch in the *New Leader* and by G. F. Hudson in *Commentary*. Karpovitch, after pointing out that Toynbee is wrong on all the things that Karpovitch knows most about, suavely admits that no doubt he is right in other fields. Hudson makes a more general attack on the entire doctrine, to which a layman can offer only a couple of corroborative footnotes. The great success of Protestant missions—not to mention a vigorous revival of Catholic missions and the beginnings of the penetration of the East by Western technology as well—came at a time when the cool skepticism of the eighteenth century had been buried under a new wave of evangelical fervor; when Protestantism was not only as vigorous but as dogmatic as the Catholicism of the Counter-Reformation. (I do not know whether

Toynbee regards Modernist Protestantism as a religion at all; but he can hardly deny that title to Fundamentalist Protestantism.)

What at present appears to be the failure of Protestantism in China seems to be due less to divine wrath at apostasy than to an intensified form of the thing that caused the eventual failure of Catholicism in Japan, when it had lost little if any of its energy and fervor in Europe—the fear of a suspicious and despotic government that religion had been merely the cover for imperialistic political intrigues. In either case there was little evidence on which to base that fear, but despots need little evidence—especially despots newly come to power, who still feel insecure.

It might indeed be argued that the West, in its relation with the East, is being punished for its sins; but the sin is not apostasy, it is too great faith. The sin that is most surely and sharply punished is a mistake—however well intended, however it may have seemed at the time the thing to do. The punishment is often delayed, and falls on the descendants of those who made the mistake; often on innocent bystanders. "Those eighteen upon whom the tower of Siloam fell, and slew them—think ye that they were sinners above all men that dwelt in Jerusalem?" We are authoritatively assured that they were not; the sin was that of the architect or the contractor, the punishment fell on people who only happened to be around. Many Europeans and Americans have suffered in Asia, and may presently suffer in Africa, for mistakes for which they were in no way responsible—mistakes made from the highest motives, as a result of faith.

For alongside the theological religion of the West, which in the past two and a half centuries has had its ups as well as its downs, there was growing up in Western Europe and America a secular religion, held as fervently by devout Christians as by rationalists—the faith in freedom, in self-government, in democracy. (Indeed the only living ex-president of Columbia University has more than once implied that only believers in a theological religion can believe in this secular religion too. The evidence for this cannot be found in history.) The Westerners who interpenetrated the East in the nineteenth century, whether missionaries, engineers, business men or administrators, mostly carried this religion with them. They made many mistakes; but it was devotion to this secular religion that led them to make what, from the standpoint of practical consequences, was the worst mistake the West ever made in dealing with the East. They educated the natives.

Not merely in the operation of modern weapons, for the greater convenience of Western powers warring among themselves; these were men of faith, faith in the whole Western culture of which this secular religion was becoming steadily a more important part. Many of those whom they educated sprang from cultures far older than ours, and in some respects more distinguished; but it was the Western culture that seemed to work; so it did not have to be forced on them; in this case they really did call us to deliver their minds, at least, from error's chain. We educated them in Western medicine and engineering, in Western government and law. And in the course of that education the pupils were exposed to the fact that there were such things as freedom and self-government and democracy—things which the educators obviously regarded as good for themselves; it was only a question of time till the pupils began to suspect that they might be good for everybody. Educate any man, of whatever race or color, in what he didn't know before and you are taking a chance; how he will turn out will depend somewhat on the education but more on his background and environment and on what was in him to start with; you may get a Nehru and you may get a Jomo Kenyatta. The one thing they have in common is a conviction that those who educated them, having fulfilled that function, ought to get out.

I have enough faith in that secular religion to believe that in the long run the consequences of this will be beneficial—as they seem to be already in the successor states of the Indian Empire.

But that is no consolation to those on whom various towers of Siloam have fallen elsewhere.

III

This digression was necessitated by the fact that the most popular of contemporary historians has offered an explanation not only for our unsatisfactory relations with Asia and Africa, but for the general dilemma of our times—an explanation which not only to me but to many of my betters seems no explanation at all. But what then is the matter with us? What have we left, if anything, that is worth saving?

The first and obvious answer, of course, is, "If we aren't worth saving, who is?" Faulty as we are, we seem infinitely preferable —by our standards—to the moral nihilism and intellectual rigidity of the Soviet system, which is competing with us for the allegiance of the East; competing indeed, though with little success outside of France and Italy, for the allegiance of our own citizens. Unfortunately, we do not always seem preferable to those among whom our missionaries, and those of the opposition, are working; and if through force or deception they have once accepted the opposition's gospel, they find that the choice is irrevocable. Rebels on the barricades would be blown to pieces by tanks and bombing planes; indeed the secret police would never let anybody get to the barricades in the first place.

G. F. Hudson—following Orwell—holds that modern totalitarian techniques would make impossible even Toynbee's last refuge for the disconsolate, wheresoe'er they languish—the creation by the internal proletariat of a universal church to compensate for the shortcomings of a universal state. "If Nero," says Hudson, "had had the resources of the MVD at his disposal, the early Christians would have been publicly confessing how in their vileness they had set fire to Rome on instructions of the King of Parthia." In the world we live in, freedom once lost is lost to stay lost. We had better remember that, in dealing with our internal even more than with our external problems.

Granted, however, that from anything that could be called an ethical viewpoint we are better worth saving than our adversaries, that is no proof that we are going to be saved unless we have the qualities that enable us to save ourselves. Faulty as was the western Roman Empire, it was far more worth saving than the barbarian tribal dominions that surrounded it and eventually overran it; but its own faults brought it down. This is worth mentioning since not only Spengler and Toynbee, but lesser men, have dealt with our predicament in terms of what befell civilizations of the past; and these analyses, however embellished with facts, or conjectures, from Chinese and Mayan and Sumerian history, all rest pretty much on the one case about which we have tolerably complete information—the decline and fall of the Roman Empire. Many historians have attempted to explain it; almost all of them, even Gibbon—even Rostovtzeff—seem to me to explain it largely in terms of their own experience and observation of their own times.

I shall not add to that confusion, but shall only point out one or two details in which our situation is different. We know now that the happiness and prosperity of the age of the Antonines, which so impressed Gibbon, was only relative—considerable no doubt compared to what had gone before and what was to come afterward; but behind the splendid front there was a dry rot inside; economically the Empire was deteriorating, and intellectually too. Economically the Western world is doing pretty well nowadays; and in the English-speaking and Scandinavian countries the problem that Rome never solved and that finally did more than anything else to bring Rome down has been solved with a fair degree of success—the problem of passing prosperity around, of seeing that everybody gets some of it. If France and Italy solved that problem too the Communist parties in those countries would soon shrink to the hard core. Our civilization, says Rostovtzeff—lately echoed and emphasized by Professor Robinson of Brown—our civilization will not last unless it be a civilization not of one class but of the masses. This is a warning that might more pertinently be directed toward the Soviet Union than the United States, in so far as what exists in the Soviet Union can be called a civilization. As for Rostovtzeff's last despairing question, "Is not every civilization bound to decay as soon as it penetrates the masses?" we can only say that we shall in due course find out. We have started in that direction and we can't turn back.

The Romans, outside of the cities, never got started; and even there civilization was a narrowing pyramid, with a hollow top. The most notable thing about the age of the Antonines was its intellectual sterility in a period of rest between calamities when the Western world might have made vast advances and fortified itself against the calamities that were to come; it is the classic case of what Toynbee calls the loss of creativity in the dominant minority. Are we losing it? Dr. J. G. Beus of the Netherlands Embassy in Washington, who has lately analyzed these forecasts of the future, thinks the Western world is still vigorously creative—not only in science and technology, but in politics, domestic and foreign, and in art and letters as well. It is perhaps fortunate that this optimistic view was set down before the recent sculptural competition in London for a statue of the Unknown Political Prisoner, where the prize was given to a contraption in wire that looked like nothing, unless perhaps a television aerial. As for letters, most of the most admired literature of the Western nations—especially the English-speaking nations—for thirty-five years past has been to all appearance the effluvium of a sick society. English literature, between wars, gave us an almost unrelieved picture of a nation in process of dissolution from its own internal weakness—a nation that would collapse in ruins as soon as somebody pushed. But the time came when somebody pushed, and it did not collapse; indeed the people who did the pushing eventually did the collapsing too.

Many American novelists have written about the late war. Most of their works would be intelligible if written by Frenchmen after 1870, or Spaniards after 1898—mercilessly candid pictures of the inner decay that led to calamitous defeat. But since we happened to win the war, something seems to have been wrong with the picture—not, no doubt, with the individual picture which each man saw, but with the total picture which few of them ever noticed.

This phenomenon is a symptom of what has been called the alienation of intellectuals from the life around them, which is taken very seriously by intellectuals. I cannot see that it makes much difference. The intellectuals wrote their books, which often sold widely; the society around them bought the books, read them, and ignored them. Indeed their authors usually ignored them when the chips were down; men who had spent their lives proving that the United States was not worth fighting for went out and fought for it like everybody else.

IV

The first condition of the survival of any civilization is that it should win its wars. Rome did, till its armies wore themselves out fighting one another. I think that from the military point of view we could win the next war, if we should have to fight it, despite the weakness of our air defense in the northeastern approaches—a matter that should be of more concern in Boston than it appears to be in Washington. Indeed there are men in Washington who might pay more attention to it if they would look at a globe, and realize that by great-circle routes Detroit is as near as Boston to enemy bases.

But to win a war under modern conditions requires more than

military strength—more even than preservation of a sound dollar. It requires political shrewdness, domestic and foreign, to a degree the Romans seldom had to practice. For five centuries after the battle of Magnesia they had virtually no need for a foreign policy, till the degenerate days when they found it necessary to make an alliance with one German tribe against another. This republic, as the *prima inter pares* of a coalition, has to deal with complexities convincingly set forth ten days ago by the President, who has had more experience in dealing with coalitions than any other man since Metternich. It would not be easy, even if he had the actual (though not the theoretical) power of a Roman Emperor; it is not so easy in a republic whose Constitution, as Woodrow Wilson once put it, permits the President to be as big a man as he can. If he cannot be or does not want to be a big man, there will be plenty of others who will volunteer to fill the vacancy.

What a civilization like ours, which is not a universal state but a coalition of independent powers, can do to insure its own continuance depends quite as much on how each state manages its own internal affairs. Here the Romans met the proximate cause of their disaster. When they had a good man at the head of the state, all went well—unless he was a good man like Antoninus Pius; perhaps the most virtuous of all rulers of a great realm and certainly preeminent in manly beauty; but he appears to have been only a glorified Calvin Coolidge, who sat there and went through the motions while the problems piled up for his unhappy successor. But when the Romans got a bad man in, there was no way to get him out except by assassination or revolution. Over a period of ninety years almost every emperor—and they were many, good men as well as bad—was got out by one or the other of those methods.

The nations which embody Western civilization are no longer subject to that danger, but their political systems have other defects. Mr. Walter Lippmann remarks that if the free world is in peril, it is not because our enemies are so strong, but because the free nations are so badly governed; and they are badly governed because of the usurpation of power by the national legislatures. Well—we must discriminate. In the nations of the British Commonwealth the supremacy of the legislature is the essence of their constitutions, and they have learned how to make it work. In the French Republic it is also the essence of the constitution; in the three-quarters of a century of the Third and Fourth Republics they have not learned how to make it work. In this republic it is in flat conflict with the Constitution, and no wonder it doesn't work. It is an old story; long before the present publicized attacks on the State Department and on the President's control of foreign policy, the principal problem of our government was Congressional usurpation, usually through committees, of executive functions. Congress not only tells administrators what they must do, which is its right; but how to do it, which is not its right and is wholly outside Congress's field of practical competence as well as of authority.

A Congress which ate raw meat during the last few years of a Democratic administration has shown that it is not going back to a milk diet just because the Republicans are in power. Nor would it do so even in wartime unless compelled as it has been compelled by every strong President. Until the question whether it would be so compelled again may arise, we might reflect that all the periods of Congressional government in our history have been periods either of bad government or of do-nothing government. There have been times when we could afford a do-nothing government; we can afford it no longer. Still less a bad government.

V

But to return from this digression into the factors that will make it practically possible—or practically impossible—to save us; back to the original question, Why should we be saved? What have we got that our adversaries have not that makes us worth saving? Our faults, God knows, are numerous and glaring enough; recognition of those faults is the chief cause of the loss of confidence that has afflicted so many people of the Western world. But we do recognize them; we do not pretend that our failures were decreed by ineluctable historical necessity; nor do we rewrite history according to the precepts of Double-think, to prove that they never happened at all.

What we have to offer, to the contemporary world and to the future, is a method, and the freedom of the mind that makes that method possible. Not an infallible method, but the best yet discovered for reaching increasingly closer approximations to the truth. It will never offer its conclusions with such assurance as does dialectical materialism—which, by a singular coincidence, always seems to produce the conclusions that are convenient for the men in power. It can only say: We have kept the door open for exploration of all possibilities, consideration of all objections, application of all possible tests; and this is what seems to be true. Maybe something else will seem more probable later on, but this is the best we can do now. Or, as the method was summarized long ago—"Prove all things; hold fast that which is good."

This method has been responsible for almost all human progress. Outside the Western world it does not exist, except in those parts of the East which have been influenced by Western thought; if it died here, it would die there too. Your late President has remarked that the right to think and question and investigate is the basic difference between the free world and the world of totalitarianism. It might well be the basic difference that would save us, if it came to a shooting war; and whether it does that or not, this one thing—the scientific method, and above all the freedom of the mind that makes it possible—is what makes us worth saving. As G. F. Hudson has observed, "To repudiate faith in freedom is to abandon Western civilization."

The founders of this republic held that faith so firmly that its guarantee was imbedded in the very first amendment of the Constitution—almost a part of the original document. Yet lately that faith has been repudiated by many of our fellow citizens, if indeed they ever held it; and in that repudiation lies our greatest danger; it is that, rather than any external attack, that might bring us down. That repudiation takes various forms and appears on various levels. One phase of it was the recent attack on the Bureau of Standards and particularly the manner in which the Secretary of Commerce questioned its objectivity. As Eugene Rabinowitch lately wrote in the *Bulletin of the Atomic Scientists*, the government has the right, if it should so choose, to subordinate the findings of science to the demands of business; but it has no right to attempt to coerce the scientists into adjusting their findings to those demands. That is Lysenkoism; it is something we had better leave to the enemy.

But far more widespread and more dangerous is the general attack on the freedom of the mind. George Kennan said at Notre Dame that it springs from forces too diffuse to be described by their association with the name of any one man or any one political concept; forces which perhaps were summarized by John Duncan Miller of the London *Times*, in the early days of McCarthyism, as a revolt of the primitives against intelligence. Unfortunately it cannot be denied that after centuries of education we still have plenty of primitives—some of them white-collar or even top-hat primitives—a sediment, a sludge, at the bottom of American society, and I am afraid a fairly deep layer at that; people who seem actuated only by hatred and fear and envy. All are the products of ignorance; for their fear is not a rational fear of a very formidable and unfriendly foreign power. I have received thousands of letters from people like that in recent years and they do not seem interested in Russia at all. They appear to regard Communism as a purely American phenomenon; what they hate and fear is their own neighbors who try to think. In the name of anti-Communism they try to strike down the freedom of the mind, which above all things differentiates us from the Communists; in the name of Americanism they try to suppress the right to think what you like and say what you think, in the evident conviction—in so far as they have any reasoned conviction at all—that the principles on which this Republic was founded and has been operated will not bear examination.

That of course is not true; but if we do not stand up and resist the people who feel that way, this movement toward suppression will be successful. I need not remind an academic community, above all, that it has already had considerable successes—though, to your eternal honor, not here. It is people who feel that way who provide the mass support for McCarthy, though of course he has an elite support as well, if it may be so termed, in the reactionary press and the Texas oil billionaires. He has already done serious injury to the United States government—especially to the State Department, on which we must chiefly rely for avoidance of war; and he has done more than any other man to encourage the spread of suspicion and distrust and hatred among ourselves, which is the best formula for losing a war.

We have now reached the point where, if agents of the FBI appear in the home town of a prominent man and begin asking questions about him, his neighbors know that he is either on his way to jail or is destined for appointment to high office in the United States government. I doubt if such confusion is healthy. I venture to remind you of the remark of a Harvard graduate of the class of 1893, Learned Hand, in a speech so often quoted that perhaps you all know it by heart; nevertheless I remind you that he said he believes that that community is already in process of dissolution where each man begins to eye his neighbor as a possible enemy, where nonconformity with the accepted creed is a mark of disaffection, where denunciation takes the place of

evidence and orthodoxy chokes freedom of dissent. If we are not
to become such a community, the friends of freedom will have
to stand up and fight.

Some men who have sentimental predilections in favor of freedom lack the guts to fight. The State Department ran out on the
appointment of Mildred McAfee Horton because it was afraid
of a fight in the Senate. The Department offered the charitable
explanation that this would have been very unpleasant for Mrs.
Horton. She didn't seem afraid of it at all; but it would certainly
have been unpleasant for the State Department, which weeps
with delight when McCarthy gives it a smile and trembles with
fear at his frown.

For the last few minutes I have been talking, not about Western civilization but about the United States. And without apol-
ogy, for we are the principal component of Western civilization,
at least in the material sense; if we go down it all goes down—
and when we confront a totalitarian dictatorship, whatever goes
down stays down; it doesn't get up again. And we shall go down,
unless we recognize what we have to fight for and have the courage to fight for it. What makes Western civilization worth saving is the freedom of the mind, now under heavy attack from
the primitives—including some university graduates—who have
persisted among us. If we have not the courage to defend that
faith, it won't matter much whether we are saved or not.

I do not think Stalin could have licked us; I do not think that
Malenkov and Molotov, Beria and Bulganin, can lick us. But
McCarthy and the spirit of McCarthyism could lick us—no doubt
without intention, but they could—by getting us to fighting
among ourselves like the Romans, by persuading every man that
he must keep on looking over his shoulder, to make sure that
the man beside him doesn't stab him in the back. There is still
enough vitality in Western civilization to save us, unless we
insist on disemboweling ourselves.

I should perhaps have begun this sermon with a text, a text

taken from the fourth chapter of the first book of Samuel, the eighth and ninth verses—the mutual exhortations of the Philistines before the battle of Ebenezer. "Woe unto us!" they said, when they realized that the Israelites had brought the Ark of God with them to battle. "Woe unto us! who shall deliver us out of the hand of these mighty Gods?" But then, realizing that nobody else was going to deliver them, they said to one another, "Be strong, and quit yourselves like men, . . . and fight." And they did fight and delivered themselves. So may we, but only if we quit ourselves like men. This republic was not established by cowards; it will not be preserved by cowards either.

RALPH J. BUNCHE

Dreams and Realities

IT is good to be again in this familiar and friendly meeting place. There was a time when I actually held classes in here in an earnest endeavor to impart learning to youth. I always felt rather inadequate to the task and have never been sure that I had much success at it. Nevertheless, the student greeting of "Prof" was always reassuring, bolstered one's confidence, and could make the most humble and ill-equipped feel a kinship with the savants. There is something thrilling about that title of "professor," a lot of dignity in it too, and even, perhaps, an element of danger. For I reckon no ego is so constantly nourished as that of the college professor, before whose trough of knowledge students stand in never-ending queue.

After all, there is something altogether unique about association with knowledge and the process of attaining and imparting it. There is, I think, nothing quite so rewarding; not, to be sure, in the material sense, but in the sense of self-satisfaction, that inner feeling which alone can signal true accomplishment. Knowledge gives, or should give, balance and perspective. For the challenge to the intellect is man's greatest challenge. What man, indeed, can fail to be humble in contemplation of the vast wisdom and

Delivered at the installation of the Gamma of the District of Columbia, Howard University, Washington, April 8, 1953.

the verities of the ages? I know, of course, that in academic as in other circles there are the bumptious ones, the brash know-it-alls who perceive themselves as the centre of the universe, because they have acquired a little learning, which, in truth, may often be worse than none. But they are neither learned nor wise, for the learned man is he who is always acutely aware of how much there is that he can never know. Humility is the mark of those who have truly communed with the goddess of learning.

My opportunities in recent years to return to the "Hill" have been far fewer than I might wish. But few occasions could be more auspicious or significant than the one which brings us here tonight. I am delighted to be present.

The installation of Gamma Chapter of Phi Beta Kappa is a historic event in the annals of Howard University. It constitutes a highly significant recognition of the University community. It is a well-deserved tribute to faculty and students alike. The University is to be congratulated, and I know that a special word of commendation is due to my good friend and former colleague, Alain Locke. For I recall that many years ago Alain Locke had the dream of a Phi Beta Kappa chapter at Howard and set to work to convert dream into reality. Tonight we participate in that reality. And I am glad that this has taken place in a university in which academic freedom has had real meaning.

I reserve my most hearty congratulations for you students to whom these prized keys have just been presented. Student vocabulary has changed since my college days and since my days as a classroom taskmaster. But I gather from listening to my college-age daughters that each of you would be aptly described in current campus parlance as a "brain." This is truly your occasion and you are entitled to feel very proud about it. For there is no achievement so worthy as that which reflects a true love of learning. Value the keys not so much as the effort they represent. You have been inducted into no cult or aristocracy, but rather into a great and democratic company of men and women who, by and large, seek after knowledge and the truth which it alone reveals.

Bear in mind always that these keys which are now yours by dint, I would like to assume, of no little effort are not an end but the beginning. They have no intrinsic merit. They testify only that you who have earned them have the ability to go very far and accomplish very much if you will continue to apply yourselves diligently and perseveringly to the pursuit of knowledge. The honor that has been conferred upon you is the reward for achievement—the only sure road of progress for individual or group.

Were this what might be called a "normal" installation of a Phi Beta Kappa chapter, I would, I imagine, make a somewhat different kind of speech from this point on. I would try to be sufficiently erudite and professorially objective to suit the occasion. But since I left these hallowed academic halls over a decade ago, I have been severely exposed to the harsh world of realities and have become, I fear, what some people like to call a "realist." Moreover, whatever embryonic erudition I may have had when I left here has become very rusty from disuse, since bureaucracy puts doing above knowing. And so I feel bound to come to grips briefly with the broad social significance of this meeting. For this is, in truth, no "normal" installation, since we are at Howard University and the University is located in Washington, D.C., about whose pattern of group relationships and democratic living much can be said, and far too little of it complimentary.

Thus I must say that it is not only Howard University and these brilliant students who are to be congratulated. Phi Beta Kappa itself is also to be congratulated. For in granting this chapter it has made a signal contribution to the evolution of American democracy. It is precisely in the realm of the intellect that democracy should find its most pure and unqualified expression. The essence of Phi Beta Kappa is the recognition of scholarly attainment. This recognition must be universal and applied to all alike on a plane of complete equality. What could be more incongruous or unjust than the erection of walls of segregation and exclusion against achievements of the intellect? Certainly nature draws no lines of colour or religion in bestowing intellect. Elated as we rightfully are, therefore, we may be pardoned for reflecting that this event, like so many events in the fulfillment of democracy's promise that eventually must come, has been too long delayed and is to be appraised in proper perspective.

The significance of this installation extends far beyond the Howard campus. It is one more important step forward in the educational advancement of the Negro citizen. It represents American democracy on the march, and that can become an irresistible force. It is a further recognition of the intellectual capacity of the Negro student. It marks a new advance toward the full integration of the Negro citizen in the life of his country. It is right that it should be done and the American conscience will be the clearer and cleaner for it.

But in our rejoicing let us not overestimate the significance of this event. To be sure, it marks progress in the application of American democracy. But only progress. The ultimate goal is still to be won. That goal is the only goal that can be compatible with American democracy—the complete integration in the life of the nation of all citizens without regard to colour or creed. If that goal were reached, no special significance would attach to this installation, and no special comment about this ceremony would be required. Indeed, there would then be no Negro or predominantly Negro colleges in which to install Phi Beta Kappa chapters. I hope to live to see that day come, and I am confident that it can and will come without too great delay.

You young men and women who tonight have been given those precious keys have a special responsibility in this regard. Through no fault of your own, you are no ordinary Phi Beta Kappas. You are good Americans and good citizens and you are grateful to the Society and to your country for the opportunity afforded you to make this promising start along the path of life. In a world in which freedom is enjoyed by far too few, you are fortunate to belong to a society whose traditions and framework and objectives are soundly democratic, despite all present imperfections in the practice. You do, I know, treasure the American way of life, with its emphasis on the dignity and rights of the individual, its concepts of equality of peoples and of equal opportunity for all, and its free political institutions.

Indeed, the Negro American, by and large, has perhaps a more lively appreciation of these American traditions and concepts than any other American, for his entire history on these shores has been a chronicle of the heroic and rewarding struggle to achieve and enjoy them. This has been the sole aim of the Negro American—to become an American in full. It is because this is so apparent that I have never felt that there was much likelihood that the Negro citizen, in any substantial numbers, could be seduced by an alien ideology which would contradict all that he has been striving relentlessly and courageously to achieve here.

You newly elected Phi Beta Kappas, I am sure, will carry on this resolute struggle and its honorable, dignified traditions with ever greater zeal. You have a solemn obligation to do so. You would not be here at all were you not already accustomed to overcoming extraordinary obstacles. You have given evidence of ability beyond the average, and your efforts will be urgently needed in the common cause. It is in your personal interest and in the interest of your group and country that you should spare no effort to eliminate every last stigma of second-class citizenship attaching to the Negro American.

You may be assured that the individual Negro can advance only as his group advances. Your interest is intimately and inseparably linked with that of your group. So long as the Negro group suffers minority status in this society, no individual Negro —Phi Beta Kappa no less than cotton picker—can ever hope to enjoy full dignity or emancipation. Negroes all, we must become full Americans all.

It is clearly in the interest of the country that the Negro citizen be quickly brought to full equality. Our American freedoms and our way of life are today more seriously challenged than ever before in our nation's history. Now, as never before, our nation needs its maximum unity—politically, economically, morally, and spiritually. Our maximum manpower potential is indispensable. Our position of leadership of the free peoples of the world requires that our prestige be unsullied. The Negro citizen is needed not as Negro but as a full-blown American standing shoulder to shoulder with all other Americans, and with free peoples everywhere, in the common, urgent causes of peace, freedom, and social justice.

There are, of course, some Americans who do not or do not wish to understand this. They say that the Negro is making progress, even too quickly, and that he ought to be patient and content. Every once in a while someone will intimate to me or say to me outright that since I seem to be getting along well enough, why do I insist on bringing up the unpleasant problem of race relations. I am glad that they do this, for it signifies that at least they are thinking about the problem and perhaps even are bothered a bit in their consciences. I tell them simply that it is inevitable that I must do so, for I am an American who believes in his country and its constitution. As a good American, I wish to see my country in these critical times as strong as it can possibly be—and to do so, it must clearly be fully democratic.

There is much bigotry still entrenched in our land, but it is increasingly on the defensive and in many places definitely on the run. We must keep it on the run by organized effort as wise as it is determined.

The practices of racial bigotry create insidious conditions. It is ironically apparent, for example, that the institution of segregation is fortified by the fact that many Negroes in many places have themselves developed a vested interest in it, and some of these are loath to see it go.

In this regard, it seems to me that those institutions of higher learning throughout the land which are Negro or predominantly Negro are today confronted with an urgent need to look into the near future and do some serious thinking about their role and their direction. When times and attitudes change, policies must change or become obsolete. As the walls of segregation in colleges and universities in the South come tumbling down—and many other such walls will inevitably follow—the ultimate impact upon the exclusively Negro institutions is bound to be seriously felt. I refer not alone to the physical fact of enrollment but to the moral factor as well. The Negro colleges, and particularly those whose primary claim to existence has been their catering to Negro students who have had little opportunity to go elsewhere, need to do some profound soul-searching. It may well be that some moral decisions will have to be made which will require great courage and a devotion to the ultimate interests of the Negro—and to democracy—above all personal considerations. The time may well be not far distant when some Negro institutions—unless radical changes in policy can be and are undertaken —may find themselves in the unenviable position of obstructing the elimination of segregation in higher education. There are signs already that some sources or prospective sources of funds for the assistance of education for Negroes are facing a prospective dilemma. They recognize a strong moral obligation to give such assistance, but they are also concerned, and rightly so, lest it develop that this assistance on occasion and in certain places may actually tend to obstruct educational integration on the higher level and thus retard the dynamic processes of democracy.

The Negro has evinced great courage in fighting against segregation. Even greater courage may be required for some to learn how to live without it. A false and shameful but somewhat comforting security has developed behind its walls.

And finally, the question which transcends all others in its importance to all of us is the basis there may be to hope for a future in which these young men and women whom we honor tonight, and millions like them throughout the world, may not have their fine intellects sacrificed on atomic battlefields.

I feel most earnestly that there is a strong basis for hope. The times are dangerous and war could come. But it need not come, and it will not come if the American people and peace-loving peoples everywhere give to the United Nations the confidence and support it merits. The United Nations way of negotiation, mediation, and conciliation of international disputes is the only sure way to peace. There have been heartening indications in recent days that United Nations efforts may again reap rich dividends of peace.

The United Nations truly belongs to the peoples of the world. It is your organization and mine. We, the people, can make it a better vehicle of peace than it is and can make better use of it. Since world atomic war is the only alternative, can we afford not to make it succeed?

The United Nations seeks a peaceful and a better world for all mankind. Despite the macabre bleatings of the prophets of doom, and they are legion, despite the skeptics and the cynics who are ever with us, and despite all of the frustrations which are endemic in these troubled times, those United Nations goals can be achieved. For the problems afflicting the world are in large measure problems of human relations. Difficult and stubborn as they may be, they are never insoluble.

It is by mobilizing the goodness that is in man, his good will and good sense, that the challenge to the future can be met and the impending catastrophe averted.

If it is a dream to envisage a world free of war, free of tyranny over the minds and bodies of men, free of racial and religious bigotry, then let us have many more dreamers.

If it is a dream to foresee an America in which all men shall walk in equality as brothers, then let us dare to dream it. For fifty years ago this meeting, and a century ago this University, would have been daring dreams.

The dream of today becomes the reality of tomorrow, if man's will is resolute, his wisdom great, and his courage unflinching. From the dreams of men all human progress is spun.

To you young members of Phi Beta Kappa I say—set your sights high, as high as your dreams, and keep them high. Fear not and be ever hopeful.

GERALD W. JOHNSON

The Provincial Scholar

THERE has been only one Phi Beta Kappa address. It is the custom for the various chapters to listen to discharges of oratory at stated times, but for 118 years such speeches have been either discourse upon unrelated topics or mere commentaries on what Emerson said to the Cambridge chapter in 1837. He was the prophet; those who have followed him are no more than exegetes, successful if they can supply a new gloss on some passage in "The American Scholar."

My own ambition does not rise even to the level of a gloss. It is confined to an endeavor to underscore certain ideas expressed by Emerson, and I make the attempt not because I claim a new understanding of those ideas, but because events have combined to emphasize their importance to our generation. I invite your attention to the Provincial Scholar, not as a discovery, but as one aspect of the American Scholar that the times have made highly important.

Emerson's definition of a scholar was Man Thinking, and the American scholar is the particular subdivision of *homo sapiens* called American, thinking. There is nothing illogical in carrying

Delivered before the Gamma of North Carolina, Davidson College, April 26, 1955.

the subdivision further and considering Southerner thinking, or North Carolinian thinking, as the Provincial Scholar.

But while it is logical, it does not necessarily follow that it is profitable. Unless it can be established that there is a significant difference between a North Carolinian thinking and, say, a Californian thinking, the inquiry must be fruitless. There is no difficulty in demonstrating that the difference exists, but that it is definable and significant is not so easy. It is self-evident that there are differences between man and man, and it is reasonable to suppose that the differences affect all man's activities, including thinking. But that they are significant is not obvious, and to make this clear one must return to Emerson's reasons for insisting upon his definition.

The point that he sought to drive home with hammer blows throughout the Cambridge lecture was that a highly significant, a supremely significant, difference exists between "thinking" and "man thinking." One is tempted to believe that his prophetic insight foresaw the invention of the electronic calculating machine, capable of performing operations that, when performed by the human brain, fall into the category of thinking. The calculations of these machines are made with incomprehensible speed and accuracy. By every objective standard of measurement they meet the ordinary definition of thinking, but they are not scholarship because they are not man thinking.

Emerson never heard of cybernetics. He died long before the word was coined. But he was well aware that under certain circumstances and subjected to a certain regimen the human brain can be reduced to the semblance of a calculating machine, operating with uncanny precision unaffected by emotion or any other factor extraneous to the problem presented. This he admitted is thinking, but he stoutly denied that it is man thinking; therefore he did not admit it within his definition of scholarship.

He said it in 1837; but hear now the words of another great thinker, spoken in 1954. At the Columbia University bicentennial Dr. J. Robert Oppenheimer, making the closing address, said, "This is a world in which each of us, knowing his limitations, knowing the evils of superficiality and the terrors of fatigue, will have to cling to what is close to him, to what he knows, to what he can do, to his friends and his traditions and his love, lest he be dissolved in a universal confusion and know nothing and love nothing." [1]

This is a more emphatic repudiation of the thinking machine even than Emerson's. Dissolved in a universal conclusion, says Oppenheimer, the man who loves nothing knows nothing. Facts in indefinite numbers can be stored in a calculating machine to be produced as needed; but if I understand Oppenheimer, he asserts that facts are not knowledge. It is the understanding of facts that constitutes knowledge, and the man completely stripped of emotion understands nothing. Thinking is a craft that can be mastered by a contraption of copper and glass and steel; but wisdom is an attribute that does not appertain to any machine.

The wisdom that enables a man to feel as well as to know has its foundation in the experiences of early life. Its basis is laid before the child has learned to read; I believe psychologists are agreed that one learns more in the first six years of life than in the following sixty; for it is in those years that one begins the study of the subject that transcends all other subjects in all the curricula of all the schools—the study of humanity. Nothing that a man learns in college or university compares in importance, or in difficulty, with the intellectual, physical, and moral discipline that engages his attention for the first few years after birth—the task of learning to be a human being.

But his progress through this immensely important period is certainly impelled more by emotion than by cogitation. It is at this time that the emotional pattern of his life is established; and the emotional pattern will always modify and all too often will govern his relations with his fellow men as long as he lives.

[1] In his *The Open Mind* (New York: Simon and Schuster, 1955), p. 144.

The child's world is extremely narrow and it widens relatively slowly, from the house and family to the street, to the neighborhood, to the school, to the town. There is no such thing as a cosmopolitan born. We all begin as provincials, and by far the greater part of our knowledge is attained by contact with people. The study of ideas comes late in the learning process, and though we continue it as long as Cato, who learned Greek at eighty, the sum of the knowledge we gain that way will not compare in magnitude with what we learned before we mastered the trick of considering abstractions.

Thus every scholar in the beginning is necessarily provincial, emotionally and intellectually. Both his affections and his knowledge are restricted to a locality and a group, and not until he has achieved most of his intellectual development does his horizon widen perceptibly. In Socrates it widens enormously, in Simple Simon hardly at all; but Socrates, as well as Simple Simon, learned the greater part of all that he knows before he was capable of understanding an abstract idea.

For the very reason that this condition is imposed upon us, alert minds have always struggled against it. The free spirit resists it, as it resists any compulsion. So the scholarly world, at least in large part, has come to accept almost as axiomatic the doctrine that provincialism is one of the stigmata of ignorance and indolence, therefore a public disgrace to be eliminated as far as is humanly possible.

Yet the very greatest scholars have always realized that the effort at its elimination can be carried too far. In the intensity of his effort to attain a world view it is possible for a man to forget entirely the parochial view, as Erasmus is said to have forgotten his mother tongue in the intensity of his study of Latin and Greek; and when one does forget the affections and sympathies that a small boy developed in a small environment, he turns himself into something closely resembling UNIVAC, the thinking machine.

276

To Emerson in 1837 this seemed to be an appalling fate, and Emerson had not a tithe of the evidence that we have. A man born with the century has still ten years to go before he can claim any old-age benefits; at fifty-five he is still middle-aged, yet such a man within his own lifetime has seen a nation that led the world in many branches of scholarship twice plunge that world into an orgy of savagery, and in the interval between holocausts perfect the technique of a new crime. The deed that is called genocide, that is, the effort to exterminate cultures as well as races, is an infamy that no tribe of cannibals ever conceived. Among savages tribe has indeed exterminated tribe, again and again, but always for revenge, or for gain, or for security, never on the hideous theory that the murder of a whole people would contribute to the betterment of mankind. This horror was invented by a nation that had carried both science and philosophy to great heights, and that had produced thinkers in almost unprecedented numbers.

Obviously there must have been a fatal defect in German scholarship, since it could not save its nation from sinking below the level of the most degraded of men. Emerson would have said that it was not scholarship at all but only learning, since it had almost eliminated what it called the "subjective," but he called the "human," element. It was thinking, but not Man Thinking. It was materialistic and mechanical. Oppenheimer would say that, loving nothing, it knew nothing, because it effected what it did not intend to bring about, namely, the destruction of Germany. Despite all its magnificent intellectual achievements, it was not yet the Sorcerer, but only the Sorcerer's Apprentice, ignorant of the incantation that would stop the ruin its half-knowledge had precipitated.

How then shall an American scholar try to profit from this frightful lesson? Oppenheimer has answered: He "will have to cling to what is close to him, to what he knows, to what he can do, to his friends and his traditions and his love." That is to say, he must maintain the flavor, without the limitations, of his original provincialism.

No young child seeks knowledge for its own sake, but only as a means toward action. Arnold J. Toynbee is certainly not a young child, but in the tenth volume of his monumental *Study of History* he has a passage that indorses the child's course. He is contrasting the Man of Action and the Man of Thought—or, to be exact, he is denying the contrast and asserting that the so-called Man of Thought is not a complete man unless and until he becomes also a Man of Action. He typifies them by Ajax, the brutal fighter, and Lord Acton, the historian whose learning was prodigious, but who never wrote a book. "Acton's calling, no less than Ajax's," says Toynbee, "is in truth subject to an inexorable law that Human Life is either action or failure; . . . for Acton, no less than Ajax, has been created by God to take action under the divinely appointed conditions of Man's Earthly Life." [2]

One of those divinely appointed conditions is that our sympathies and affections are rooted somewhere in some particular locality, although we may spend our lives in a distant part of the world. As a rule the spot where we first became aware of things outside ourselves is the place where our roots are fixed; and as long as they are firmly in the earth, our sympathies and affections will not wither, however far distant may be the place where they blossom. But the quality of their native soil will affect their color and perfume even on the other side of the globe; while if the roots are torn up, they will almost invariably grow pallid and scentless.

My point is that the scholar, who learned to be a human being in North Carolina before he learned to read Sanskrit perhaps in the University of Paris, will remain a North Carolinian as long as he remains a human being. He may spend his active life in Hong Kong and die there, but at the end, as the college song

[2] Arnold J. Toynbee, *A Study of History*, X, 38.

has it, when he dies he'll be Tarheel dead. His only alternative is to be a dead Grammarian, such as Browning celebrated in his famous lyric, who was not a human being but only a Grammarian. There are no citizens of the world, for the man whose allegiance is exclusively to the world is not a citizen of anything; but there are citizens of North Carolina with a world outlook, and it is upon the development of more and more such citizens that the hope of the world depends.

If then some local coloration of his thought is what makes a thinker a man thinking and therefore a scholar, the practical question before the scholars of any region is not to eliminate local color, but to turn it to advantage. Specifically and for this specific audience, the question is one of making a North Carolina heritage an intellectual asset.

It can, of course, be a liability. To the extent that it restricts one's mental horizon, clouds one's understanding of other men, blunts one's sympathies, parochialism is an evil and the ruin of true scholarship. But it does not necessarily have any such effect. I make the assertion flatly and boldly, for I have seen the proof, not once but repeatedly, right here in North Carolina. I have known a number of men whose scholarship was made sounder and better by their close attachment to Southern soil; and to move from the general to the particular, I invite your attention to two whose work was done in this state. I refer to the late William Louis Poteat, biologist, and the late Howard Washington Odum, sociologist, both men worthy of the words of Ecclesiasticus: "Leaders of the people by their counsels, and by their knowledge of learning meet for the people."

Poteat's early work on the Arachnidae was distinguished enough to procure him an invitation to Yale, but he declined because he had found in his native North Carolina opportunity to deal with something more important than spiders. It was to serve as an interpreter to young men of the new learning that at the time was revolutionizing biology.

279

Nearly twenty years after Poteat's death, at the beginning of this year, I found in Toynbee's concluding volume published a few months ago a statement that had a curiously familiar ring. In summing up his work Toynbee said that "he meant by History a vision—dim and partial, yet (he believed) true to reality as far as it went—of God revealing Himself in action to souls that were sincerely seeking Him."

After some search I found what it was that made that seem like an echo in my mind. It was in a baccalaureate address that Poteat delivered to the graduating class of Wake Forest in 1926, eight years before Toynbee published his first volume, and nearly thirty years before he published his tenth. Poteat said, "I think of science as walking to and fro in God's garden, busying itself with its forms of beauty, its fruits and flowers, its beast and bird and creeping thing, the crystals shut in its stones and the gold grains of its sands, and coming now at length in the cool of the long day upon God Himself walking in His garden." [3]

I do not see how anyone can claim that the vision of the great English historian is a whit broader than that of the relatively obscure North Carolina biologist, for they both saw God at the end of the vista, which is the culmination of all men's seeking.

Howard W. Odum was not in fact North Carolinian by origin, but he was Southern, and his Georgia environment was very similar to this state. He had none of Poteat's mastery of musical prose; on the contrary, he was notorious for his use of the jargon of sociology to the confusion of the lay reader. But his poetic insight was at least equal to that of Poteat; and in his curious rhapsody called *Rainbow Round My Shoulder* he used the language of a Negro manual laborer to convey shards and fragments of broken visions that William Blake would not have disdained.

[3] Included, with other speeches and articles, in *Youth and Culture* (Winston-Salem, N.C.: Wake Forest Press, 1938).

But it is neither as writer nor as savant that he should always be held in grateful remembrance by this state; it was as the man of action, always in arms against injustice, which he believed almost always originated in ignorance. Odum was twice a Doctor of Philosophy, once from Clark University, once from Columbia, but there never was a man further removed from the dry and bloodless scholar immured in his library. On the contrary, anything and everything that happened in North Carolina interested him more than anything he read in books; and if it was a movement that promised any addition to the general welfare, he was always in the thick of it working hard.

What made him superb, however, was neither his learning nor his energy. It was his ability to spend a long life fighting for righteousness without any touch of the moral arrogance that is the besetting sin of most crusaders. Odum would have repelled with unfeigned horror the suggestion that he was a better man than the lowliest of his neighbors; which brings him, of course, within that wonderful definition in the Gospel according to St. Mark: "Whosoever will be great among you, shall be your minister: And whosoever will be the chiefest, shall be servant of all."

I cite these two examples to illustrate what I mean by the Provincial Scholar; it is a man whose intellectual activity may range to the furthest frontier of thought, but who somehow contrives to bring it home to enlighten and help the man next door. This college is located in the state of North Carolina and the county of Mecklenburg. If the scholarship of Davidson College can lead Mecklenburg County into new understanding of truth, depend upon it, that scholarship will be listened to, soon and respectfully, in the halls of Oxford and Upsala and the Sorbonne.

It is my belief that the scholar whose roots are in Southern soil has at this juncture in the world's affairs a unique value, if he will exploit it. He is the only American whose emotional development as a child was tinged with bitter memories of defeat, invasion and conquest. He should therefore be the man most immune to what D. W. Brogan calls "the illusion of American omnipotence." What other men's heads alone tell them we know both in our heads and in our hearts—that an American army can be defeated and that an American victor can be ruthless and bitter and unfair. Therefore we should possess the political maturity that comes only through suffering, and at this moment political maturity is more to be desired than much fine gold.

It is not politically mature to proceed on the assumption that we hold a monopoly of wisdom and virtue and that all others must be brought to our ways of acting, if need be by force of arms. It is not politically mature to assume that what is un-American is by definition unrighteous. It is not politically mature to think that all who oppose us do so because they are saturated with Original Sin; it is so far from mature that it is the style of those primitives whose only name for a member of their own tribe is the word meaning "man," implying that members of all other tribes are something less than human.

So much will be admitted by any rational American, but it is felt most keenly by a Southerner. What some people of other regions apparently neither think nor feel, and certainly will not admit, is that our discoveries in the art of self-government are not final, but partial and tentative, and that the most important task before us is not the preservation of what we have but the discovery of unknown truth. But your Southerner, whose grandfather died boasting that he was still an Unreconstructed Rebel, is conditioned emotionally, as hardly any other American is, to accept the truth that the American government is not perfect and that the first duty of patriots is to perfect it, because the effort to perfect it is the best means of protecting it.

It is not to be denied that Southern provincialism can run, and sometimes has run, into sterile ancestor-worship. But that occurs only among the intellectually undeveloped; it is only remotely a danger to a man thinking. Upon him its effect is confined to some slight coloration of his thought, and I dare assert that it is heresy to maintain that completely colorless thought, unstained by the slightest tint of emotion, is scholarship. It is a mechanical process in which the human brain is as inferior as is the human hand to the precision of the machine.

We Southerners learned under "the red-hot rake of war" that being American is not a status but a process. It is a man not enjoying but seeking the good life and in the search willing to accept truth wherever it may be found. It is a man knowing that some fragment of the truth is often to be found even in the camp of the enemy; a man who has followed Cromwell's advice by learning that it is possible for him to be mistaken; hence a man intent upon understanding, not upon conquering.

Such men are desperately needed at this period of the world's history. Modern advances in science and technology have been so tremendous that adjustment to them puts an almost intolerable strain upon education. Chaucer's complaint of "the lyf so short, the craft so long to lerne" is far more poignant today than it was when he uttered it; so the temptation to reduce thought to a mechanical process increases daily. Yet yielding to it would mean going the way that Germany went; and the men best able to resist are those whose thought may range along the outmost boundaries of knowledge, but whose emotions are firmly rooted in some particular spot of earth that is their spiritual home. For they alone are secure against falling into that lowest level of the Inferno, that hell of ice where men are "dissolved in a universal conclusion, and know nothing and love nothing."

RHYS CARPENTER

Learning and Living

MY initial anecdote goes back thirty years, yet it still retains its pertinence to my theme for this occasion:

Two archaeologists were imbibing the matutinal cup of percolated coffee when a sudden pensiveness overtook the one, which prompted the other to inquire into its cause. Said the one, "Something wrong with the coffee?" Said the other, "It's not the coffee; it's the percolator." Said the first, "Something wrong with the percolator?" Said the second, "Nothing wrong, exactly; only, I believe that it must have been designed by Dynamic Symmetry!" Toast, jam, and coffee were forgotten on the instant, while calipers were produced and all possible measurements of lid, spout, and body were taken, recorded, and converted into intricate calculations to determine whether the twentieth-century commercial product did indeed conform to the imaginary structural law for ancient Attic pots. I have forgotten how the final verdict ran; but the point of the anecdote is that the breakfast was cold when this archaeological pair returned from their theoretic spirit-world to the hard (or rather, chill) realities of Boston. A gap had opened between learning and living.

Of course, a practical-minded person could have healed this

Delivered before the Zeta of Pennsylvania, Haverford College, June 1, 1955.

particular gap with the thoroughly practical suggestion that one should always drink one's coffee first and measure the percolator afterwards; but even thus rectified and removed from the breakfast table, the gap would have remained spiritually as a deep and perhaps unhealable cerebral dichotomy, in which the wretched percolator would play a double role—once on a lower level as a mere utilitarian source for the purveyance of hot coffee, and again in a more spiritual and almost Platonic form as a no less ebullient source for an immaterial draught of Esthetic.

There can scarcely be any question that the realm of learning and the realm of living are not superimposable identical areas; and hence to occupy both of them, simultaneously and continuously, smacks of the unreal behavior of four-dimensional existence. Yet I hope to show that there is no truly irreconcilable antagonism between the two, and that, if any in a four years' sojourn on a college campus have caught the contagion of giving their present time to the vanished past, this is no warrant for supposing that they have thereby unfitted themselves for the future, just because learning and living move in opposite directions.

What I have to say applies to almost every course of study that has no immediate practical application—history, literature, abstract mathematics, philosophy, many of the natural sciences. But I choose deliberately the most patently useless subject in the entire college curriculum—useless even to those who intend to become artists—the History of Art. For here, flagrantly apparent, we shall be able to put a finger on an opposition between learning and living, between the study of Art and the practice of Life.

Interest in the factual past of the fine arts can hardly be due to mere curiosity for the sake of exploring an unfamiliar subject, nor yet for mere acquisition of encyclopedic information. To be sure, there is a "social fringe" to art, made up of those who acquire some superficial knowledge in order to seem cultured and be in a position to contest the intellectual superiority of others. But this is seldom the motive for its choice as a subject of major attention on a male college campus. The true incentive to devoting time and energy to such a study is a realization that the fine arts are in sober truth "fine"; that Italian paintings are admirable in their own right, for what they are as paintings; that the Gothic cathedrals are superb, precisely and uniquely as buildings; and that Greek sculpture is in no need of further excuse than its own vivid presentations of physical vitality in subtle conversion to marble and bronze. If we sought for a single word to say what all these things were to us, beyond being things for our brains to grasp and our minds to remember, we probably should have to fall back on the rather uncertain, much overused, and hence rather lame word, "beautiful." Had they not strongly appealed to you as beautiful on their own account, you might well have hesitated to give them so much of your time amid the pressure of a college curriculum which offered courses of study many times more extensive than the available eight semesters of a bachelor's lifetime.

As a direct result of this special coloring to the study of the fine arts, when the college term is over and you have acquired your B.A. diploma and very probably within a few years a single wife and more than a single child, there will still cling to you not merely the slowly evaporating fumes of your college lecture notes, growing fainter and perhaps sweeter as they fade, but also more enduring scents—or, to spell it a trifle differently, sense—of artistic beauty, in real presence when it chances to be about you, or in regretted absence when you fail to find it in your surroundings. Deliberately evoked in art, it will henceforth be expected in life. Whether or not you had specifically asked for it, you will find that you have in your hands a measuring stick which you cannot drop or lay aside, but will have to use.

Your own town with its public buildings, its streets and parks and open places, its freight yards and its waterfront—will these be "beautiful," as things that have been planned by men's brains and laid out by men's hands can be beautiful? Your own house with the carpeting on the floors, the wallpaper, the furniture, the patterns and colors—do these measure up to the measuring stick which you have brought with you? Only too often, there will come the regretful negative answer and, with it, a feeling of opposition between the possible and the actual, between the might-have-been in terms of what once was in Italy or Greece or China and the really present in our own communities and environment, in our own land and our own lives. And so inevitably the gap will open up and prove to be not just once again the familiar break which is always caused by distance in place and time, but a gap in fundamental human terms, a wound with a feeling of hurt in it.

Supposing that for some reason we must live amid ugliness— and that is the destiny in store for most of us—would it have been better never to have learned to suspect that it was ugly? More convenient, perhaps; less galling, certainly; but better? I doubt whether many of you would honestly agree to such a proposition. And is it necessarily true that everything that does not match the accepted beautiful in art is therefore ugly? And even if one felt it were, does the esthetic vision involve nothing more than a fatal direct comparison between Velázquez and the illustrations in the weekly magazine, between York cathedral and the parish church, between the Greek way of life and the slums across the railroad track? Granted that most good art is idealistic and therefore in some sense unreal and inactual, very little good art is quite as inactual or as completely unreal as such a judgment would imply. Surely the artist's way is at bottom a way of seeing what is really here, of shaping actual materials into actually existent realities—Shelley's

> But from these create he can
> Forms more real than living man,
> Nurselings of immortality.

When art has been most active and has meant most to its day, it has not been a way of retreat, a gilded cage, an imaginary escape from the real world, so much as a deeper penetration or a radical reconversion of physical and sensible actualities.

How pitiful was the crazy redhead, *"le fou roux,"* as they called him, in his painter's shack in Southern France! Yet it was Van Gogh who taught us to see the ordinary world around us in new terms of luminous solid shapes which certainly exist, but which the normal process of seeing does not utilize. It would have been difficult to find anything much uglier than Van Gogh's material environment during most of his unhappy life; in many instances it might be said that nothing could be uglier than the things which he set out to reproduce in paint on his canvases. But when he had finished, a gap almost as deep as human consciousness had somehow been bridged.

My contention would have to be that by studying art we can acquire a special way of looking at things, which may be called for convenience "esthetic vision," and that, rightly employed, this esthetic vision is not merely a carping and critical way of disliking things, as though from weighing everything in the scales of supernal perfection everything had in consequence been discovered to be wanting and worthless. Esthetic vision is a creative act (like most seeing that is not mere recognizing or gaping). Like eyeglasses to the nearsighted, it gives access to a world otherwise remaining invisible—a real enough world, but one that requires to be seen. These glasses need not be either rose-tinted or rainbow-colored: they may be just clear powerful lenses, stepping up normal vision.

For example, could anything be more picturesque than a group of locomotives conversing together between puffs in a roundhouse? Now that they are in imminent danger of becoming old-fashioned and even a little ridiculous, perhaps we can manage to take a new interest in them as though they were bison threatened with extinction on our great plains.

And though I think that the wabbling wire gadgets which their playful inventors have the impertinence to thrust under our eyes as examples of modernist sculpture are pretty silly things, they can stimulate us to see what their childish creators have been seeing—the wonderful tridimensional patterns which (quite accidentally) have been built up and brought to our attention by modern machinery. A great turbine installed and at work in a powerhouse is a magnificent work of art—or would be, if it had been consciously created as such. At least, it may be so seen by anyone who has the eye to envision it.

Most certainly, the immediate result of beholding the world in esthetic terms is not an unmitigated abhorrence of its ugliness. The Oscar Wildes of the 1890's and the self-appointed disciples of Walter Pater were guilty of despising reality and abandoning it for an artificial realm of pained aloofness in which they dwelt exquisitely in deliberate superiority to the annoyed, uninitiated commoner. Such a gap between life and art cannot be healed, because it is kept intentionally open. If it produces suffering, it is with a sadistic appreciation of the elegance of one's own misery. The highly superior young man with his poppy or his lily in his medieval hand deliberately closed his horizon on himself. His passage through life was inside a scented sedan chair with the silken curtains drawn. The succeeding generations have long since rescued us from such unpardonable myopia, and modern life gives us boundless opportunities to expand our powers of artistic experience. Imminent and immediate ugliness can almost always be dissipated in the framework of a larger setting, and our esthetic experience can be made into a creative striving for such a framework. American small towns are losing their drabness as color is flooding more and more freely through them. The crowding traffic of our city streets, the extraordinary patterns and kinetic forms of the huge swaying buildings, the ramped highways and bridges with their twisting approaches over interlacing railroad tracks, wharves and piers at dusk and in the illuminated darkness—all these we can be taught to see as the artist sees them, without preciosity or affectation.

And even though heightened powers of observation and attention and the judgments incident to the education of artistic sensibilities make inevitable a conflict between our own taste and a tasteless environment or a philistine situation, it is not essential to our survival that we should insist on emphasizing the unpleasantness which assails us, lest we make an organ point out of every discordant note. It is not necessarily a proof of the integrity of our taste and training to make public announcement of our unfavorable reactions; and I do not think that it seriously injures our artistic sensibility if we refrain from applying it promiscuously to every act and every object in our environment. *"Perdidi Musam tacendo"* ("I have lost my Muse by keeping silence"), says the late Latin poet of the *Vigil of Venus;* but sometimes much more is lost by too much eloquence. In Athens a tiny and delightful Byzantine church, immeasurably too small to cope with the modern community which had grown up around it, has been overshadowed by a new metropolitan church built immediately next to it, as huge as it is hideous. Large letters over the entrance doorway of this tasteless monster proclaim in New Testament Greek with unexpected and quite startling frankness, "How aweful is this place!" That is the sort of esthetic judgment which one does not need to express quite so openly or so insistently.

The real gap is not between the beauty of art and the lack of beauty in life. A more genuine and deep-seated difficulty can reside in the impassivity of artistic contemplation, its quietism and impracticality, as against the lack of any contemplative context in the performance of our daily tasks. I dare say that this is not as aggravated in the recent college graduate as in the professional practitioners of art or in teachers, writers, and thinkers for whom the gap between learning and living is more gapingly open. Rightly or wrongly, we form a habit of screening out of our attention most things which we dislike. I should be the first to admit that I have been wrong, through most of my life, by sticking this plaster of inattention over the gap between learning and living. Having done so myself, I can warn you against the habit. The notorious absent-mindedness of my profession is merely an indication of our overconcentration on mental interests which by their very nature have no connection with our daily environment. In a small German city there lived an archaeologist whose features bore a remarkable resemblance to those of quite another citizen. One morning, while waiting for his bus, he descried inside the approaching vehicle the familiar face of his Double pressed against the pane of a window. "Well, well," said he, "I must have got on at the other stop this morning!" and turned back home, still pondering his morning's lecture.

The anecdote does not record any further details, but we have heard enough to recognize a sad discrepancy between learning and living.

In a milder form the discrepancy exists for all of us who see with the mind as well as with the eye and hence employ more than merely pragmatic vision. Walt Whitman was of the opinion that a mouse is miracle enough to stagger sextillions of infidels. Yet none of us can take the occasion to review our theological convictions when confronted with the spectacle of a mouse in our larder. Still more distressingly, if our vision is esthetic also, the contemplation of a charming long-eared little fellow just in from the fields, regarding us from the pantry shelf with a look of unabashed curiosity, is hard to reconcile with our cold-bloodedly calculated and murderous behavior towards his innocent desire to share our food and lodging for the winter. But this is basically a moral issue which has been aggravated by esthetic convictions. Our normal human hesitance to kill is made more poignant when crossed with an aversion to the destruction of a beautifully constructed creature. But once again, as we go through life, slaying and destroying, few of us can draw the conclusion that it would have been better never to have discerned any beauty in the living things whose annihilation we occasion.

Perhaps you have already decided that my field mouse must be the *ridiculus mus* which came out of the mountains' travail in Horace's line, and that I have diverted our present discussion into mere whimsicality. Yet the real issue comes quickly enough to light whether we talk of mice or men. It is easily delimited and once identified will be met in every context, great or small. In order to argue that the discipline of seriously studying the history of art for most of the years of a college course has been a detriment or embarrassment to normal later life (and that, I take it, is fundamentally the issue which I have set myself to examine), you would sooner or later be forced by the logic of the debate into the position of having to deprecate and decry the power of a trained discriminating eye. For it seems to me obvious that esthetic vision, as I have been calling the act of seeing the world with an artist's interest in what it may offer, does not merely involve the perennial judgment between the beautiful and its opposites, but is in itself a heightening of the act of seeing.

Probably there is such a thing as seeing too much; but I doubt if it is possible to see too well. And since it is the mind and not the retina which really does the seeing, it should not be surprising if an educated person can see better than an uneducated one, or if a student trained to the analyses of the art historian can discover more significant detail in the great painted canvas which is life.

No matter what the enterprise or undertaking, to see analytically, to mark differences and detect identities, to work with patterns (which usually betray functions and organic groupings) is to approach one's problems with a key to their comprehension. If you decide to breed dogs, you will breed better dogs than your competitor if you can truly *see* the dogs which both of you breed. If you join a civic committee, you will bring eyes where others may bring only tongues. If you can pick out patterns amid disorder, you can organize your household or your community. Surely, the eye is the pride of the senses; and to the keenest goes the prize.

Will you overlook the focus directed on myself, if I move in from the student of art to my own immediate profession of archaeology? In 1940, when the next-most-recent war came on, we archaeologists were eyed askance. The physicists were hurried off to specially equipped laboratories, little guessing perhaps the atom-splitting destiny which awaited some of them; and most of the other scientists were in heavy demand. The historians were shifted readily enough from the mess which was Europe under Napoleon to the mess which was Europe under Hitler. The experts in political economy and government seemed to think that they were predestined to be ambulance chasers hastening from one national accident to another. The practitioners in modern languages made out a plausible case of utility for their services (to the rather pointed exclusion of their dead and buried colleagues in Greek and Latin). But there was only pity for the archaeologists, the most patently useless of all intellectual idlers, who by their own admission could not touch a civilization until it was over and done with. In the remote future beyond the war, when Europe should be in ruins and only stray military police should be wandering over the face of the land, like jackals in the desert nightfall of humanity, perhaps the archaeologists might find something useful to do, poking around with the jackals; but for the immediate emergencies of warfare?—never! The walls of Babylon and Nineveh could not help to decide the contest between Maginot and Siegfried; men were not shifting Bronze Age relics, but struggling for their lives against an Age of Steel; even a firsthand knowledge of the attributable painters of Attic red-figured vases could not be considered much of a recommendation at GHQ. The archaeologists were patently campus-bound for the duration.

I must confess that this devastating verdict would not, in my biased opinion, have proved anything more serious against the pursuit of archaeology than that its matter and mentality were thoroughly alien to the prosecution of modern warfare—a decision that a humanist might accept with equanimity. Yet it turned out that the verdict was wrong: the archaeological mind was of very real value, and when that value was realized, it was widely put to use. England had been aware of this ever since the preceding Lesser World War had brought it out, and England in 1939 accordingly impressed her archaeologists into immediate service. From England, America rather dubiously learned the tidings and hesitantly followed the lead. It turned out that the mind successfully trained in the archaeological disciplines had developed a knack for recognizing evidence in very fragmentary and almost invisible clues and for logically reaching conclusions by combination and elimination, which made it singularly capable of coping with a variety of problems in military and civil intelligence. In the course of the great skirmish, my college received an official request that one of our archaeological candidates for the doctorate be permitted to postpone her examinations for several years longer on the plea that her type of mind and equipment of training had made her signally successful in a confidential branch of the service for which she was not replaceable from any other profession or source of supply. Greatly surprised and somewhat incredulous, Bryn Mawr granted the request.

There seems to be, therefore, the possibility of raising the plea that not merely is the archaeological eye a piece of mechanism such as should be worth anyone's while to acquire, even if it is to be used solely in the routine of private life, but that there is also such a thing as the archaeological mind or brain behind the eye, and that this too is highly specialized in its behavior and may be valuable for its capabilities. Whether it is an admirable possession, in the sense that it will evoke much admiration among bystanders, is a topic beyond my competence. I suspect that it may not always be an endearing capacity: a candidate for political office would be more liable to election without it. The ability to make whole things out of fragments and to spot the significant trifle amid the mass of unimportant accumulations, which is the trained archaeologist's typical attainment, would not invariably be a gift comfortable either to its possessor or its vicarious victim. Yet undeniably it would be useful; since to see the whole vase in the sherd, the statue in the fragment, the building in the broken block, and the civilization in its casual remnants, borders on the less material but not altogether different gift of being able to see the grown man in the child, the entire person in the chance remark, and the trend of the times in a shift in social manners or political allegiance.

And though by definition the archaeologist deals only with material things such as can be touched, handled, and examined, before he has finished his task, he ascends to immaterial levels.

To what has physically survived he has mentally added whatever else is missing and has perished: the fragmentary pot or painting, statue or building, has yielded to him the original, full and entire, from which the piece has sprung. And all the pots and pictures, statues and buildings, the broken lamps and locks, the tools and *trivia*, which chance and fate have swept into his ken, have yielded the still broader view of the towns and cities, the traditions and customs and typical behavior of an entire period or phase of human existence on our planet. That is the archaeologist's technique—to fit the existent sherd into the nonexistent pot, the pot into the artist's factory or the household's use, and finally the artist and the household into their time and place in the cultural history of mankind. It may not be easy to do, and somewhere in the process there will usually be a slip or an outright failure; but at least this is the ideal objective, and in so far as the archaeologist succeeds, this is what he achieves. And if he does this by profession, he can hardly help doing it also by daily habit. His eye behaves differently from the eye trained in art, since it reassembles quite as normally as it analyses, being more interested in the reconstructive synthesis than in the passive impression or emotional judgment. Such as it is, let us remove it from its normal professional environment and drop it into ordinary civil life, to see what it would do. How does it bridge the gap between learning and living?

The lowest level of archaeological activity deals exclusively with physical and material problems. On this level the archaeological performance in ordinary life would probably not be very edifying. It would hardly rise above visiting the village dump and returning home with a fairly accurate idea, gathered from broken china and discarded kettles, where in the community there had been recent domestic accident, what families were going in for replacements and therefore perhaps had been inflating their income; perhaps even it would culminate in a shrewd differentiation between wealth, prodigality, and commonplace carelessness among the various families thus exposed naked to our archaeological Peeping Tom. Inside the four walls of his own household, the archaeologist's discoveries might prove to be even more disconcerting; but I warned you that I never recommended him for popularity. Nor am I now very seriously commending him to your attention as a prowler and petty sleuth.

If it be truly a prerogative of divine contemplation that a thousand years will seem but as yesterday, then to this slight extent something of divinity may lie within the grasp of the archaeological mind; for it is schooled to use the centuries as its measuring stick and to pass without dizziness from millennium to millennium. And though it may never be permitted impiously to aspire to that ultimate vision which sees, according to the magnificent Latin phrase, *sub specie aeternitatis*, it can at least claim that it regards both the past and the present *sub specie saeculorum*.

Since nothing ever comes from nothing, it is false to think that anything ever begins or that the proximate cause is ever the true cause. To see the world only in terms of the present, whether that present be the fleeting moment of time or the almost equally brief span of an individual experience, is to see with such short-sightedness as almost not to see at all. For to see is to recognize, and how can we recognize what we have not seen before? An infant cannot properly see because it can do nothing with the intricate arrangement of light which it catches on its retina. Past memory has to invade present experience before any world of objects can be built up. So in a much larger sense the spectator who sees only in terms of the present stares without truly seeing anything. At a symphony concert several thousand ears in the audience may all hear the same sounds, but they do not all hear the same music; and the chances are that the brain with the most complete musical past experience is the brain which hears most. To be sure, the archaeologist who sees *only* the past may get little benefit from living in the present; but the archaeologist who sees also the present in terms of a continuous past may reasonably hope to see more than his fellows. Let me illustrate my point by returning to one of the fields about which I am supposed to speak out of professional knowledge—the history of painting.

How puzzling have been the weird productions of the futurists, cubists, surrealists, and abstractionists to those who have formed their taste and likings from paintings with a preponderance of naturalistic illustrational content! The perspective of the general public without artistic historical experience is too short to include under a common focus both the traditional painters and the modernists. If the work of one of these groups is to be classed as art (they feel), that of the other is not; and they are apt to have a strong conviction as to which of the pair ought to be excluded. That is bad enough, if nine-tenths of the public on whom the artists necessarily depend for material and spiritual support cannot make the step into modernism; but infinitely worse is the situation of the modernist artists themselves, whose brevity of vision allows them to see clearly enough what they are revolting *against*, but only very vaguely what they are striving *toward*. Ultimately, of course, it does not much matter whether or not they know whither they are going, since if they are on their way, they cannot fail to move and sooner or later to arrive at their predestined goal; but they could spare themselves (and us) a great deal of agony in the meantime if they would only sight their objective and aim at it a little more consciously, instead of thrashing around like crashed fliers trying merely to keep afloat until rescue arrives.

Under the archaeological perspective the phenomenon of modern art is readily explained. For the past thousand years our West European culture has insisted on the illustrative function of painting, by which I mean nothing more recondite than that painters and public have consistently assumed that pictures were necessarily pictures *of* something. Hence these painters have tried to show real (or possible) people and things, in a real (or possible) environment, with every appropriate detail in actual form and correct color. Now, an ordinary mirror or a piece of ground glass can perform that same trick to perfection, with most magical accuracy taking the three-dimensional world of solid things in boundless space and somehow reproducing them on its flat surface inside its fixed border. But for a man to take a blank piece of material and an assorted collection of pigments and perform the same little trick that the mirror does with such ease, so as to make the outside world somehow stick on his little square of paper or canvas—that is indeed a formidable task and a tremendous achievement. *Ars longa, vita brevis est:* one man's lifetime is far too short, starting at scratch without hint or help or precedent, to work out the secrets of this miracle. Generations of artists, each apprenticed to begin where its predecessor left off, can work out the geometric rules of perspective and foreshortening, the indications of lights and shadows, the illusion of atmosphere and distance, the corrections for focal definition and blurring, and the many, many other matters whose forms and formulas must be mastered before the world on the painted surface is a fair rival to the world on the silver mirror. Five hundred years is not a bad working average for the complete process. It could be done in much shorter time if that were all that man had to do; but with this and that to keep him busy in his curious fuming and strutting and quarreling, he seldom succeeds in keeping his mind on what he is doing long enough to get it done. However, so long as there is still some evident advance waiting to be made, some refinement to add, some technical problem or process to master, a specific direction for his efforts is dictated to the working artist. But when the entire process has been elaborated as completely as material barriers permit (for apparently there cannot be the achievement of an absolute illusion whereby we are so deceived by the painted appearance that we think ourselves actually inside and part of its spatial world), then the painters have nothing on the technical side of their craft which they can do except repeat their predecessors' behavior and their own; and it soon transpires that where all the technical resources have been explored, the emotional resources too will soon all have been discovered and exploited. Hence to the twentieth century came that sense of baffled repetitiousness which has coined the inelegant phrase "same old stuff!" with which to greet any and every exhibition (however meritorious) of work in the accepted tradition.

The attainment of the technical goal of realistic representation after six hundred years of undiverted effort and almost unbroken advance has happened to fall precisely in our own lifetime. It is remarkable that the event should chance to occur in your generation and mine, I grant you; but, like the atomic bomb, it was bound to happen *sometime*. Ancient classical painting, starting about 700 B.C. at a much more primitive level than did Giotto at the start of our own West European cycle, took a couple of centuries longer to reach the final stage of realistic illusionism, so that it is not really so extraordinary that, with this classical pacemaker available for comparison, the critical final phase of European painting should have occurred in the twentieth, rather than some other, century: perhaps the more surprising accident is that it was precisely you and I who also happened along at just this time.

But why and whence, you ask, comes modernism?

Sub specie saeculorum, which is to say from the archaeological point of view, modernism is merely a sample of a very natural but rather crude attempt to reason the matter out logically. When the painter's technique has become so perfected that he can successfully hold his own against the mechanical magic of the mirror or the camera, a great disillusion dawns. There is really no human spiritual merit in mirrors and not terrifically much in cameras—no matter what the daily press and *Life* magazine may think. If we set up a large mirror out of doors so as to revolve on a pivot and watch with what marvelous agility it rearranges its world of colored shapes as we turn it, never misdrawing a foreshortened form, never mismodeling a luminous appearance, we should soon tire of the marvel and, within ourselves, cease from wonder. Looking-Glass Land is less interesting than its prototype, since we can only gaze at the one, whereas we can live and act in the other. So also, seemingly, with the painter's magic. The technical feat, wonderful as it is, cannot be adequate justification for its performance; indeed, it can hardly pretend to supply the reason why the task was ever attempted. It is inconceivable that the ineffable wonderland created for our eyes by Giorgione, Titian, Velázquez, Rubens, and their brethren is really only a more or less successful Looking-Glass Land for us to gape into. We shall be sure that it was never really trying merely to be that, if we consider the vastly superior realism of the inanimate kodachrome and the soulless technicolor. When we start to review the great six centuries of European painting, we see instantly that success in the technique of reproducing the veritable aspect of the living world is no measure of success; for

300

otherwise, with so consistent a trend in its history, we should have to say that the later the date, the better the painting! Despite the fact that in the earlier times none of the artists could produce atmospherically correct outdoor scenes or impart any persuasive impression of uniform, continuous, and unrestricted space extending from our eyes to the disappearing horizon, we still prefer Bellini to Bouguereau, and even, perhaps, Van Eyck to Van Dyck. If we prize paintings for what we feel and not, as in a child's picturebook, merely for what we see and recognize, it must be that it is not the pictorial content which makes the painting, but something in the way the painter fashions it— the pattern perhaps, the flow of color, the movement of the lines or of the surfaces, something suggested by the imagined masses, in short, emanations from some scarcely suspected universe of esthetic forms. Then *these* must be what the great painters really were working with; *these* are art's true resources and riches; *these*, and not the mirror's technique of illusion, are the final objective! Such reasoning is quite possibly deplorable logic; but it is the logic of modernism. Cubism, futurism, vorticism, the various devices of abstractionism, surrealism, all are nothing but variations on a single theme: they are all only so many different approaches to an attempt to isolate the esthetic and emotional mechanism from the illustrative content in which traditional art embodied it. And their ambition (the one thing which for all their voluble differences they completely share) coincides with the only apparent avenue of escape from the monotony of the fully attained technical achievement of illusionistic realism.

As this flight from realism has been organized and attempted during the past forty years, it has been a terrific medley of hit-and-miss experiments and impostures; often it has moved on the level of kindergarten and clown; and it is very generally characterized by a moronic obstinacy which refuses to admit that a *reductio ad absurdum* is automatically in itself an *absurdum*. But it is, for all its vagaries, an exploration of the not-yet-understood, it is a delving into genuinely vital factors in artistic emotion, and (short of a refuge in an arbitrary symbolism such as perhaps only a great religious movement could vitalize) it is practically the only thing for art to do, because art, like life, must keep moving, and further progress down the six-century-old track of the Great Tradition was barred when the track itself came to its end. Hence, wrong as they may be in the application of their ideas, the modernists are basically right in their main theory. Let it be granted that, in the short perspective of two generations, they are mainly a source of truculence on their part and exasperation and ridicule on ours; but that is only because Queen Victoria and Salvador Dali could never share the same *Lebensraum* or, shall we say, cabinet? But in the tolerant contemplation of an archaeological perspective, there is enough that is well with their peculiar world to give us serene confidence in the adolescence which must some day mature out of their present puerility.

My conclusions are not too astonishing:

The eye which has been sharpened and refined in a discipline demanding intelligent use will continue to function more finely, provided only that its possessor will insist upon its exercise and not permit it to slip into dullness. And the mind which has dwelt intimately in the past is better able than its contemporaries to endure and comprehend the present, provided that it does not take the past merely for a place of refuge, but has schooled itself to see how the Present is only, and precisely, the still-living, the everliving Past. Put into his proper place in the long rise out of the neolithic into the technologic age, that outrageous creature, mid-twentieth century man, will no longer seem so abnormally violent, so unexpectedly cruel and stupid, nor yet for the first time in his racial history will he appear perplexed, bewildered, forlorn, and pitiable.

And so the gap between learning and living closes at the touch of the probing fingers of Understanding and the healing hands of her still finer helpmate, Sympathy.

BRUCE BLIVEN

The Mid-Century Pessimists

THE present era can be characterized in many ways. We might say that it is the age when the atom turned on man and bit him. It could be called the time when the wheel came to Africa. It is the age when the automobile exploded the family all over the landscape—a revolution promptly counteracted by television, which drew them back into one room again, but no longer as the family of old. Today they sit silent and zombielike in a row, ghastly and livid under the gray-green light from an illuminated rectangle in the corner. But more than anything else, it seems to me that this is the Age of Fear. Never before were so many people so badly frightened for so many reasons. Never before was nostalgia such a potent political and social force, as millions of mid-century pessimists look back wistfully upon a halcyon earlier day.

Among the fears of today there are four that seem to me particularly important. First of all, of course, is the fear of another world war, using the new weapons of destruction. The civilians are back in the front line again, where they had always been until a few centuries ago. We all know the awesome power of the hydrogen bomb. Even more terrifying, in some ways, are

Delivered before the Beta of California, Stanford University, June 16, 1956.

the new poison gases; a quart or two, dropped from an airplane, can in a few moments kill every organism in a wide area, while leaving all man-made installations—houses, factories, railroads, power plants—intact and safe for the use of the conqueror a few days later when the air is pure again.

Another common fear, at least in a certain element of the population, is the dread that our culture is somehow being debauched by cheap jazz, comic books, bad movies, and especially by bad television. Those who share this fear in its more extreme form are alarmed (or perhaps are fascinated) by the prospect of the day when people will have forgotten how to read and will sit in front of the television screen as much as possible, day and night, except when they are out being juvenile or adult delinquents. The Cassandras of this school of thought believe that honor and discipline, honesty, filial respect, prudence, and obedience are all going down the drain.

Closely allied with this general fear is a specific one that democratic political institutions cannot survive in the technological age upon which we are now entering. They see what the dictators, in Italy, Germany, Russia, China, and, temporarily, Japan, were able to do in the way of wholesale hypnosis, using the instrumentalities of mass communication and the secrets of human behavior that the psychiatrists have lately learned. They fear a new, more skillful, telegenic Huey Long, and what he might do in this volatile, excitable country of ours.

A fourth fear is confined as yet to a fairly small section of the people, though an important one. It is the fear that burgeoning population may outrun dwindling resources to the point of catastrophe. Modern science has reduced the death rate by about two-thirds in a few decades, while leaving the birth rate in some parts of the world almost untouched. World population grows by more than 80,000 a day; some countries, like Ceylon, already desperately overcrowded, double their population every twenty-five years.

To be sure, the scientists talk about new sources of food from the sea or from algae, synthetic proteins, artificial photosynthesis; but the pessimists feel that these things would only postpone and not prevent the crisis. They see many millions of acres of land destroyed through improper cultivation—destroyed so thoroughly that to bring them back into production would mean an enormous expense. They see the whole United States, to name only one country, running badly short of water. Even that most seemingly inexhaustible of all resources, the air, is now polluted in some regions to the point of grave danger. It is not generally known that several thousand persons died as the indirect result of bad smog in London in a single weekend a few years ago.

These fears of today must be read in the light of several profound disillusionments of the past century. It is now ninety-seven years since Darwin first gave the world the doctrine of evolution. After the first, brief struggle with the Fundamentalists, this doctrine was generally accepted by the Victorians as the automatic guarantee of human progress. Everything in the world was to get better and better, from man's point of view. There were to be no more wars; disease would be conquered and so would poverty. Around the corner were two chickens in every pot, Utopia for everybody—except perhaps the chickens! Alas, we know today it is not that simple. The law of the survival of the fittest still holds good to some degree, but we are less sure than we once were how to answer the question, fittest for what? or that this sort of evolution bears any close relation to the aims of human society as of this moment.

Before mankind had had a chance to recover from this shock, it was confronted by another disillusionment. The Victorians believed that human nature is highly stable and fundamentally good. Now we have come to realize that nothing is more malleable than what we call human nature: it changes from culture to culture and from time to time, endorsing with equal alacrity cannibalism, polyandry, and the zoot suit, asking only that they have the approval of the majority at the moment. And then, along came Freud to tell us that fundamental human nature is far from being the noble thing the Victorians supposed; on the contrary, it is powerfully egotistical and by native impulse immoral. Try to curb the instincts too ruthlessly, and you get into trouble: when we say, "Get thee behind me, Satan," we may be working up for a cardiovascular lesion.

The angry, vengeful God of the Old Testament has for better or for worse disappeared out of our firmament; and with Him has gone the authoritarian, all-powerful father of the family. When that family disintegrated as an economic unit with the coming of the factory system and the end of cottage industry, the father's autocratic power began to evaporate. This is certainly nothing to deplore, but it has meant a long, hard period of readjustment.

A final disillusionment that has been severe for many people who are hardly aware of it has come in the four decades since November, 1917. For centuries, men had been constructing imaginary Utopias; even if you rejected each of them in turn, you did not necessarily reject the idea that Utopia might some day be possible. Ever since 1848, Utopia building had centered for many people around the vision of the future that was dreamed by Marx and Engels. In 1917, one-sixth of the land area of the globe was taken over by a group professedly dedicated to bringing that Utopia into existence; yet before long the realization slowly seeped into world consciousness that what was being witnessed was no Utopia, but in most of its important aspects a slave state on all fours with ancient Sparta. The degree of disillusionment corresponded to the degree to which you had invested your hopes in this new Utopia. For some it was disaster; but for everyone—including those who had always vigorously repudiated the collectivist ideal—it represented some blackening of the skies.

Behind the specific forms taken by the pessimism of the day there is the general fear that technological advance is outrunning social organization. People even propose the fantastic impossibility of a moratorium on science, a ten- or twenty-year halt to technological achievements until the world can catch up. Others make a distinction between progress in the physical sciences, which is bad, and progress in the social sciences and the arts, which is good. Lewis Mumford is one of many who have recently described much of the progress in invention as mere gadgetry, destroying wholeness and peace in the spirit for the sake of unimportant alleged improvements in living. Such critics are made unhappy by the fact, of which they appear only partly aware, that this is an Elizabethan Age in science, a Restoration Age in art. It seems to me obvious that what we need is not less science but a more rapid pace in social transformation. That rapid pace is itself made possible by science, and especially the new aspects of science that seek to probe the recesses of the human soul.

I don't want to err as far on the side of optimism as the mid-century pessimists do on theirs. Certainly no guarantee exists that man will not destroy his civilization or even, conceivably, the human race itself, which will then join the many thousands of other species now extinct. But I see no valid reason to believe that this will happen and some arguments which appear to me impressive that it will not. In the last analysis I think humanity has enough intelligence not to commit suicide.

While the danger of a catastrophic war is still great, I believe it is somewhat less than it was a few years ago, and is decreasing. If we can get through the next few decades without a conflagration, I think the chances are good that there will never be another major war—and I know how many times in the past this prediction has been made and has proved wrong.

Many informed persons believe today that the horrors of hydrogen bomb warfare are so great—for the victor, if there is one, as well as for the vanquished—that the weapon may never be employed. We have already one small bit of historical evidence for such a situation in the Second World War: even the half-insane dictators did not use poison gas, under circumstances where it would have been a useful tactical weapon, as in aerial bombardment far from the boundaries of the user's own country.

The greatest world danger is certainly the fanaticism of the Russian leaders—a fanaticism strikingly similar to that of the Mohammedans of the seventh century A.D. While the danger from Russia is still great, it seems clear that it will diminish as time passes, as a new generation of leaders arises, and as the effort to keep the Communist bloc encapsulated from the rest of the world breaks down, as it is bound to do.

The wars of the past have been fought for the personal aggrandizement of kings, for religious ideals, for gold, land, and slaves. Today world public opinion opposes the ruler who starts a war to maximate his own ego. Luckily, modern combat on a big scale is so expensive that even a successful war is likely to cost more than the loot it accumulates is worth. Religious fanaticism like that of the Communists is still a menace; but as indicated, I think it is a diminishing one.

Some of the other world dangers that have been partly created by science are moving toward scientific solutions. Tremendous strides have been made in many parts of the world toward undoing the soil destruction that came about with the invention of the iron plow, and as this situation is rectified, the water table tends to rise again. The increase in world population is a very difficult problem, complicated as it is by religious inhibitions; but even here there are hopeful signs. India, whose desperately poor population increases by more than five million annually, is facing up to the problem as no other country in the world has yet done. Everywhere the colonial so-called backward areas are being industrialized; it is a process no outsider can stop and no insider wants to. Colonialism itself is on its deathbed; the best proof of this is the fact that all the relatives have been called in to asseverate that it never looked better. With industrialization there comes, almost always, a marked drop in the rate of population increase as well as a loosening of the religious, cultural, and other ties which previously encouraged a huge birth rate.

We are probably far from the day of large-scale production of synthetic or other new types of food; yet a review of the literature shows that progress has been amazingly fast. Here in California great insight has been achieved into the miracle of photosynthesis. Edible yeasts and algae have been bred, and are already part of the daily diet in public institutions in certain tropical countries. Raising fish for food, as farmers raise meat animals, is a significant development, already widely practiced in southeastern Asia.

As for the fear that our culture is rapidly going down the drain, the pessimists here justify themselves only by selecting certain facts and omitting others. The first and biggest that they overlook is the tremendous experiment, still less than two centuries old, of teaching everybody to read and write. On the total scale of human history, this only began an eyewink ago. It is far too soon to write it off as a failure. To be sure, there are bad books, magazines, and newspapers, inferior television and radio programs, dull and vulgar movies; but good things are also being done in all these media.

America spends more money on good music than all the rest of the world combined. Through the efforts of a few magazines, with *Life* at their forefront, we probably know more about the great art of the past than the people of Italy, France, or any other part of the world. You cannot laugh off a civilization that buys 1.2 million copies of Shakespeare's works every year, as America now does in paperback editions. You can't laugh off television, when more people saw a single performance of *Richard III* on TV than had seen the play in its whole history, in all countries, in all languages. Mass culture tends to upgrade itself, partly because the manipulators are born in the Puritan tradition and try to do a little better than they need to, partly because the public tires of the meretricious but in the long run never tires of the good. It is not without significance that the sharpest critics of our mass culture are those who proclaim with pride that they never have any contact with it.

The rapid urbanization of our culture has certainly, for the time being, got somewhat beyond our social control; but already countermeasures are beginning to be taken. The great explosion into the suburbs is an indication that people realize cities drowned in automobile traffic are less inviting than they were; when bad planning makes life in the suburbs also obnoxious, forethought and care will begin to be applied there as well. An expenditure of one hundred dollars per automobile for an afterburner—since cars are the chief offenders—would go a long way toward bringing the smog problem under control. And who knows what tomorrow's technology may bring? In Palo Alto there has been invented the "flying manhole cover," a miniature one-man plane guided by leaning forward or back, to right or left. In mass production it will cost no more than a Ford. If the commuters start using them, we may see the freeways glistening white and empty under the morning sun, while aerial traffic cops wrestle with the problem of airborne swarms, like human gnats, each complete with briefcase.

The aggressive instinct will never be bred out, or talked out, of the human animal; and it is well that this is so. On the other hand, the blind, overcompensated aggressions that lead nations into war are a type of mental sickness about which psychiatry has learned a great deal in recent decades. Those who know most about it, like Dr. Brock Chisholm, recently Director of the World Health Organization, believe that in time we may be able to cure this sickness, which produces so many criminals at home as well as reckless warmongering leaders of nations. These experts tell us, too, that the fundamental stuff of our youth today is as good as it ever was, that juvenile delinquency ought to be described for what it is, as adult-caused delinquency.

I am told that many of the present younger generation feel a defeatism about the manageability of the world into which they are now emerging. I don't know whether this is true or not and I suspect the reports are exaggerated, as reports of bad news always are. But if and to the extent it is true, I think it is wrong. Man's troubles are self-made; what he has done that is bad, man can cure.

In a fight, it is always a mistake to break off the battle, a maxim pointed out to me during the Second World War in a way I shall never forget. At one time in that war the British were being pushed back by the Germans across North Africa from west to east. Not far behind them was Egypt, where they had almost no reserves at all, and the Middle East where they had none. A pincers movement was shaping up, with Hitler's armies in the Balkan countries preparing to strike downward and join forces with their comrades somewhere beyond Suez. The British situation seemed hopeless, and talking one day with a high official of the British government, I suggested to him as an armchair strategist that perhaps the army in North Africa ought to be evacuated from the Egyptian ports to save as many men and as much *maté-riel* as possible.

The official shook his head. "The first rule in military tactics," he told me, "is never to lose touch with the enemy if you can possibly help it. Many times a situation that looks desperate turns out to be far less desperate than it seems."

This proved to be a good rule in North Africa, where only a few weeks later the Germans were stopped and rolled back. I suspect that it is a good rule in life.

FRANKLIN L. BAUMER

Religion and the Sceptical Tradition

THE twentieth century, particularly since the Great War of 1914–1918, has been called a number of things more or less appropriate: "age of uncertainty" and "anxiety," "age of unreason," "age of suspicion." But from the point of view of religion, which I propose to treat chiefly in this lecture, no term more exactly hits the mark than "age of longing."

This is the title of a recent novel by Arthur Koestler, and to lay my foundations I shall have to describe its central *motif*, if very briefly. *The Age of Longing* is a religious book, not in any narrow or creedal sense but in the sense that it deals with what are essentially religious themes, faith and doubt, death and pain, and apocalypse. The scene is Paris in the 1950's, the *dramatis personae* are a heterogeneous group of people, mostly intellectuals, from all parts of the Western world. What these people all have in common—with the signal exception of Fyodor Nikitin, the Russian cultural attaché—is a longing for faith, faith in a

Delivered before the Kappa of New York, Syracuse University, in May, 1956. Previously given, in 1955, as a Lawrence Lecture at Connecticut College, it was published in the Henry Wells Lawrence Memorial Lectureship Series, Volume IV, Lecture 2.

meaningful universe. "We are the dispossessed," says Julien Delattre, the poet of the company, "—the dispossessed of faith; the
physically or spiritually homeless." "LET ME BELIEVE IN SOME-
THING" is the agonized cry of Hydie, the American girl who
had been educated in a convent but who had since lost her faith.
It is this longing for faith that draws her to the Communist
Nikitin as to a magnet. He at least believes in something, even if
it is only a utopia measured in terms of kilowatt hours, bushels,
and tons. In the end Nikitin's faith repels Hydie, but it is her fate,
and it is the fate of the others too, not to be able to crawl back
into the sheltering womb of traditional Christianity. "I won't
have any of your patent medicine," says Delattre to the Roman
Catholic priest, Father Millet. "What you ask of me is the un-
conditional surrender of my critical faculties."

Koestler's book is obviously at once an allegory and a parable.
Under a fictional guise it seeks to represent real people and a real
situation in the Western world today. Koestler, who as much as
any contemporary writer has seen and personally experienced
the agony of Europe over the past thirty years, describes in his
book what is essentially a new species of *homo sapiens:* the hollow, homeless, dispossessed man, the spiritually displaced person
if you like, who drifts—like the characters in Aldous Huxley's
novels of the early 1920's, but also unlike them in that he is painfully conscious of drifting and of longing not to drift. The story
also points a moral. This, says Koestler, who obviously does not
belong to the art-for-art's sake school of literature, is not a
healthy state of mind to be in, and to the extent that it has captured the intellectual and political leaders of society, it threatens
to pollute the very springs of Western civilization. People who
have no faith but who long for a faith become schizophrenic,
and their creative faculties and even their will to resist tyranny
dry up. When this happens on any large scale, civilization itself
succumbs to a longing for death, the Freudian death-wish. What
can be done about it? Well, says Delattre, who often seems to

speak for Koestler, the only hope lies in the emergence of a "new transcendental faith," not identical with the old religious faiths, which will nullify the false religion of "Society" by which Western man has been living for several hundred years. Who will invent this "new transcendental faith"? There is the rub, for "religions are not invented; they materialise." We shall just have to wait for it to happen.

Now doubtless Koestler exaggerates, not only in order to point his moral but also because he is an ex-Communist, for it is a fact, I think, that ex-Communists are prone to see too much faith on one side of the iron curtain and too little on the other. It is well to remember too that Koestler has mainly Western Europe in view, and not North America. Yet he did not dream it all up either, of that we can be reasonably sure. There is external evidence, much of it circumstantial perhaps, to show that this *is* in reality an "age of longing." I can barely allude to the evidence here: the spiritual odysseys, in part autobiographical, like Huxley's *Ends and Means* and C. E. M. Joad's *The Recovery of Belief;* the psychologist Carl Jung's discovery of "modern man in search of a soul"; hollowness and loneliness as a major theme of modern literature (Koestler is by no means the only writer to report the longing of modern man); the "anxiety" and "forlornness" described by the atheistic existentialists; the "escape from freedom" of countless people to the totalitarian systems which supply a faith of sorts; even some sociological evidence, such as the remarkable survey of religious belief in England made by Rowntree and Lavers shortly after World War II. Perhaps the best evidence comes from ourselves, for how many of us can truthfully say that we do not share in some degree the longing of Delattre and Hydie.

Assuming, then, that at least to some extent Koestler mirrors a real state of mind, we want to know *how* this state of mind crystallized and *what* if anything can be done about it—not out of idle curiosity, but because it is an existential problem, a prob-

314

lem of deep personal concern to all of us. In this lecture I propose to take up these two questions, not with the idea that I can fully answer them—the time is too short even if I had the knowledge and wisdom to do so—but in the conviction that the historian is peculiarly fitted to throw light upon them and to make suggestions. For the historian sees, as people without historical training do not always see, that the two questions are interconnected. That is to say, *what* to do about any given situation depends to a large extent upon *how* that situation developed historically. As Edmund Burke pointed out *à propos* of the French Revolution, men and nations are what they are because of their history and to achieve workable solutions to their problems they must think and act within the framework of their history.

Now the first question—the "how" question—resolves itself into two subsidiary questions: (1) Why does the prodigal son—the Delattres, the Hydies—find it so hard to return home to his ancestral faith? and (2) Why, at the same time, does he long for a faith? The answer to the first of these subsidiary questions is *the sceptical tradition*. The prodigal son cannot go home, or at least he can go only part of the way home, because he is the heir of a tradition which at fundamental points challenges the religious tradition, the Judaeo-Christian tradition, of the West. Whenever he takes the notion to pack up and go home, the shades of Voltaire and Ernest Renan and Sigmund Freud and many other eminent sceptics rise up around him and persuade him to stay where he is—wherever that is. This sceptical tradition had its origins long ago in headwaters of the late Middle Ages and the Renaissance. These headwaters emptied into rivulets, and the rivulets, coming from all directions, eventually flowed together to form a mighty river which swept innumerable people before it, at first mostly the educated classes, but later many from the masses too.

It is convenient to think of the sceptical tradition as developing in three main stages. "This plague," says the American colonel in Koestler's book, "must have started in the eighteenth century" ("plague," incidentally, is the colonel's word for it, and not mine). Actually, the eighteenth century marks the second, and not the first, stage in its history. The trial of the Christian God by the rationalists and self-styled "philosophers"—the "intellectual *cause célèbre*" of the eighteenth century, as Carl Becker called it—could never have taken place without an initial stage in which philosophical and scientific sceptics, most of them sincere Christians, prepared the way for religious scepticism by dismantling traditional conceptions of nature and knowledge. Nevertheless, the colonel was basically right. The eighteenth century was the first great age of religious scepticism, in the sense that it then became the talk of the town; that is to say, fashionable not only in esoteric intellectual circles, but also in café-society, among the middle and upper classes. Even the powers that be took a hand in the trial of the God of the Catholics and Protestants when at the end of the century several determined attempts were made at the top to dechristianize revolutionary France.

In the nineteenth century the sceptical tradition moved into a third phase. The majority of the eighteenth-century dechristianizers were not, after all, anti-religious, at least not on the surface. Voltaire's battlecry "Crush the infamous thing" referred, not to religion as such, but to a particular kind of religion, revealed religion, Christian orthodoxy. He could not conceive of nature without a God to create it, a watch without a watchmaker. Robespierre, at the Feast of the Supreme Being in June, 1794, not only applied the torch to a symbolic figure of Atheism but also tried to substitute for the old established religion a new religion of the Supreme Being. And he was by no means the only revolutionary leader who could not conceive of a society without some kind of organized church to uphold morals and civic spirit. In these respects the majority of the religious sceptics of the eighteenth century looked backward as well as forward.

But in the next century men in ever increasing numbers contrived nothing less than the "death of God," as Nietzsche so dramatically phrased it, and not merely the Christian God. The century of Auguste Comte and David Friedrich Strauss, of Ludwig Feuerbach and Karl Marx, of Sir Leslie Stephen and Sir James Frazer, witnessed the triumphant march of agnosticism (the word was invented by Thomas Henry Huxley, and it signified suspended judgment), of materialism, and perhaps most ominous of all, religious indifference. Religion, in the traditional sense of belief in the gods, was debunked in countless new definitions: religion is the opiate of the people, religion is myth, religion is self-projection, religion is anthropology; religion is what man eats, an instrument in the class struggle; religion is childishness, a phenomenon now outmoded in man's evolution toward control of nature, and so on. The new breed of intellectuals were not loath, moreover, as so many of their eighteenth-century forbears had been loath, to discuss religion before the servants, and there is evidence to show that the servants were beginning to learn their lesson. In view of this sceptical drift, is it any wonder that the prodigal son left home in the first place and afterwards found it difficult to go back, however much he might desire to do so? Throughout the three stages, of course, Christianity was by no means obliterated; indeed, at times it showed a remarkable ability to counter-attack, as in the Methodist and evangelical movements in England and in some phases of the so-called romantic movement. Yet there can be no doubt that for the first time in its history Christianity—and not only Christianity, but religion in general in the nineteenth century—was forced to beat a serious retreat and to yield considerable territory to a powerful enemy.

It is impossible in one lecture to detail this development. I shall therefore confine myself to several broad observations which are pertinent to my final thesis. First of all, it is important to recognize that the scepticism of which we have been speaking was not a plot, nor, with regard to its effects, altogether a "plague." The eighteenth-century sceptics and their opponents, the Christian apologists, often attributed to each other the lowest of human motives. Priests and kings were said to have invented revealed religion for their own greedy advantage. On the other side, the sceptics were contemptuously labelled "Cacouacs," a tribe descended from the Titans, who emitted poison whenever they spoke. This was, of course, a gross misrepresentation. The sceptical tradition was the result, not of a diabolical plot, but of righteous indignation and honest doubt, and failure to recognize this fact at the outset can lead to some very false conclusions about the present-day religious situation. Furthermore, this doubt was not the result of abstract thinking, or at least it was not wholly so. As I see it, great changes in the human consciousness never come about in just that way. Change is, so to speak, from the bottom up as well as from the top down, or from the outside in as well as from the inside out. The intellectuals articulate the change—who else?—but they do so as much and more because they live in a life-situation as because they cogitate on the logical possibilities of an intellectual problem. That is to say, events in the world around them incite them to radically new ways of thinking which in another kind of environment might never have occurred to anyone.

How then, if not as the result of a plot, was modern religious scepticism generated? To answer this question satisfactorily we should have to subject the first stage of the sceptical tradition to a much more complete analysis than we can do here. We should have to assess the effects upon religious thinking of such apparently far removed events as Western Europe's contacts with extra-Christian cultures and the warfare between the sects within Western Christendom; the creeping secularization of the Roman hierarchy in the late Middle Ages; the clash of rival philosophies and theologies during the Renaissance and Reformation which stimulated the pyrrhonism of a Michel de Montaigne, the minimal theology of a Sebastianus Castellio, and the incipient deism of a Lord Herbert of Cherbury; the tendency of the Reformation, on its Zwinglian and left-wing side, to empty the world of its religious symbolic content; the rise of a middle-class culture with its inevitably new attitude toward work and man's rational control of his environment; the reduction of the world to mathematical categories by Copernicus, Galileo, and Descartes; etc.

From the complex interplay of these and other factors there gradually grew up in men's minds a new idea of nature, a new conception of knowledge, and a new vision of time, all of which militated against the old religious interpretation of the world and man. The modern world has produced two ideas of nature which have been damaging to the cause of religion in the long run. The first of these ideas pictured nature as a machine; the second described it as red in tooth and claw. What these two ideas had in common was that they provided a naturalistic, as opposed to a teleological or theological, explanation for physical and biological events. By the "mechanical philosophy," as Robert Boyle dubbed it in the seventeenth century, all natural effects could be explained by the laws of local motion, without having recourse to final or formal causes except, possibly, in the first instance. Back of this philosophy lay an understandable desire to control nature which could be achieved only if science was divorced from theology and metaphysics, principally Aristotelian metaphysics. But whatever its origins, its result was to drive purpose and ultimately intelligent design too out of nature, and to encourage what I like to call naturalistic thinking—by naturalistic thinking I mean the habit of supposing that the naturalistic explanation accounts for everything, that "nature" is all that there is, that nature in no way points beyond itself. In a world increasingly dominated by science and scientific concepts this habit inevitably spread to other realms of thought, notably to psychology, political theory, and history.

It could never have proceeded to such sceptical lengths, however, if it had not soon become intertwined in people's minds with a sceptical conception of knowledge. "The foundation of morality," Thomas Henry Huxley wrote in 1889, "is to have done, once for all, with lying; to give up pretending to believe that for which there is no evidence, and repeating unintelligible propositions about things beyond the possibilities of knowledge." Huxley's statement epitomizes the empirical theory of knowledge which descended from John Locke through David Hume and the Positivists, and which by Huxley's day had become an inveterate habit of thinking among educated people. Extreme empiricism limited knowledge to ideas derived from sense impressions, *i.e.*, the physical world, and checked by experiment; everything else was set down as opinion or misguided "enthusiasm." It demanded sensible evidence for everything, and Hume, for example, showed how there was no reliable evidence for miracles or even the engineer-God whose existence most of the early mechanists inferred from the wonderful order of nature. Historically, this empiricism represented an attempt by men of peace and common sense to reach firm ground in a world of conflicting philosophies and orthodoxies. But it also registered a profound shift of interest from metaphysics to physics, from "vain" speculation to knowledge that could be useful to man in this world. In Locke's phrase, "we shall not have much reason to complain of the narrowness of our minds, if we will but employ them about what may be of use to us; for of that they are very capable." The ultimate effect of this kind of thinking was to promote religious agnosticism, for it denied the human mind access to that "vast ocean of Being" upon which all true religion depends. In Huxley's day, it should be noted, agnosticism was reinforced by still another conception of knowledge which was born of the growing historical consciousness of the nineteenth century. Truth, it was being said, is relative to a particular time, place, and social group, and Ernst Troeltsch, among others, was rightly worried about the problem which this historical relativism posed for religion.

Perhaps, though, the principal factor in the rise of scepticism lies deeper still, in the new vision of time which fired Francis Bacon's imagination and which is already so pronounced in the great quarrel between the "Ancients" and the "Moderns" at the end of the seventeenth century. In Carl Becker's description,[1] this vision, at least as the Enlightenment understood it, was dedicated to the following propositions (significantly, Becker calls it "the religion of the Enlightenment"): "(1) man is not natively depraved; (2) the end of life is life itself, the good life on earth . . . ; (3) man is capable, guided solely by the light of reason and experience, of perfecting the good life on earth." This was substantially a vision of power, born in an age when new vistas of power were opening up to Western Europeans through geographical and economic expansion and with the development of modern science.

On the surface the "Kingdom of Man," as Bacon called it, does not appear to be unreligious, and, indeed, the social gospellers of the nineteenth century seized upon it as the ideal expression of Christian love on earth. But look a little beneath the surface and I think you will see that at essential points it outflanked the religious position. The principal end of mankind was said to be "happiness," and in few of the many books written on that subject in the eighteenth century was anything said about misfortune, suffering, or tragedy as part of the permanent datum of things here on earth. Moreover, the means to the end was "change from without" rather than "change from within." It was assumed that man did not need to be changed inside, that new and better methods of knowledge and education, better laws and better political and economic institutions—in a word,

[1] Carl Becker, *The Heavenly City of the Eighteenth-Century Philosophers* (New Haven: Yale University Press, 1932), p. 102.

social engineering—were the thing. Thus, the active virtues were rated above the passive and contemplative, and philosophy itself, in proportion as it became imbued with this vision, devoted itself to instigating social change, to getting things done, as opposed to reflecting upon the meaning of what had been done (as in the "philosophy" of the Enlightenment, which revolted against the metaphysical systems of the seventeenth century as well as the Middle Ages; and Karl Marx, who revolted against the essentially contemplative philosophy of Hegel). Perhaps the most important thing about it was its focus on society—in Koestler's phrase, the horizontal "Man-Society" relationship as opposed to the vertical "Man-Universe" relationship. The article "Philosopher" in the great *Encyclopedia* of the eighteenth century expresses this relationship neatly. "Civil society is, so to speak, a divinity for him [the philosopher] on earth; he burns incense to it, he honors it by probity, by an exact attention to his duties, and by a sincere desire not to be a useless or embarrassing member of it." The vision of the Kingdom of Man was in reality a substitute faith which a religious man could hold, at least in its entirety, only at his peril.

So much for the reasons why, as Edward Gibbon once put it, "in modern times a latent and even involuntary scepticism adheres to the most pious dispositions." Principally for these reasons the sceptical tradition had reached a high water mark in the "infidel half century," as George Bernard Shaw called the age of Darwin. But already the tide had begun to recede somewhat, and it is a matter of record—allusion has already been made to some of the documentary evidence, and that is all we can do here—that it has continued to recede down to our own times. Basil Willey speaks of a "counter-drift toward religion." This is undoubtedly too strong, and even Willey qualifies his statement by remarking that it has not occurred on any general scale. As I see it, what has been happening more and more in recent years is that the will to doubt has become intermixed in people's minds with a new will to believe—I mean, of course, "believe" in a religious way. There are good psychological, philosophical, and existential reasons why this should be so. William James once wrote to an English rationalist friend of his:

Your bogey is superstition, my bogey is desiccation. . . . In my essay [he refers to his famous essay on "The Will to Believe," delivered in 1896] the evil shape was a vision of "Science" in the form of abstraction, priggishness and sawdust, lording it over all. Take the sterilist scientific prig and cad you know, compare him with the richest religious intellect you know, and you would not, any more than I would, give the former the exclusive right of way.[2]

The interesting thing about this statement is that it repeats, in its essential thought, what Mme de Staël, Samuel Taylor Coleridge, and other romantics had said a hundred years earlier about the "cold doctrine" of the Enlightenment. In both ages there have been people who expressed fear lest the empirical theory of knowledge lead to "desiccation" of the human heart and imagination.

The new idea of nature suggested by quantum and relativity physics has also provided fuel for the will to believe; or at least it has done so in certain quarters. I think I can best show the connection which some people have professed to see between the new idea of nature and the will to believe by citing two remarkable statements, one by a scientist and the other by a philosopher and historian. It will perhaps be said, Sir Arthur Eddington once wrote, "that religion first became possible for a reasonable scientific man about the year 1927" (his reference was to the overthrow of strict causality in Heisenberg's principle of indeterminacy or uncertainty in nature). "Modern scientific leaders," observed R. G. Collingwood, "talk about God in a way that would have scandalized most scientists of fifty years ago." What

[2] Quoted in Ralph Barton Perry, *The Thought and Character of William James* (Cambridge: Harvard University Press, 1948), p. 215.

lies behind these two statements is a conviction, now fairly wide-spread, that it is not possible to construct a mechanical model of nature. Matter, it appears, is energy and not inert atoms acted upon by mechanical forces; the behavior of individual electrons cannot be certainly predicted; space and time are relative to the observer, etc. In other words, there is more to nature than science used to think. Ergo, perhaps nature is, after all, an "organism" with a creative purpose, or a symbol of a wider reality, or a thought in the mind of God, or something like. At any rate, so we are told by the likes of Alfred North Whitehead, Eddington, and Sir James Jeans.

But at bottom, of course, the new will to believe traces to an existential situation. I need not belabor the point since it is so very obvious. The Kingdom of Man which the eighteenth century promised by the twenty-first century at the very latest does not seem to be materializing, just the reverse, in fact, if the Spenglers and Orwells are to be believed. The twentieth century, especially in Western Europe, has had a great shock. All the external machinery of which Western man had such great expectations has turned against him, just as Matthew Arnold and Samuel Butler predicted that it might. Another way of saying the same thing is that it is now understood, after two world holocausts and the recrudescence of barbarism in Nazi Germany and elsewhere, that machines can be used by men to evil as well as good purpose. It is also widely understood that evil is not simply the result of bad social conditions but that it is, to quote C. E. M. Joad, "endemic in the heart of man." These revelations have knocked the props out from under that substitute faith which, as I suggested, had become the working philosophy of a great many modern people. As a result there was bound to be much longing for a faith, and the way would seem to have been opened for a fresh exploration of that inner world where pre-eminently man meets the gods.

But Western man—I speak generally, of course—had learned not to believe in the gods. And so we are back again to the problem posed at the beginning of this lecture. The Delattres and Hydies—or generically, modern man—are on the horns of a dilemma. They long to believe, they even will to believe, but what to believe in is a problem for them. Two traditions, the sceptical tradition and the Judaeo-Christian tradition, pull them in opposite directions and even checkmate each other. What if anything can be done about this situation?

There are, it seems to me, four logical possibilities and all four have advocates in contemporary thought. The first possibility is that in the realm of religion Western man has reached the point of no return. On this view the spiritual longing observable in the Western world today represents a "failure of nerve." It will pass, or at any rate it ought to pass, for religion clearly belongs to the infantile stage of human evolution, and progress depends upon putting it behind us and growing up. In Sigmund Freud's classic summary, "Criticism has nibbled at the authenticity of religious documents, natural science has shown up the errors contained in them, and the comparative method of research has revealed the fatal resemblance between religious ideas revered by us and the mental productions of primitive ages and peoples." The trouble with this statement is that it is a half-truth only. It is correct as far as it goes, but at bottom it constitutes a serious misreading of history. Militant agnosticism of this kind ignores the possibly ontological validity of tradition, specifically the religious tradition, which for all its mistakes and even arrogance may after all be found to have preserved deep insights into the nature of being. It also ignores the evidence in history for the religious nature of man. I know that I am on debatable ground here, but I am impressed, as I believe most students of history must be impressed, by the sprouting up in the modern world of new religious or pseud-religious cults to take the place of the old cults. It is as if there were something in man's nature which makes him ceaselessly seek objects of devotion outside himself, objects which, moreover, are located in a metaphysical order of some kind. It might be argued pragmatically that in the long run failure to find such objects stunts the imagination and reduces the vital powers and thus affects adversely the history of civilization.

The second possibility is a return to the religion of grandmother. Arnold Toynbee aptly calls this way "archaism," and it is exhibited at the present time in the new supernaturalism, in the theologies known as Neo-Thomism and Neo-Orthodoxy. These theologies are not without wisdom, but it is extremely doubtful whether they speak effectively to the condition of modern man. If the sceptics underestimate the value of religious tradition, the neo-supernaturalists overlook the necessity of change. They speak as though it were possible for people to go back to a view of the universe which originated and flourished in climates very different from our own, and to accept that view upon authorities which modern man cannot accept. As we have seen, Julien Delattre resisted Father Millet's persuasions on this score. They speak, moreover, as though the sceptical tradition were easily circumvented, as though it did not raise genuine problems about nature, knowledge, and time. As Toynbee says,

Archaistic religious movements are intellectually indefensible because the antecedent Rationalism that has driven a traditional religious faith off the field does not in reality just come and go like the fog. . . . Souls that have once had the experience of intellectual enlightenment can never thereafter find spiritual salvation by committing intellectual suicide; and, though the quest of recapturing their lost faith is in itself both intellectually and morally legitimate, agnostics who embark on this quest will not find themselves able to worship God again in spirit and in truth if they seek to open for themselves a homeward spiritual path by deliberately closing their mind's critical eye. . . .[3]

Unfortunately, Toynbee has no alternative to suggest, except to "cling and wait." This, however, is a third possibility, and it too

[3] *A Study of History,* IX, 631.

is a fairly common attitude today, to be found, for instance, in persons as unlike as Toynbee and Koestler, Simone Weil and Karl Barth. I have already cited the passage from *The Age of Longing* in which Julien Delattre argues the need for the emergence of a new transcendental faith which would reestablish relations between Western man and the universe.

"Who is going to invent it?" asked Hydie.

"There is the rub. Religions are not invented; they materialise. . . ."

"And all we can do is to wait for it to happen?"

"Oh, one can always go on fiddling with programmes and platforms. But it comes to the same thing."

Theologically, this "waiting" is construed as the dependence of "gravity" (*i.e.*, the sin that holds man to the earth) upon grace. Modern man cannot simply will a return to religion, says Simone Weil; he can only wait for belief to percolate down through his scepticism. In other words, it is modern man's fate to live in a state of religious indecision and waiting, which will be relieved, if we are to believe Toynbee, only after a "painful period of probation" and when the Holy Spirit listeth and not before.

There is still a fourth possibility, however, which Toynbee does not develop but which deserves to be developed. This is an attitude which attempts to combine religion and scepticism; a *via media*, so to speak, which steers a course between the two traditions. Such an attitude would hardly land the homeless in a new age of certainty, but it would provide them perhaps with some temporary shelter from the elements and give them something to do while they were waiting.

Looking back over Western man's spiritual odyssey since the seventeenth century there would appear to be two chief stumbling blocks to the creative flow of religious life. One comes from the side of traditional religion, the other from the side of scepticism. On the one side traditional religion—I mean the religion of the churches, the orthodoxies—claimed to know *too much*. Largely on the authority of an external revelation it claimed to know, in detail, God's attributes, how his will was done, why the world was created, and how it would end, the decisive events of history, etc. Simultaneously, the sceptical tradition claimed to know *too little* about what Herbert Spencer called the "Unknowable." It began, as we have seen, with a great profession of unknowing which simply did not permit human access to metaphysical planes of reality. Between these two extremes there could be no meeting ground at all, as the great "warfare between science and theology" in the nineteenth century clearly showed. But suppose we were to admit frankly, with the sceptics, that what the theologies say about God and the world is myth, image, symbol, that is to say, that it is neither the literal nor the whole truth, not the thing-in-itself, but a poor human attempt to express the inexpressible. Suppose we were also to hold, however, as our existential situation might now prompt us to hold, that these myths and symbols are not merely human projections, not illusions, but reflections of mankind's deepest psychic experience. Might these twin admissions not open the gates and portals to a kind of religion which would satisfy twentieth-century man's spiritual longing without at the same time necessitating the surrender of his critical faculties: a religion which avoided both theological overstatements and sceptical aridity; a religion based upon psychological experience but which made a bridge from psychology to metaphysics; in a word, *an experiential religion.*

There has been a groping toward this kind of religion in recent years. One calls to mind, for example, Professor Basil Willey's lectures to the divinity school of the University of Cambridge in which he argued for a Christianity based upon the unshakable foundation of "repentance and rebirth" rather than "assent to doctrines and propositions." Willey claimed descent from such thinkers as Coleridge and Sören Kierkegaard, for both of whom, although in very different ways, Christianity signified "life" as opposed to a theory or a concept. He might also have mentioned Coleridge's contemporary, the great German theologian Schleiermacher, who tried to reconstruct Christian theology on an empirical basis, deducing doctrine not from an external revelation nor from metaphysical principles, but from man's emotional needs and feelings. Willey's own contemporary, the psychologist Carl Jung, explores farther than Schleiermacher and finds that religion is experience of a side of life—he calls it the "collective unconscious"—to which the conscious mind does not usually have access. Jung's formulation is particularly helpful in the current religious dilemma. For he speaks as a scientist and yet takes an affirmative attitude toward religion. He not only recognizes the therapeutic value of religion but concedes that in the religious experience man may have contact with a suprapersonal and even metaphysical order of reality. But at the same time he doubts that religious dogma ever corresponds to objective facts of the universe. For Jung, as for Coleridge, religion is not so much an idea as an experience which can never be captured successfully or accurately in words; it can only be projected in symbols.

As I have suggested, this kind of experiential religion may be the beginning of an answer to Hydie's desperate plea, "LET ME BELIEVE IN SOMETHING." Doubtless, in her pessimistic frame of mind she would reiterate that religions are not invented and that there is nothing for it but to wait. But I am reminded at this point of something William James once said about waiting. What James said was, to be sure, in rebuttal of a somewhat different position, that assumed by the so-called "rugged and manly school of science" which advocated living in complete suspension of judgment in religious matters, but it applies as well to the Hydies of the twentieth century as to the W. K. Cliffords of the nineteenth. Said James:

This command that we shall put a stopper on our heart, instincts, and courage, and *wait*—acting of course meanwhile more or less as if religion were *not* true—till doomsday, or till such time as our intellect and senses working together may have raked in evidence enough,—this command, I say, seems to me the queerest idol ever manufactured in the philosophic cave.

No one wishes to be duped, least of all the modern heir of the sceptical tradition. But as James also remarked, unless people meet the religious hypothesis half-way, they may never make the gods' acquaintance.

I would interpret "half-way" to mean that there are things that the sceptic can do while he is waiting. He can, for instance, do the very thing that Toynbee says he cannot do, namely winnow the chaff out of the traditional religions. This is what the German Protestant theologian Rudolf Bultmann has recently attempted to do with his program of "demythologization." Bultmann believes that the old mythological mode of thought which represented God in human terms, and as interpenetrating nature and history, is "finished"; modern man, brought up to think of both the world and the human personality as closed systems of causality, cannot accept or even grasp such a view. He therefore advocates, to the dismay of Karl Barth and other right-wing critics, the radical demythologization of Christianity and its reinterpretation in existential rather than in mythological or historical terms. On this interpretation, the Easter faith ceases to be a faith in a cosmic or historical event which occurred approximately two thousand years ago in a mythological universe; it becomes an understanding of man's situation here and now, and indeed at all times and in all places: man fearful, lost in a world of impermanence and death; man vainly striving to overcome his forlornness by reliance upon self and, failing in this, finding his redemption at last in an experience of the saving grace of God.

To sum up, the modern sceptic, whether he takes the demythologizing way of Bultmann or the mythologizing way of Jung or some other way, *can* take stock of his religious position in the light of the two traditions of which he is the heir. This stocktaking involves, above all, the reassessment of his religious tradition in terms that are meaningful to him, the decoding and rewording of ancient concepts which in the course of time have all but lost their meaning. Probably this is a task primarily for laymen—especially laymen with a pronounced sense of history— rather than clergymen whose vocation commits them to an orthodox position.

Yet the historic churches too can help in this endeavor, principally by assisting the sceptic to develop personal habits and mental attitudes upon which all profound religious life would seem to depend, but which have been lost sight of amidst the complexity and perplexity and noise of modern life: to wit, participation in the great cycle of the religious year; reestablishing a connection with the "world of silence," as Max Picard would say; and recovering the ancient, contemplative attitude toward work and leisure, which still another European Catholic, Josef Pieper, urges us to do. These are things which the modern sceptic *can* do toward satisfying his longing to believe. Whether he *will* do them, in such measure as to make any difference in his personal integration or in the integration of Western civilization, is a moot question. The historian cannot say that he will do them. For unlike the scientist or the prophet the historian knows better than to predict what will happen and what will not happen.

WILLIAM G. CARLETON

The New Conservatism
and the Mass Society

THE work and values of American intellectuals of the 1920's
and 1930's have been under critical fire since World War II.
But what of the intellectuals of the 1940's and 1950's? Perhaps
by now it is not unduly presumptuous to begin attempting to put
the American intellectuals of mid-century in some kind of historical perspective.

First, a word about the intellectuals of the 1920's and 1930's.
The present generation tends too much to regard American
thinkers and creative artists of those years as "radical." True,
many of them were excited by the constructive possibilities of
the Russian Revolution and enormously interested in the Soviet
Union as a laboratory for vast social experimentation. However,
as Granville Hicks and others have repeatedly pointed out, very
few of America's intellectuals of the 1930's were Communists.
Even among those who went pretty far to the left, there were
many who survived their earlier enthusiasm to make valuable
contributions to democratic thinking in the 1940's and 1950's.

Delivered before the Alpha of Alabama, University of Alabama, in
1957. Published as "American Intellectuals and American Democracy"
in The Antioch Review, Summer, 1959.

Some of these—Edmund Wilson, Malcolm Cowley, Robert Gorham Davis, Hicks himself, and others—reveal an awareness of twentieth-century realities, born of their earlier probings and experiences, too often lacking in our younger contributors. Others, with the God-that-failed mentality, having become disillusioned with the authoritarian "truth" of the left, have been searching ever since for some brand of authoritarian "truth" on the right. These embittered futilitarians, often extroverts in their personalities, have been among the leading assailants of their own generation.

It is my own feeling that the intellectual temper prior to World War II was more in harmony with the dominant American tradition than is the intellectual temper today; and more, that in general the intellectuals of the earlier period were coming to grips more realistically with the central problems, domestic and international, of our time.

Much has been written about how we were "betrayed" by the intellectuals of the 1930's. But as we move deeper into the twentieth century, we may find that it was the intellectuals of the 1940's and the 1950's, and not those of the 1930's, who departed more widely from the American tradition—at the very time, too, when that tradition needed to be reinterpreted, and applied to the realities of today.

I

What is the dominant American tradition? It is optimistic, democratic, rational, experimental, and pragmatic. It maintains that men are not the slaves of social conditions and blind historical forces, that to a large extent men can rationally mold their own institutions, without an hereditary or a privileged elite to guide them, and within the value-framework of human dignity and individual freedom. Although this tradition is often rationalized in terms of Locke, the Enlightenment, and Rousseauean humanitarianism, it came out of the historical interplay of creative man and indigenous American conditions: vast land and resources and a relatively small population; the relative absence of feudal, manorial, communal village, guild, and internal mercantilistic practices and traditions; the lack of aristocracy, priesthood, status, and "orders" generally; frontier realities; and the obviously howling success of the American experience.

America's Declaration of Independence boldly proclaimed the equality of men, regardless of birth, status, race, or religion. It was a revolutionary document when proclaimed, and it is a revolutionary document today. The Constitution of 1787, "struck off by the mind of man," created a government structure so contrived as to guarantee liberty; it set an example of how man might literally "make" his own institutions. Even the Transcendentalists, in revolt against rationalism, were optimistic and practical idealists. Like the older American rationalists and the later American pragmatists, they were ready to make a future to order. "Why should we not also enjoy an original relation to the universe?" asked Emerson. As H. S. Commager has pointed out, the Transcendentalists, with all their faith in *a priori* truths, took a chance that the heart knew better than the head and labored heroically to make the good come true. Even the most lasting impression of Darwinism on the American mind was not the rationalizations of the Social Darwinians, glorifying the plutocrats as the "survival of the fittest," but the assurance that there is constant change; and change, to most Americans, was something that could be directed to the good, be made "progressive." And at the turn of the century came William James's pragmatism, that marriage of American optimism and practicality with the bright promise of science. Pragmatism harmonized with American tradition and practice, for it emphasized the importance of experimentation, breaking with the past, rejecting custom and habit, trying new methods, creating a future on order.

American intellectuals of the 1920's and 1930's were in the

dominant American tradition. John Dewey emphasized the plasticity of man's instincts, the malleability of human nature. Truth was what worked out not only for the individual but for society. Individuals sought, in common with their fellow men, for secular, immediate, and particular truth that had meaning for the community. Thorstein Veblen, fusing economics, sociology, and anthropology, and posing as an objective, if ironic, observer, sought through an analysis of the conflicts between business and industry, between technology and the price system, to realize the possibilities of the new technology. Charles A. Beard and Herbert Croly saw in the marriage of Hamiltonian centralization and Jeffersonian democracy solutions of contemporary industrial problems through democratic national planning. Vernon L. Parrington wrote passionately of the history of American thought as the history of an evolving revolutionary liberalism; the central theme was that of the battle between conservatism and liberalism, reaction and revolt, with liberalism and revolt triumphant; the American tradition emerged as the identification of Americanism with democracy. Roscoe Pound, Oliver Wendell Holmes, Jr., Louis Brandeis, and Benjamin Cardozo were in revolt against legal abstractionism and scholasticism, and were busy infusing the law with pragmatic values and social realism. Sinclair Lewis was writing of the ugliness of commercial civilization; Dos Passos and Steinbeck and Farrell were portraying social injustices; but in all of these writers, even in the determinism of Dreiser and Darrow, there was the unspoken assumption that man could overcome ugliness and evil by changing his environment. Even Wolfe, at the close of his life, was groping toward a recognition of something larger than himself.

In contrast, the most vocal and conspicuous of the present generation of American intellectuals have surrendered to non-involvement or non-commitment, or retired into formalism, or become obsessed with techniques, or retreated into the individual psyche, or fled into the non-rational and the irrational, or seri-

335

ously distorted the American democratic tradition, or sought to substitute for evolving and fluid democratic values the fixed values of status and aristocracy. Exponents and exemplars of each of these points of view have all played down the wondrously rich diversity and flexibility of American life.

Now, of course, the older trends have not disappeared; the dominant points of view of the 1920's and 1930's still have creative exponents today; and vistas opened by earlier thinkers continue to be explored. In some areas, notably law and jurisprudence, pragmatism and social realism continue to make notable gains. Also, it must not be supposed that the new conservative points of view are entirely new; all of them had antecedents in the 1920's and 1930's and even earlier. Nor can it be denied that some of the work of America's uncommitted and conservative thinkers and creators of today is deepening insights, sharpening tools and techniques, penetrating psychic mysteries and complexities, intensifying aesthetic perceptions, and in some aspects of thought and life making Americans a more discriminating and sophisticated people.

What is novel in the current situation is the popularity of non-involvement and non-commitment and of conservative and aristocratic values. Conservatism is being proclaimed as the truly traditional attitude of Americans. Conservatism, it is said, has been our dominant tradition all the time; what is new, it is claimed, is our belated recognition of conservatism as our national tradition.

Let us examine some of the values of the New Conservatism and kindred schools of thought popular today, inquire into the authenticity of their claim to be our national values, examine whether they square with today's social realities and the facts of contemporary society, and suggest some of the consequences likely to follow were we to accept them as our "traditional" and guiding values.

336

II

Many intellectuals of the post-war generation have fled from all values whatsoever. They have taken refuge in non-commitment and non-involvement and called it objectivity or sophistication or wisdom. The great vogue among textbook writers and publishers for anthologies and collaborative works which acquaint the student with "all points of view" is today a much-used way of escaping integration and commitment. Sampling opinion, taking polls, and compiling the results of interviews constitute another way of escaping commitment by merely tabulating statistically the relative opinions and values of others on comparatively surface or safe questions. More and more, authors of books and magazine articles merely report opinion, but do not express an opinion of their own. They indicate trends, but seldom pass judgment on them. And as for moral judgments— these are to be avoided as "hortatory" and "evangelistic." There is not even a commitment to eclecticism, to an avowed defense of a society in which the existence of plural and diverse values is taken as a positive good, the hallmark of a healthy, vital, free, and infinitely fertile civilization. This would be a defensible position, for it may be that the American society has in fact become such an eclectic society. But few contemporary intellectuals are committed to eclecticism as a positive value in itself.

Closely akin to the trend to non-commitment is the emphasis on form, technique, and methodology. One way of escaping commitment in subject matter is to concentrate on form. In all the intellectual disciplines today, even in the humanities and the social sciences, there is a growing concentration on forging methods and techniques that will make the discipline truly "scientific." Now, of course, nobody objects to sharpening the tools of investigation and research, but an excessive concern for methodology may also be a way of avoiding all substantive

337

import. For instance, had Kinsey waited to "perfect" his methodology, or retreated into a minuscule area of investigation, or confined himself to a safe aspect of his subject, or been frightened by the moral and social implications of his researches, we would have been denied one of the few illuminating works of our time.

In literature, too, there has been an almost obsessive preoccupation with form, with style. If the 1920's and the 1930's represented a revolt from formalism, the present generation is characterized by a return to formalism. T. S. Eliot and the New Critics began the trend to form; today, form has become the vogue and most of our influential writers have been molded by the canons of the New Criticism. Norman Podhoretz has commented on the high stylistic polish, the precociously sophisticated craftsmanship, of our rising young novelists, even when these have little to say.

In matters of substance, many of this generation have retreated from social considerations into the individual psyche. There is an enormous preoccupation with individual man's motivations, love life, sex drive, frustrations, complexes, and neuroses; and there is a neglect, even an ignoring, not only of social considerations and problems but even of the impact of society and environment on individual man himself. Podhoretz has also commented on the concentration of today's young novelists on the individual's psychological drama. To our rising novelists, the supreme fact is personality and the main business of life is love. There is an almost total lack of awareness of the social environment as a molder of character and as a maker of the traumatic situations themselves.

In even many of our mature novelists and playwrights, life has been reduced to the individual's viscera, his gonads, and an eternal contemplation of his navel. There is, of course, a certain insight and fascination in the plight of the neurotic hero enmeshed in his own complexes and in the interplay of his little circle of family, friends, loves, and hates. But is this the ultimate wisdom in art? On this question, Arthur Miller eloquently writes:

What moves us in art is becoming a narrower and narrower esthetic fragment of life. . . . The documentation of man's loneliness is not in itself and for itself ultimate wisdom. . . . Analytical psychology, when so intensely exploited as to reduce the world to the size of a man's abdomen and his fate equated with his neurosis, is a re-emergence of romanticism. It is inclined to deny all other forces until man is only a complex. It presupposes an autonomy in the human character that, in a word, is false. A neurosis is not a fate but an effect.

Is all of this an escape? Miller suggests strongly that it is, that we actually are more aware than previous generations of the impact of the city, the nation, the world, and now of the universe on our individual lives; yet we persist in refusing to face the consequences of this in art—and in life.

The degree to which non-social and even anti-social attitudes have come to prevail in literature and humanities faculties of our colleges and universities today is perhaps realized only by those of us who teach in them. Recently, by way of illustration, it was argued in the humanities staff of one of our state universities that Steinbeck's *Grapes of Wrath*, which for many years had been required reading in a course in twentieth-century literature, should be dropped from the readings because it was "only a social tract and not literature." The book was dropped.

Historians and biographers, whether they have the training for it or not, increasingly use the psychoanalytic approach in writing the lives of famous leaders. This method is also used by Harold Lasswell and his followers to analyze the careers of prominent politicians. When this is the approach, the tendency is to emphasize personal motivations, often running back into childhood, and not the social consequences of the leader's mature activities. Since conservatives are less "troubled" than liberals, radicals, and rebels, they usually come off as more adjusted and normal, whereas the non-conservatives, being more "troubled," are likely to come off as agitators, extroverts, and cranks, as victims of frustration, complexes, and neuroses. This method, which minimizes the larger social setting of a leader's work and the social results of his work, tends to reduce all leadership, conservative and liberal alike, to the trivial and the commonplace, to rob it of its historical and social significance.

During the 1920's and 1930's, advances had been made in treating the leading philosophers and political and social thinkers in terms of the historical time and social milieu in which they did their thinking. Many intellectuals of this generation are in revolt from this. Exponents of the "great books" approach, the Neo-Thomists, and, among others, David Easton in political theory argue that this method reduces thought to a mere sociology of knowledge. There is now a new emphasis on "pure thought," on theories separated from their historical and social context, on sheer logical analysis of the ideas themselves in an attempt to discover absolute truths. However, the emphasis does not seem to be on all the acknowledged ranking thinkers in the Western tradition. All too often greater emphasis seems to be placed on the thinkers in the Plato-Aquinas tradition, in the *a priori*-deductive-authoritarian tradition, and less emphasis placed on the equally important thinkers in the skeptic-nominalist-inductive-empirical-pragmatic tradition. Now, intellectuals engaged in this business are certainly not running from commitment. On the contrary, these are seeking, through a new exegesis and a new scholasticism, absolute commitment and eternal verity.

III

Many of today's intellectuals are putting a new emphasis on non-rational values. The rationalist values of the Enlightenment are more and more under attack. This is particularly true among the New Critics, the Southern Agrarian Romantics, and the increasingly influential Neo-Thomists. Arnold Toynbee, who has a greater vogue in the United States than anywhere else, speaks disparagingly of the Enlightenment as turning its back on the Christian virtues of faith, hope, and charity, and emphasizing the Mephistophelian maladies of disillusionment, apprehension, and cynicism. A political scientist, Eric Voegelin, is writing a gargantuan work, an attempt to build "order" in history and politics on Thomist thought. It seems that the apple of discord appeared with the Greek skeptics and early Gnostics.

Now, of course, rationalism is not enough to explain history and life, but neither is non-rationalism. In order to be aware of the importance of the non-rational, one need not embrace non-rationalism completely; indeed, a rational respect for non-rational values may be the beginning of wisdom. Our society today, conscious of both, has a better chance of reconciling rational and non-rational values—of balancing the Apollonian and the Dionysian (to use Ruth Benedict's terms), the prudential and the passionate (to use Bertrand Russell's terms)—than any society which ever existed. But this new balance and this new wisdom will not be attained by denunciation or rejection of rational values.

Closely connected with the revolt from rationalism is the revolt from democracy and the bold affirmation of the values of an aristocratic society. The intellectual revolt from democracy had its origins in the 1920's with H. L. Mencken, the New Humanism of Irving Babbitt and Paul Elmer More, Southern Agrarian Romanticism, and the New Criticism. Ortega y Gasset's *The Revolt of the Masses*, which appeared in 1930, has had a tremendous, though often unacknowledged, impact on non-democratic and anti-democratic thinking in America. Today, Southern Agrarianism lives on in John Crowe Ransom, Allen Tate, and a number of younger votaries. The Neo-Thomism of

Mortimer Adler has increasing influence. And the New Criticism of T. S. Eliot, Ezra Pound, and Kenneth Burke has become the dominant influence in literary criticism. "America," according to Burke, "is the purest concentration point of the vices and the vulgarities of the world." The New Criticism has been summarized by Robert Gorham Davis as a way of thinking in which "authority, hierarchy, catholicism, aristocracy, tradition, absolutes, dogmas, and truths become related terms of honor while liberalism, naturalism, scientism, individualism, equalitarianism, progress, protestantism, pragmatism, and personality become related terms of rejection and contempt."

In his *The Conservative Mind*, Russell Kirk finds in conservatism a unified movement and a consistent body of first principles from the time of Edmund Burke right down to the present. He sees these first principles as belief that a divine intent rules society; affection for the mystery of traditional life; conviction that society requires orders, classes, status, social gradations, and hierarchy; persuasion that property and freedom are inseparably connected; faith in prescription; recognition that change and reform are not identical. This, of course, is a far better description of traditional European conservatism than of American tradition or even of American business "conservatism."

Peter Viereck, in his *Conservatism Revisited*, finds in Metternich and in the Metternich system of 1815–1848 a sagacious attempt to conserve the traditional values of Western civilization and to bridle the forces of liberalism, nationalism, and democracy, which, according to Viereck, have led in the twentieth century to the mass man, fierce class and international wars, and totalitarian statism. A defense of the Metternich system is something novel in American historians, for up to this time every school of American history—Federalist, Whig, and Democratic—has seen in the Metternich system mostly obscurantist reaction. Many American specialists in international relations are searching in the Metternich system and the diplomacy of the reactionary Castlereagh for techniques and methods for coping with the revolutionary ferment of our time.

There is a disposition, too, to import from anthropology the "tenacity of the mores" as reason for resisting change. "Respect for the mores" played its part in the decision to retain the Mikado in Japan; it is being employed to sabotage new racial adjustments in the South. A century, it seems, is hardly long enough to allow Southern whites to adjust to the changes of the Civil War. Anthropology, of course, deals with the ways and techniques of change as well as with the resistances to change, but the emphasis of the conservative intellectuals who go to anthropology for rationales is on resistance to change.

America's New Conservatives describe the European past in too glowing terms; they romanticize it; they hearken back to a Golden Age which in fact never existed. They minimize the good of an industrial society. They do not give enough credit to the enormous gains made by industrialism over poverty, ignorance, disease, and personal brutality. They make conservatism both too comprehensive and too simple. They tend to appropriate for conservatism the whole humanistic tradition of the Western world, whereas, of course, that tradition has become a part, in somewhat varying ways, of Western reaction, conservatism, liberalism, radicalism, and socialism. Again, a consciousness of tradition, habit, and the organic continuities of social life are in themselves not so much a matter of conservatism as of the maturity and profundity of one's social understanding. The New Conservatives see in historic conservatism a consistency, a unity, and a continuity it never had in fact. If the need today is to weld aristocrats, businessmen, Catholics, and Protestants into a common front against Marxism, such was not the case in the past; indeed, such a combination represents a putting together of historic enemies. The contemporaries of Metternich did not consider him an impartial mediator between aristocrats and bourgeoisie; they knew him to be the friend of

343

aristocracy and the enemy of the bourgeoisie. Very often these New Conservatives think of conservatism as being above the battle, as being the wise judge composing conflicting interests, snugly fitting moderate change into social and historical continuity. They too often forget that conservatives, like everybody else, are motivated by their interests. Conservatives are likely to overestimate the virtues and underestimate the injustices of an existing order and of their own position. As William Lee Miller has pointed out, "relative justice" will usually not be found with the conservatives, however cultured or humane or "new," but with their opponents.

The New Conservatism is an attempt to substitute European conservative values for the American liberal tradition. It is as transparent a fraud as the Southern antebellum feudal dream of Fitzhugh, Harper, Ruffin, Holmes, Hughes, Dew, DeBow, Tucker, Bledsoe, and Hammond. (How many Americans, how many Southerners, remember these names today?) Kirk and his cohorts are attempting to foist Burke's traditionalism on America, and as Louis Hartz has acutely pointed out, Americans, including Southerners, cannot become Burkian traditionalists without becoming Lockians, because the predominant tradition Americans have had is that of Locke.

IV

Some other thinkers are guilty not of falsifying the American tradition but of distorting it. Frederick Hayek, who has had an influence on contemporary American thought, erects free enterprise into a rigid system and decries all departures from it as "the road to serfdom." Walter Lippmann, in his *The Public Philosophy*, takes natural law concepts, which are capable of both a liberal and a conservative interpretation, and gives them a conservative Thomist slant. (Lippmann himself is an illustration of many of the older generation who have travelled spiritually from left to right. Lippmann has moved from democratic socialism to liberalism to conservatism—and to the urbane observer above the battle.) Louis Hartz, Clinton Rossiter, and Daniel J. Boorstin emphasize the private property drives of Americans to the point of distortion.

Americans have believed that they began in revolution and that by a continuous process of experience and free experiment they have been in a continuous revolution, a "permanent revolution," ever since. Hartz gives American history a different twist. He contends that Americans have never had a revolution, that they were born free. Unlike the European, they escaped the feudal-manorial-guild society, the society of aristocracy, status, and fixed orders, and were literally born into the new society of the free market. The result was a property-owing, middle-class society which took Locke for its patron saint; and if Locke had never existed, this society would have had to invent him. Now, of course, there is much truth in this, but it overstates the ease with which the American society came to birth and maturity and it understates the difficulties of building and maintaining a free and democratic society in the face of constantly recurring tendencies in the human situation to privilege, complacency, stratification, and ossification. In spite of the relative absence of an inhibiting cake of custom from the past and in spite of the favorable conditions of the American environment, a free society did not just occur automatically. Even in America, inhibiting left-overs of the European past were considerable. To realize the possibilities of the new environment, to mold America's free society and adapt it to constantly changing conditions, required vision, imagination, and humanitarian impulse; it required the experimental and pragmatic spirit; it required struggle and the willingness to do battle; it required innovators and fighters and innovating and fighting movements.

Kirk claims that the American Revolution was "a conservative restoration." Viereck calls it a "conservative revolution" in the pattern of the Revolution of 1688. (This would indeed be a surprise to Macaulay, who described the American experiment as "all sail and no ballast.") But Hartz says it was no revolution at all. (How "hot-house" all this would have seemed to the expropriated and exiled Tories!) The American Revolution, with its Declaration of Independence and its sweeping away of Old World legal, political, economic, and social "vestiges," *was* a revolution, a revolution of considerable radical propensities.

Even though most of the subsequent political and social drives in American history represented "merely" a further breaking down of the status society, an extension of the free market, and a more widespread distribution of private property, they also showed a continuing humanitarian and innovating spirit. The great mass movements to abolish indentured servitude and imprisonment for debt, to enfranchise the propertyless, to emancipate women, to educate the masses at public expense, to abolish slavery, and to insure social justice in an industrial society are not to be set down as merely putting the finishing touches on a system preordained by indigenous American conditions. The struggles between theocracy and independency, Old World tyranny and New World freedom, seaboard and frontier, federalism and republicanism, agrarianism and capitalism, slavery and freedom, industry and labor were hardly picayune. Even the party battles of Hamilton and Jefferson, Clay and Jackson, McKinley and Bryan were not the hollow shams a whole host of young historians and political scientists are now "demonstrating" them to have been. While the drive in America to private property, to "American Whiggery," and to Horatio Algerism, so emphasized by Hartz, is undeniable, so also have been the drives to the freedom of the mind, equality of opportunity, and relative social justice—as exemplified in varied ways by Roger Williams, Daniel Shays, Franklin, Paine, Jefferson, Benjamin Rush, Jackson, Dorothea Dix, Horace Mann, Emerson, Greeley, Theodore Parker, Ellery Channing, Wendell Phillips, Lincoln,

Whitman, Peter Cooper, Henry George, Edward Bellamy, Peter Altgeld, Susan Anthony, Jane Addams, George Norris, John Dewey, and scores of others.

Hartz raises some basic questions about the very nature of the political process. Are the conflicts of politics, even in Europe, rendered meaningful only when they involve class and the dialectics and ideology of class? Cannot problem-solving and the clashes of group interests, as distinct from those of class, also be meaningful? Granted that American politics have involved little class and ideological conflict, have not the clashes of America's amazingly diverse group interests over the distribution of the benefits of the American economy been most significant? Was the New Deal any less significant because its approach was non-ideological, that of "mere" problem-solving? Cannot Americans make decisive contributions to the underdeveloped peoples today by a problem-solving rather than a dialectical-ideological approach?

The Hartz thesis, that America has had no feudal and aristocratic right, no Marxist left, but only a liberal center, does much to clarify the difficulty Americans are having in understanding the "isms" abroad. But in playing down the humanitarian and the experimental elements in American life, Hartz and other conservatives are making it more difficult to bridge the spiritual gap between Americans and the non-Communist social-democratic revolutionary forces abroad. We cannot bridge this gap by harping on America's "monolithic liberalism," but we may bridge it by emphasizing the innovating, pragmatic, and basically non-doctrinaire nature of Americans and American society.

V

Those Americans writing about the American economy in a large and significant way—and beginning with World War II these have dwindled in number—are guilty of one kind of distortion or another.

A. A. Berle, who with Gardiner Means in the 1930's wrote a most meaningful book about America's big corporations, has now become an apologist for the economic concentrates. In his *The Twentieth Century Capitalist Revolution,* he likens the big corporations to the feudatories of old and to the modern sovereign state. Indeed, Berle sees the modern corporation taking over some of the functions of the state. According to him, we need not fear this corporate power because the big corporations will check one another, and they will go a long way toward checking themselves because of the sense of benevolence and social responsibility they are developing, the self-restraints of natural law, and the infusing spirit of a kind of twentieth-century City of God. Berle's distortion is that of optimism.

C. Wright Mills, in his *The Power Elite,* sees big business and the political state as merged, and the United States as a monolithic oligarchy ruled by the corporate rich, the high political directorate, and the war lords. These orders of the American society have an interlocking membership and transfer among them takes place at the top. But what is the common goal of this elite? What common interest holds its parts together and gives it a common direction? Mills develops no concept of class which might hold this elite together, and he suggests no other bond of unity. What, then, prevents rifts and conflicts in the elite itself? The truth seems to be that the American society is more complex and diverse and has more vital conflicts and clashes on all levels than Mills will concede. America's elite is not as exclusive, concentrated, and unified as he makes out, and its decisions are not as free from the influence of Congress, political leaders, political parties, group associations and pressures, mass organizations, journalistic opinion, and public opinion generally as he contends. Mills's distortion is that of oversimplification and pessimism.

J. Kenneth Galbraith, until recently, strongly suggested that we may enjoy the economic benefits of oligopoly and at the same time escape the evils of concentrated power because of the operation of what he calls countervailing power, new restraints on economic power which have come into existence to take the place of the old competition. The new restraints appear not on the same side of the market but on the opposite side, not with competitors but with customers and suppliers. Galbraith admits that under the inflationary pressures of demand, countervailing power weakens and then dissolves. But even in the absence of inflationary pressures, countervailing power is not pervasive but sporadic, because while in our economy some customers and suppliers are large-scale and organized and able to exert countervailing power against original power, others are small-scale and unorganized and unable to exert countervailing power. Galbraith suggests that government step in and create countervailing power where bargainers are small-scale and unorganized. But government is not something isolated from society, above the battle, forever standing ready to act in a disinterested way to correct imbalances. Government itself is subject to pressures. Why doesn't government encourage the countervailing power of small business to oppose the original power of the concentrates? Because the concentrates have access to government, too; they can put pressures on government; indeed, their pressures are likely to be more effective than those of small business. Galbraith's distortion is that of seeing too much symmetry and balance, of substituting countervailing power for the old "unseen hand" as a built-in regulator, as an automatic balancer.

However, one can scarcely classify Galbraith as a conservative. In his more recent *The Affluent Society*, he has revealed some skepticism about his own concept of countervailing power, and he has emphasized the importance of the public sector, the area of government-produced goods and services, in our economy.[1]

Is it not strange that in the avalanche of publications that pours

[1] This paragraph was added after the Alabama address because of the subsequent publication of *The Affluent Society*.

from the American presses there are so few studies of our business concentrates, those huge institutions that lie at the heart of our economy and our society? There is no end of studies in the classical market tradition, but there are relatively few which deal institutionally and pragmatically with our big-business economy. Every year our universities and foundations sponsor all sorts of studies on threadbare and peripheral subjects in all the intellectual disciplines, but how few studies there are that deal with the actual operation and administration of our giant corporations. Just how independent are these corporations? What is the nature and effectiveness of their controls over the economy? Why have not the trained personnel in these big corporations, more and more of whom are specialists from our graduate schools, taken advantage of their positions inside these corporations to give us realistic studies of their actual workings? (At least after they have retired or gone on to other employment.) Until more of these studies are made and then synthesized, much of what we say about the American economy—and the scope and nature of power in America today—will be inadequate, unrealistic, and speculative. Impressionistically, our economy seems to be amazingly mixed; but whether there is a preponderance of power and where it is, or what are the more important loci of power and whether and how they are balanced, are questions which cannot be answered yet.

VI

Perhaps the most pervasive distortion today is the belief that we live in a completely mass society and mass culture and that these are evil. Many intellectuals and aesthetes, and their numerous imitators, speak rather glibly of mass man, organization man, the crowd mind, group conformity, "togetherness," nonautonomous man, stereotyped man, the other-directed society, and the monolithic society. This conception may be selling our

liberal society short. On the other hand, this may be sympto-
matic of a growing awareness of the importance of cultural
freedom, in addition to political and economic freedom, a manifestation of a cultural revolution which is already far along the
way. People were not so conscious of agrarianism's narrow limitations and its non-autonomy, but at least we are now increasingly conscious of the non-autonomy produced by industrialism.

The truth seems to be that while in some of its aspects our
society is more integrated than the pre-industrial societies of the
past, in some other aspects it is less integrated. In its economic
and political areas it is more integrated, and there are threats to
personal autonomy in these areas. However, we are increasingly
conscious of them, and it is precisely in the political and economic areas that the American liberal tradition is strongest. This
liberal tradition needs to be reinterpreted and then applied to the
new realities. Certainly, rejecting the liberal tradition at this time
would be a surrender to the forces of impersonality and not a
challenge to them.

But in many of its other facets our society is less integrated.
People in an industrial society have been freed from the old
restraints of localism, from customary status and class, from the
traditional primary groups of family, neighborhood, and parish.
They are mobile. They can escape to the anonymity of the cities.
There is a much wider range of choice in careers than there was
in the past. And all people, no matter what they do, work less
and less and have more and more time on their own. But do they
escape the old fetters only to be absorbed in the crowd? There
is escape into privacy and into sub-groups of one's own choosing
as well as absorption into the crowd.

W. H. Auden, in his *The Dyer's Hand*, observes that advanced
technological society, by putting at our immediate disposal the
arts of all ages and cultures, has completely changed the meaning of the word "tradition." It no longer means a way handed
down from one generation to the next. It means a consciousness

of the whole of the past of all societies—with their infinite ways and values—*as present.*

In our society, all sorts of values—pre-industrial and industrial, rural and urban, non-scientific and scientific, non-rational and rational—compete and jostle within communities, neighborhoods, families, and even individuals. (In some individuals, this produces neuroses; in many others, it produces personal emancipation and cultural enrichment.) In their personal lives, Americans display a wide variety of recreational, aesthetic, religious, moral, and sex values—perhaps the widest variety in the history of human societies. The amazing variety of attitudes and practices in sex found by Kinsey would likely be found also in other aspects of personal living, if these were given similar scrutiny.

The mass media, which are often said to impair autonomy and creativity, are in fact Janus-faced. They widen the outlets for banality and mass vulgarity, but they also widen the outlets for good reading, good drama, good art, good music, knowledgeable interpretation of events, and live history-in-the-making. Actually, in consumption, there seems to be at the present time more discriminating connoisseurship in food, drink, clothing, dress, housing, sex, entertainment, travel, reading, music, and the arts than there was in the days before mass advertising and the other mass media. And in production, creativity, far from drying up, has never been so alive. Never before has it been so easy for so many people to have careers in research, scholarship, science, and the pure arts. Since 1901, American scientists have in each successive decade been receiving a larger and larger portion of the Nobel prize. Since the 1920's, Americans have had five winners of the Nobel prize for literature. We may deplore the current avoidance of social realism by our contemporary American writers, but we can only applaud their increasing sophistication and craftsmanship. And the practical arts grow and multiply. There has been an enormous expansion and proliferation of the service industries, of applied social science and psychology (like social and personnel work and psychiatry), of applied writing (like public relations, trade journalism, criticism), of applied art (like architecture, landscape gardening, commercial art, dress design).

A self-confessed middle-brow, Russell Lynes, comes closer than any intellectual to summing up the nature of our culture:

Ours is a "You-name-it-we-have-it" kind of culture. It is a vast market place of conflicting tastes, conflicting ambitions, and conflicting needs. In guaranteeing "the pursuit of happiness," we recognize that not every man's happiness is measured by the same yardstick. We may do our damnedest to convince him that our yardstick is better than his, but we do not beat him over the head with it. . . . Out of the crowd that the *voyeurs* of culture call "the mass," many single voices are heard. So long as this is true, what we have is not a "mass culture," but neither is it an aristocratic culture. It is a highly competitive culture.[2]

Is not ours a society without a metaphysical base? Is not ours an amazingly diverse, pluralistic, and eclectic society held together by a kind of humanistic pragmatism? And is not ours the probable prototype for other advanced industrial societies of the future?

To discover the actual nature of our society, the individual must for the most part look to the realities about him and trust to his own observations of life. Our researchers are currently bogged in methodology, minutiae, timidity, and bureaucracy; and our humanistic and literary intellectuals, with a passion for monistic unity, symmetry, conceptualism, and abstraction (most of all the New Humanists, the Neo-Thomists, the New Critics, and the New Conservatives), are busy constructing some homogeneous pattern for our society and culture, a pattern which simply does not exist. In a recent issue of *Commentary*, Robert Gorham Davis has pointed out how during this century American literary critics, with thorough Judaeo-Puritan-Brahmin book-

2 *The Tastemakers*, p. 170.

ishness, have given the whole American literary tradition a homogeneity which in fact it does not possess.

VII

It would be a cruel paradox if we Americans failed in the world contest of today because we had succeeded too early and too well in developing the industrial society of the future. Our very wealth, as a society and as individuals, is producing a spiritual and psychological gulf between us and the world's poor folks which under the very best of circumstances is going to be difficult to bridge. Most of the world is in revolutionary ferment. The anti-imperialist revolutions in Asia, the Middle East, and Africa are the most important political event of our time, and these revolutions are seeking not a rationale for the *status quo* but a justification for basic change. They may find that justification in Marxism. They may find it in the dynamic, democratic, libertarian, experimental, and pragmatic tradition, the dominant tradition of the American society. But they will never find it in the non-rational, non-democratic, anti-democratic, aristocratic, authoritarian, and ritualistic attitudes of America's New Conservatism. Politically, the attitudes of the New Conservatives make sense only if the United States is about to undertake to erect a Neo-Metternich system to underwrite a conservative and reactionary *status quo* in the world or to build an outright American empire. But if the United States is to win the anti-imperialist revolutions from the Marxists and put itself squarely at the head of all those forces determined to build a future democratic world, then the New Conservatism is working untold damage to American foreign policy, even to American survival.

The New Conservatism distorts and even falsifies the American tradition. It does not square with the facts of our modern industrial society. It is playing into the hands of the Marxists. It is giving verity to the Marxist theory of history that a bourgeois society, when confronted with the Marxist challenge, must necessarily commit suicide by going reactionary. It is damaging America's appeal to the revolutionary, but democratic, forces abroad, and weakening the democratic attitudes in America necessary for a sustained and successful democratic appeal abroad.

On the other hand, America's optimistic, democratic, libertarian, rational, experimental, and pragmatic tradition is the dominant and authentic American tradition. Moreover, it is the only tradition ample and flexible enough to allow and give meaning to our culturally heterogeneous and eclectic society produced by advanced industrialism. And this authentic American tradition is the only one available to us Americans that will appeal to foreign peoples in revolutionary mood, justify their drives for basic change outside a Marxist framework, and give sense to the kind of societies their new industrialism will eventually evolve.

HAROLD W. DODDS

On the Place of the
Intellectual in America

IN speaking of the place of the intellectual in America, I am fully
aware that with all the valor of ignorance I shall be venturing into
deep waters in which historians, philosophers and social scientists,
colleagues whose lives have been devoted to learning, navigate
with assurance and competence. Nevertheless, I cannot resist the
temptation to share some impressions, as possibly the best response I can make to the flattering invitation to speak at this
meeting of our own chapter of Phi Beta Kappa. For the function
of an intellectual in American life is a controversial subject with
which any college president of a few years' standing can claim
to have had some practical experience, and it is on this basis that
I speak.

Contrary to good academic practice I shall not attempt my own
definition of an "intellectual." Indeed, I have never heard a satisfactory definition of this loosely used term. One in my files asserts that he is "a person of spurious intellectual pretensions, lacking in common sense." A less hostile commentator describes him
as a man of high verbal aptitude who expresses many opinions in

Delivered before the Beta of New Jersey, Princeton University, March
28, 1957. Published by Princeton University Press, 1957.

writing, some of them favorable. A more sympathetic definition is that he is a "person who tends to tackle a problem by exercising his powers of reason on the basis of known and proven evidence." The saving word in this definition is "tends," for, as Alexis Carrel remarked many years ago, there is no such thing as a purely intellectual person. Moreover, if artists and writers, indeed if research scientists, are to be included among the intellectuals, it must be under a broader definition which pays due regard to creative imagination. Perhaps Percy Bridgman's is as good as any: "A person who likes to use his mind better than anything else he can do" is an intellectual.

In the writings of some self-confessed intellectuals, one encounters a wistful comparison between the role of the intellectual in Europe and in the United States, to the disadvantage of the latter. Among Europeans, they remind us, the intellectual enjoys a special prestige which sets him apart as a member of an elite. Americans, on the other hand, it is said, continue to resist the whole idea of an intellectual elite. Replicas of Rodin's "Thinker" may be found in front of our public libraries, but few people, it is charged, take them seriously. As I was putting these remarks on paper, I read a B.B.C. Third Program address by an American university professor who asserted that "the life of the mind has never had the place of authority in my country that it has in yours." The speaker was right in a way—but in a way that calls for explanation and definition of broad social values. I doubt whether he really wishes that we had in America the historic British social structure which established this authority, a structure in which a university education was a recognized class privilege and conferred a special social status, and still does to a degree unparalleled in the United States.

The concept of an "intellectual" as a person belonging to a special category, and therefore meriting a special sort of respect, is not native to America. It is an importation from abroad; and intellectuals have suffered in America and, to a lesser degree in

357

England, from the application of such foreign notions. In recent years, particularly, the glamour which Russian communism possessed for a few who boasted of their intellectuality worked injury to the position of men of learning in all English-speaking countries; more in America, it is true, than among the British. The behavior of the well-publicized World Congress of Intellectuals at Breslau in 1948, for example, was notable for a startling absence of that rational treatment of world affairs by which some American delegates had hoped to forge a new link in the ruptured chain of international understanding. Granville Hicks in his account of his conversion from communism back to American liberalism makes clear that the failure of the intellectuals who espoused the Russian ideology was not that they thought too much but too little, and under party orders renounced their duty to keep on thinking—but this was too fine a point for many of our people to grasp.

However, America's consistent refusal to recognize an "establishment" of intellectuals in the Continental mold roots in causes deeper than the much-advertised defection of a small few to Soviet Russia. Rather does it run to a national unwillingness to accept what John Fischer has caustically termed "a self-conscious privileged Mandarin Caste," a vivid figure of speech to describe a limited group which feels that its superior mental equipment establishes it as a class apart. Whatever arrogance of this sort may be found on the Continent, certainly it is not representative of academic scholarship in America, although American scholars are not immune to it.

Continental Europe, especially France, offers the classic example of a people who have traditionally supported an "establishment" of intellectuals. Some writers have made a great deal of diverse national characteristics as revealed by different popular attitudes towards men of thought in contrast to men of action. Madariaga years ago observed that English-speaking peoples reflect in order to act. "A Frenchman," he wrote, "sees in prospective action an excellent opportunity for setting problems before his mind." Kenneth Douglas summed up in one sentence his view of the situation in France: "Since the time of the Revolution, it has seemed natural to the French to turn to professors and literary men, not only for the expression but even for the enactment of their political ideals."

That the world has profited richly from French thought and French art and letters, no one will question for a moment. But deep preoccupation with theory divorced from practice, which characterized the intellectual elite in France, spread beyond the universities and diverted public attention from the crass but real need to build factories, modernize industry, and maintain economic, naval, and military strength. The proposition that I have heard in years past advanced by lecturers on this campus, that "the French think; the Americans act," with the clear implication that action is an inferior human function, earned prestige for France in artistic and bookish circles; but it was to the injury of the health of the body politic and the nation's power for decision. According to one eminent student and friend of France, one consequence, so far as French politics are concerned, has been a separation between the government, including Parliament, and the mass of the people.

It does not seem to me, as a political scientist, too far-fetched to relate in some degree the multiplication of splinter parties and inability to sustain a stable French government to a refusal by the governing groups to surrender intellectual pride in fine distinctions and shades of meaning, despite the need for action in times of grave emergencies.

Other nations, including Napoleon's despised shopkeepers, have fared better. To paraphrase Sir Harold Nicolson: It is neither ignorant nor foolish to argue that the stresses of history can better be endured and surmounted by a community possessing a large component of "ordinary common sense" in its government than by a community governed by self-conscious intellectuals. When Nicolson turns from politics and administration to "art, music, architecture and letters," he deplores, as we all may for America, that so many of his countrymen "should be indifferent to the things of the mind [and] should take a sort of pride in their indifference." Yet it may be interpolated here that the scholars in the arts and letters must accept their share of responsibility for this indifference. Moreover our people seem to be advancing culturally, despite their critics. One example does not support a generalization, but the number of paid admissions to classical concerts of symphony orchestras has come vastly to exceed the number of paid admissions to professional baseball games, which are supposed to represent the great national pastime.

Turning to the Germans, it seems to me that they have shown a greater respect for the intellectual than we have, but not so all-embracing as the French. The prestige which still attaches to the *Herr Doktor* knows no counterpart with us. In particular, the ranking of the university professor continues to be high. Yet I had an earlier impression confirmed by a visit to Germany last summer. It was that this prestige, which is guarded so carefully by the class-conscious professors themselves, and the protection which it affords against accountability to the public, have not been good for the professors, or for the universities, or for the nation. Time will not permit elaboration of the grounds for this impression, but I suggest that German universities are being hampered in their adjustment to a new and more democratic world situation by the inflexibility and class consciousness of the professors. I suggest that our American professors may be closer to the great truths because they are closer to the people than some of their Continental colleagues.

To return to our own country, America, as a United States senator once sharply reminded me at a committee hearing, does not favor an aristocracy of brains any more than an aristocracy of inherited wealth or noble blood. Although the senator himself was no candidate for an American aristocracy of brains, had there been one, he did speak for millions of voters. The man of thought rightfully claims parity of esteem with the man of action, and is properly resentful when it is denied him, as is all too common in the United States. But I wonder if he should not in part be blaming himself as well as our "Rotarian" bourgeois culture. America sadly requires the services of the man of thought; but if he takes an attitude of aloofness, our society will hold him aloof. He must go to society if society is to come to him. He can exert his full influence in the United States only if he is a conscious and willing member of the society about him.

More and more, for good or ill, the man who wishes to devote himself to the intellectual life in America associates himself with a college or university. If there is a true "establishment" of intellectuals in America, it relates largely to the organized academic profession of which the university is the corporate manifestation. Therefore it is not unreasonable today to assimilate the position of the intellectual in America to that of the professor as the professional custodian of thought and culture.

Even as late as the nineteenth century, Dr. Abraham Flexner has reminded us, many philosophers and scientists went their way with no formal connection with any institution of learning whatsoever. In Great Britain for example "a banker (who never attended a university) was the author of the greatest history of Greece up to his time," and "a gentleman of leisure made in *The Origin of Species* the most upsetting contribution to science and philosophy. Neither Ricardo nor J. S. Mill was a university professor."

Today all this has changed substantially. The base of operations of a modern Francis Bacon would probably be a university rather than a government office in London. When Einstein published his first statement of the theory of relativity he was employed in the patent office in Berne, but within four years he became a professor in a university.

361

In short, for good or ill, the advancement of learning in America is becoming more and more professionalized within a university frame of reference. The humanistic scholar, critic, or artist who subsists without a formal university connection nevertheless avails himself of university associations, a university research library and university fellowships, and gladly numbers professors among his friends. He may even welcome appointment to a visiting professorship now and then! Writers and artists who accept the title "creative" are beginning to find places on college and university faculties. Industrial laboratories find it profitable to settle in the neighborhood of a university, and both private and governmental research agencies are careful to cultivate friendly relations with academic people. There are losses as well as gains in this trend toward the professional channelization of the search for knowledge, and we may all hope that the day will never arrive when the guild of university scholarship will not be under challenging competition by the independents.

With all its foibles and shortcomings, the university, as it has developed since the Middle Ages, has become our chief institution for discovering and sharing truth. The centuries have proven how sharing stimulates discovery, and how discovery invigorates sharing. No alternate form of organization has appeared which provides such fertile soil for the pursuit of learning and which culminates in a fuller knowledge of the whole man.

A generation ago, Santayana complained that there existed in the United States "a separation between things intellectual, which remain wrapped . . . as it were under glass, and the rough business of life." Unhappily this separation still exists, although it can be exaggerated to the point that the man of thought is made to appear a very lonely figure indeed, despite the fact that many Americans do sustain an interest in the "things intellectual" with which scholars are concerned. Woodrow Wilson as a young man exposed the bent of his mind in an early essay addressed to the "perennial misunderstanding between the men who write and the men who act"; in other words, between those whose professional role is to be men of thought and those whose role is to translate knowledge into action. He was wiser than Santayana, for he went on to point out that the misunderstanding was not solely the fault of the men involved in "the rough business of life."

It is greatly to America's interest, as well as to the interest of the universities and the life of learning which they sustain, that Santayana's "separation" be narrowed, that Wilson's "perennial misunderstanding" be reduced. This can be accomplished only through improved communication between professional men of thought and professional men of action.

The first step is to appreciate that the man of scholarship and the man of action follow two distinct vocations. The function of one is to be tirelessly curious and critical in sifting old knowledge and in discovering and sharing new; the function of the other is to get the world's business done. Each pursuit demands its own special talents and operates under its own set of responsibilities. In a perfect world, each calling would fully understand and support the other. Unfortunately in this less-than-perfect world each tends to distrust the other, to the grave impairment of the contribution which each might otherwise be rendering.

The business or professional man who depreciates the role of the scholar "because he is a theorist who has never met a payroll" misconceives the nature of scholarship; for it is the duty of the scholar to be academic, to be an "armchair" scientist or philosopher or economist, to be concerned with the very subtleties and refinements of expression which to the practical man are apt to seem unsubstantial. By contrast, for the man of business no decision is "academic" or "armchair." Nor can he afford the luxury (for him) of long contemplation of delicate shades of meanings in which the scholar rightfully delights. His success relates to his talent for simplifying his problem, for concentrating on the few most fundamental elements, in order to come to a prompt decision that will stand up in practice. His success relates to his capacity for ready decision and willingness to accept the risks and responsibilities which decision entails. A fluent flow of logic and excellence in formal presentation of a case are valuable assets for a businessman, or a college president, but they will not compensate for a decision that experience does not sustain. The evidence which for the man of action adds up to wisdom is heavily empirical. Sensitive to the lessons of experience, the practical man tends to be conservative. According to Huxley's famous *mot*, he is on this account one who "repeats the errors of his forefathers."

On the other hand, the man of thought entrusts his career to new ideas—by a process which his profession knows as creative scholarship—long before they are tested by experience. There is a story to the effect that during the mastership of Sir J. J. Thompson at Trinity College, Cambridge, the fellows of the college were meeting to elect a new member. One fellow pressed the claims of one candidate by saying that "when he has written on a subject, the last word has been said." To which the Master replied, "That may well be, but perhaps we are looking for the young man who says the first word."

Whatever may be the practical applications of pure science and pure scholarship, and they are numerous these days, the fact remains that one essential function of a university is to sustain the search for more knowledge for its own sake. Consequently, it is a place which not only entertains dissension but actually encourages it. As Mr. Conant has remarked, it is from the quarrels of scholars that truth emerges.

The service of scholars is to pose questions and propositions which challenge experience and accepted practice. Because of the very nature of his work, the professional in the field of new ideas is bound to be a social irritant. New knowledge is apt to be painful, even on occasion to college professors themselves, for most of us lose early in life childhood's avid, if annoying, zeal for asking questions. New truth does not bring repose, said Emerson. Therefore it is not strange that American popular opinion should find it difficult to grasp the essential idea of a university.

One service of the scholar that a "free enterprise" businessman often fails to grasp is that, in a world of what he terms creeping authoritarianism, the scholar supplies nature's prime example of the individualist. The scholar resists authoritarianism even when dignified as "team play." Although much modern research calls for group action, the university investigator demands broad room for individuality in himself and his associates. Thus the profession of scholarship renders a collateral social service by sustaining a vigorous concept of individual dignity and human freedom in an age of expanding governmental and other social restraints over individual behavior and enterprise. America cannot afford to undervalue the island of independence which academic freedom maintains for our society in general.

It is the scholar's insistence on the preservation of his integrity as a free individual that has led some honest conservatives in recent years to suspect him as a subversive agent busily engaged in undermining the foundations of freedom. If he has heard of Crane Brinton's thesis that the four great revolutions of history were preceded by the desertion of the intellectuals from the social order of the time, our conservative friend may worry as to whether the man of learning has deserted the contemporary social order. As Brinton remarks, the intellectual customarily takes a critical attitude toward the daily routine of human affairs; he is therefore exposed to the charge of rocking the boat when he should be pulling an oar. "An intellectual," he adds, who was "as satisfied with the world as with himself would not be an intellectual," and this can be quite irritating to people who are satisfied with the world the way it is. Yet Brinton concludes, and I most heartily agree, that he has not deserted. At bottom American intellectuals for whom university professors speak "share the faith of their fellows" in our free way. "They are not really alienated," he concludes, "from bankers, businessmen and politicians, in the way the intellectuals of the revolutionary times were alienated from kings, tsars, nobles, gentry and prelates." In other words, while the American man of thought may occasionally sigh for a place of honor such as his Continental counterpart enjoys, at least he has tended on the whole to remain one of the people. To a degree greater than may appear from superficial observation, he has succeeded in maintaining contact with his society. May it always be so.

That the general public does not comprehend adequately the historic function of scholarship is not entirely the fault of the public. On its part the profession of academic scholarship *as a profession* has paid too little attention to its lines of communication with the public, to its duty to share with society as well as discover. How shall society be able to digest the discoveries of science, for example, which are now so promptly seized and developed by technology, if scholars in the humanities and the social studies elect to remain aloof from the layman's world of affairs and fail to communicate with it? For quite obvious reasons, the work of interpretation of scholarly production should not be left to popularizers alone, however scrupulous they may be in their reporting to the public, or however carefully they may guard against misleading headlines.

It is true that many of the most creative scholars do not seem to be able to communicate with others than members of their guild, nor is it necessary that all should possess such capacity or seek to cultivate it. Nevertheless the guild should cherish qualified members who can interpret recondite matters to the public. I do not suggest for a moment that scholars should deal only in terms and concepts readily intelligible to laymen, although I should urge them to be on their guard against the temptation to develop technical jargon purely for the sake of verbalizing. Least of all do I suggest that ideas should be diluted or softened because they are hard to express except in the vocabulary of scholarship. While I believe that in fields related to human conduct and values care should be exercised to see that the data should include the conditions of action, I should not call from his cubicle the scholar who belongs there, nor seek to divert anyone from his pursuit of "abstract thought." Indeed a proper university is under a solemn duty to do just the opposite —to promote, not merely tolerate, pure science, pure scholarship, in season and out, against the pressures of the short-sighted, the practical. The university is society's guardian institution of philosophy in its broadest and deepest sense.

Although a professor is a citizen with the right to participate as a citizen and qualified often to make substantial contributions to the world of action, his calling imposes no imperative on him to rush out and be a man of action. It is important to remember that the scholar's first *vocational* obligation is to be an intellectual, and it is the business of the university to support and protect him in the practice of his vocation. Scholarship's chief participation in events is exercised through the communication of ideas to the minds of men. Strengthened by the knowledge that ideas constitute power and that the men who wield them are our ultimate rulers, the scholar need not yield an inch on his right to be heard. Our civilization is moving too rapidly from one radical technological change to another to permit us to spurn, or even to neglect through sheer inattention, the vast intellectual resources of our universities.

Whatever may be the future of the intellectual in America, it will be closely tied to the fate of our universities. There are critical days ahead, days which carry a direct threat to scholarship in the area of the liberal arts, including, to a somewhat less degree than in the case of the humanities, pure science. The anticipated doubling of student enrollments within the next fifteen years will create heavy strains all along the line. The American people have a strong sense of ownership in their colleges and universities, both state and private, and are quite ready to substitute their discretion as to aims and operation for that of university faculties. Sometimes in moments of discouragement I have envied the protected social position of the universities of free Europe, which renders them more remote than we are from popular pressures. For example, despite vastly increased government support, Parliamentary inquiries, investigations by Royal Commissions, and multiplication of state scholarships, the average English businessman is far more inclined to trust the universities to look after themselves than is his counterpart in America. Nevertheless, I always return to the realization that it is fortunate for our society that our colleges and universities are of the people, not merely for the people.

But in the near future unless strong counteracting measures of popular education are instituted, standards of instruction and opportunities for scholarship will suffer severely under the popular compulsion to accommodate three million more students. The necessary counteracting measures will be unpopular among large segments of the voters. But by the application of intelligence and imagination I am sure that ways can be found to meet the crisis without deterioration of standards, and that in fact the crisis itself will offer a challenge and an opportunity for American intellectuals to assert and establish even more firmly their place, not as a class apart, but as vitally contributing participants in our national life.

PAUL B. SEARS

The Steady State: Physical
Law and Moral Choice

THE dream of universal harmony is an ancient one. Often it has taken the nostalgic form of a Golden Age, long past. Again it appears as future promise. The dreamer who looks ahead often sees it all very simply. Let him and all who think alike with him have their way. Never has this been better set forth than by Dr. Rabelais.

"Then, ah then!" continued Homenas, ". . . then plenty of all earthly goods here below. Then uninterrupted and eternal peace through the universe, an end of all wars, plunderings, drudgeries, robbings, assassinates, unless it be to destroy these cursed rebels, the heretics."

In an earlier chapter Rabelais had given us a glimpse of a far nobler harmony—that of the Abbey of Thélème. Peopled by the generous and enlightened who could trust each other and tolerate differences, its motto was *Do What Thou Wilt*. But in the Prophetic Riddle just following he pictures a world disordered, too much like the present for comfort. It is here that one may

Delivered before the Triennial Council of the United Chapters of Phi Beta Kappa, August, 1958. Published in *The Key Reporter*, January, 1959.

see, if so minded, a brief, graphic, uncannily prescient forecast of the revolution that was to come less than three centuries later.

There are today four times as many human beings in the world as when those words were written. Old and stable social orders have broken up. New powers, through new knowledge, are at man's disposal. He has, in truth, become a geological force. The dream of ultimate harmony still persists, but the old cleavage remains. There are those who think the blessed state must come by eliminating all who do not think as they do. There are others who hope for a condition of mutual tolerance and restraint, founded upon some measure of common understanding.

These are moral problems, using that term in its broad and classic sense. But morality today involves a responsible relationship toward the laws of the natural world of which we are inescapably a part. Violence toward nature, as the Tao has it, is no less an evil than violence toward fellow-man. There can be no ultimate harmony among our own species in defiance of this principle. But more than that, we can find in certain concepts of natural science an invaluable guide as we struggle to attain a better order in our own affairs.

A disturbing paradox of this scientific age is the fact that its most profound implications have not sunk into our minds and become manifest in our behavior. Commonly—too commonly— we hear such glib phrases as "man's control of nature," "the necessity of an expanding economy," and "the conquest of space." As Ortega y Gasset has said, the effect of the industrial revolution has been to create an illusion of limitless abundance and ease, obscuring the ancient doctrine that effort and struggle are the price of human survival.

Thus in one sweep are brushed away the lessons of history, the wisdom so painfully gained through disciplined thought and intuition in the fields of ethics and aesthetics, as well as those aspects of natural science that could afford us perspective, rather than immediate convenience. A subtle and dangerous symptom of this last is the recurring objection to physical and biological analysis of man's estate.

Whatever else he may be, a human being is a physical object and a living organism. He is by no means an inert particle, nor is he exempt from physiological limitations. Enough of us have been caught, afoot or on wheels, in traffic jams, have been hungry and thirsty, and are sufficiently familiar with birth and death to appreciate these facts. To mention them is not to say that human beings are mere particles or mere animals. Yet certainly one must be free to weigh any consequences that may result from a particular quality or property of mankind, without being condemned for applying physical or biological analogy to the demigod, man.

There is precisely here a most delicate and important job of identification and discrimination. Could we clarify it, it might help lower the costly barriers that hamper free intercourse between scholars in the humanities and those in science—indeed, among scientists themselves.

An initial difficulty comes from confusing analogy with proof. Yet no matter how much the role of analogy may be abused, its importance as an aid to scientific investigation is very great indeed. Wisely selected parallels, or analogies, are the source of models that science can then test. A new situation, structure, or process suggests a familiar one, and we go on from there. The brown discoloration of a peeled apple suggests oxidation, and so it proves to be.

We can also isolate certain qualities in a system and study them profitably on their own merits. A notable instance is afforded with respect to mere increase in human numbers within a finite space. Obviously we cannot apply the laws that govern the dynamics of gas molecules strictly unless we are all playing blindman's buff with motion at random. This we are not doing, for eyesight and judgment enable human beings to pick open pathways, which molecules cannot do. Yet the general principle that freedom tends to diminish (or stress to increase) as numbers multiply applies not only in theory but in historical fact.

The application may be pressed still further. When energy is introduced into a system, the stress increases. This obviously applies to the molecules in a kettle of heated water. I am unable to see why it does not apply with equal rigor to modern man, who, through the internal combustion engine, is drawing upon the fossil energy of oil deposits, now being consumed at an estimated rate one million times faster than they have accumulated. By virtue of this process the average American moves, I should judge, some ten times faster than he did in 1900, and if so, covers one hundred times more territory. The evidence of stress as a function of numbers and energy is manifold. Yet we have reassuring voices telling us not to be disturbed, because the earth can support an indefinitely increased population.

Perhaps, with so much at stake, it is time to make certain we understand what science is, and what is its role in human affairs.

Science is the discovery and formulation of the laws of nature. In our enthusiasm we may forget that a law not only tells you what you can do, but what you cannot do. When we use our knowledge of natural law for specific problems we are practicing technology, not science. And because scientific technology has placed an estimated minimum equivalent of three dozen servants at the disposal of the average American, we are, quite naturally, more inclined to listen to promises than to warnings.

Yet the necessary warning can be stated quite simply. *The applications of science must be guided, managed, controlled, according to ethical and aesthetic principles and in the light of our most profound understanding.* Unfortunately we cannot set up an equation to show that because a thing is possible, it is necessarily wise and proper. If we could, it might simplify matters.

Certainly the application of science has been selective. An astute student of cultural processes, examining the Western world, would note that science has been applied in spectacular fashion to the elaboration of consumers' goods, the reduction of mortality rates, and the tapping of fossil energy. He would also note certain consequences of this situation. Among them would be an explosion of human population without known precedent in the biological world, a lessening of the need for muscular effort, increased leisure, a startling multiplication of the rate of individual movement, dissipation of non-renewable resources, and disruption of natural cycles in the landscape. Nor would he be likely to overlook the signs of increasing tension upon the individual and the disintegration of value systems, which, whatever their limitations, have always exerted a stabilizing effect on human societies.

Our observer would find the question of man's relation to environment relegated to the fringes of serious scientific inquiry. He would uncover a widespread belief in the possibility of and necessity for a perpetually expanding economy. He would find economists well pleased if they could look ahead twenty-five years while a few scientists try honestly to peer much farther into the future. He would see that a great deal of effort is being given by the latter group to estimating the maximum number of human beings that could possibly be kept alive on earth, such estimates ranging from three to ten times the present population. Concerning the quality of existence possible under such conditions he would discover a strange silence broken only by such bold prophets as Orwell, Huxley, and Sir Charles Darwin, the physicist.

Persisting, he would recognize other interesting conditions. Although the devising of means of human destruction continues uninhibited, frontal attack on the control of population pressure —difficult enough for technical reasons—is largely taboo. So are suggestions that human happiness might well be possible under a far less wasteful and consumptive economy. And while analysts

373

are beginning to demonstrate that, beyond a certain limit, the expansion of any urban center means economic loss, not gain, their warnings carry little weight.

Modern society seems incalculably rich in means, impoverished in ends. The dazzling success of science in placing facilities at our disposal has left us all, including the scientist, a bit confused. Yet wisely enough the editor of a recent collection of studies on population points out that while the scientist possesses no special magic or superior methods for reaching policy decisions, he can offer sound knowledge, highly relevant to the making of value judgments.

There appears to be some consensus on one point: that an improved level of living for mankind is desirable. Such a blanket statement covers a multitude of possibilities, of course, although it clearly implies adequate nutrition, a better distribution of benefits, and relief from unnecessary hardship and suffering. But on the means of attaining this objective, we find ourselves in a bipolar atmosphere of world politics. One doctrine holds the individual generally competent to take part in decisions and provides elaborate safeguards to ensure him this privilege. The other sets up a monolithic structure in which the individual is submerged, ostensibly for his own good.

It would clarify, if not resolve, matters if we were to admit frankly that our Cold War is the third great religious conflict of the Western world. The two previous ones were abated, not simply by military means, but more basically by concession to the idea of survival through dynamic equilibrium. Hope today lies in arriving at some similar agreement in principle, powerful enough to carry conviction, broad enough to tolerate the inevitable diversity that should enrich rather that impoverish human culture.

This brings us inescapably to a well-worn topic—the need for a better entente between the sciences and the humanities. Granting freely that science has frightfully disturbed the orderly world of the humanist, the latter has not, in my judgment, risen to the full opportunities that are his.

One cannot generalize about either humanists or scientists with any assurance, good manners aside. But this restriction does not apply so strictly to the fields they represent. A safe proposition is that neither of these vital activities should be carried on in isolation from the other.

Complicating the situation is the prevailing conviction that science holds the key to man's future. Julian Huxley has described this mood as "the airy assumption that 'science' will surely find a way out," a mood intensified by recent developments in the exploration of outer space. Yet it is clear enough that the fundamental problems of mankind are no longer technological, if they ever were, but rather cultural.

The need, in this neotechnical world, for the best that the humanities can offer is well-nigh desperate. It is the business of science to minimize the areas of uncertainty in human affairs. They remain large enough when this is accomplished. At this point we must begin to draw on the accumulated experience and wisdom of mankind to formulate, refine, and dramatize the ethical and aesthetic values that will guide us.

Values are the business of the humanities, and values clearly determine the direction of human effort. With incalculable powers at the disposal of mankind, the need for responsible control is correspondingly great. People shape their values in accordance with their notions of the kind of universe they believe themselves to be living in. The basic function of science is to illuminate our understanding of that universe—what it may contribute to human ease and convenience is strictly secondary.

Personally I am far less interested in guessing how thickly mankind can be amassed on this planet and still survive than I am in the optimum quality of existence for those who do. It is on this issue that the humanist must not desert us. We need his tempered judgment, his knowledge of great human achievement,

375

his sensitive awareness of the creative human spirit to help us understand what, indeed, constitutes the good life. Doubtless this is an issue that can never be completely settled, but with each step that clarifies it, we shall have more guidance in our quest for a worthy goal.

Yet this goal must be sought with a realistic understanding of the natural world of which we are a part. We must know its possibilities and respect its limitations. We must scan it for hints and models, remembering that the organized system of life and environment has been operating more than a thousand times as long as the experience of our own species. Our knowledge of the vicissitudes of geological and climatic change, of organic competition, conflict, even extinction, should not blind us to the essential order behind it all. In our consumptive age we hear much talk of the danger of depleting our environment. A far more profound threat lies in our power to disrupt its orderly transformations of material and energy.

The confidence with which the physical scientist faces his task rests essentially upon a few basic assumptions with respect to the orderly behavior of energy and matter. One of the important concepts corollary to these principles is that of the steady state. Systems tend toward conditions of minimum stress and least unbalance—that is, toward equilibrium. Energy flowing into a system operates to upset this trend, unless the system is so organized as to transform that energy in orderly fashion, using it meanwhile to keep the system in good working condition. Such a system, that is, an open steady state, is approximated in living communities. Green plants utilize solar energy to build carbon compounds that sustain themselves and animals as well, while complementary processes return materials for fresh re-use.

The heat from a stove—energy—will keep the pot boiling so long as there is water in it. But it will not replace the water when it is gone, nor mend the pot when it melts. By contrast, an organized pattern of living communities is self-maintaining if energy is available.

These circumstances have long since caught the imagination of men. Harrison Brown and other analysts point out that if man continues to increase in numbers and per capita requirements his fate will depend on his success in tapping additional energy sources rather than on lack of materials. For example, the mineral content of a ton of granite or a cubic mile of sea water is most reassuring. The hitch comes in the energy cost of reclamation, yet the literature abounds in optimistic assurances that man is clever enough to turn the trick. Now and then, but not always, we see the added proviso that he must first learn how to behave himself better than he does. On a less responsible plane we continue to hear talk of an expanding economy, the conquest of nature, and man's unlimited future.

Poking about such an imposing edifice of technological statesmanship is creepy business, not unlike that of being near neighbor to a high-tension wire or an unguarded atomic pile. Yet certain naive probings seem unavoidable. Why not, for example, divert more of our scientific enterprise to studying the model that is before us, that has operated for more than a billion years, and has made our own existence possible?

Again, why continue, not only to tolerate, but to sponsor reckless and irresponsible multiplication of human numbers? Why accede to the notion that in a world where millions are hungry and malnourished through failure to apply the knowledge we now have, industrial enterprise must concentrate so largely on the mass production of what a philosopher would consider toys for adults?

Why worry so much about the other side of the moon when our cities, bursting at the seams, are erupting into an unplanned chaos? Why dream of escape to other planets when our own would respond generously to kinder treatment? Right and proper

377

it is to push knowledge to the uttermost limits, but why not use what we have to clean the open sewers we call rivers, purify the air we must breathe, slow down the tragic waste of human ability, and get things about us shipshape? We are sweeping too much stuff under the bed, locking up too many closets.

Probably men will always differ as to what constitutes the good life. They need not differ as to what is necessary for the long survival of man on earth. Assuming that this is our wish, the conditions are clear enough. As living beings we must come to terms with the environment about us, learning to get along with the liberal budget at our disposal, promoting rather than disrupting those great cycles of nature—of water movement, energy flow, and material transformation that have made life itself possible. As a physical goal we must seek to attain what I have called a steady state. The achievement of an efficient dynamic equilibrium between man and his environment must always, in itself, have the challenge and the charm of an elusive goal. The infinite variety and beauty of the world about us, the incalculable facets of human experience, the challenge of the unknown that must grow rather than diminish as man advances in stature and becomes at home here—these are sufficient guarantee that a stable world society need never be a stagnant one.

HENRY A. MURRAY

Beyond Yesterday's Idealisms

MR. PRESIDENT, Ladies, and Gentlemen: The list of orators
since the first performance of this rite in 1782, the blaze of famous names, was blinding to one who as an undergraduate was
never on the Dean's list but often in his office, blinding to one
who has been fumbling in the dark for many years, in the under-
ground of mind, well below the level of luminous rationality
sustained by members of this elite society. From the parade of
annual orations one receives imposing views of the diversity of
elevated thinking in America, challenging yet humbling, I would
guess, to pretty nearly anyone your President might pick to add
another theme to this medley of reflections.

Happily for a man in this predicament there are transfusions
of courage to be had from a host of predecessors, especially, as
you well know, from those wondrous emanations in 1837 of the
Platonic Over-Soul of Ralph Waldo Emerson. To this apostle
of self-confidence I attribute whatever stamina is required to
speak freely to you today, some 120 years beyond his yesterday.
Here my cue comes from Emerson himself, who reminded his
enthralled audience that each age "must write its own books."
"The books of an older age will not fit this."

Delivered before the Alpha of Massachusetts, Harvard University,
June, 1959.

379

Emerson's preoccupation was Man Thinking, or, to be more accurate, Mr. Emerson Thinking, serene and saintly, solitary and aloof, residing in his own aura without envy, lust, or anger, unspotted by the world and impervious to its horrors. My preoccupation will be a little different, a difference that makes all the difference: men and women thinking, privately and publicly, in the teeth of an infernal, lethal threat that will be here as long as our inhuman human race is here.

In the realm of thought, Sigmund Freud—who, on the question of innate, potential evil, concurred with St. Augustine—Freud marks the great divide which separates us irrevocably from the benign atmosphere of the untempted, unhurt, and unmolested sage of Concord. Also separating us from that tall, angular, gentle, blue-eyed mystic, who saw evil at such a distance that he could dismiss it and condone it, and who, in so doing, as his admirer Santayana pointed out, "surrendered the category of the better and the worse, the deepest foundation of life and reason"— separating us incurably from that justly venerated poet-thinker are the blights and blasts of more than forty lurid years of enormities and abominations perpetrated by our fellow men on the sensitive bodies and souls of other men. Before the occurrence of this global epidemic of lies, treacheries, and atrocities, most of us Americans were temperamentally with Emerson, strongly inclined to optimism, and so to shun or to deny the fact that human creatures were still capable of surpassing all other species as callous and ferocious torturers and killers of their own kind. But now that we have seen all this, the darker vision of the once-rejected Herman Melville resonates with more veracity in some of us.

Would that I could offer, out of my well of joy, a nicer prospect, more appropriate to this festive week! But were I, with bland, buoyant, or urbane ideas to indulge both you and me, I would deserve the label that Melville, on second thought, attached to Emerson—Confidence Man.

You see there is still danger that out of shallowness and the desire to be pleasant at all costs—two of our besetting sins—we may rid consciousness of the unflattering knowledge we have gained and, by so doing, cancel the possibility of ever reaching the conclusion that the present degree and aim of certain of our dispositions and certain states and aims of our various societies are definitely out of date, unsuitable for survival. It looks to me as if we must transform or fall apart.

The inevitable decision is that the eminent Yankee seer was right: the books of *his* age, his *own* books—imperishable as they surely are—are not in all respects fitting to *this* age. The present age and your coming age must write its own books.

I suppose that most of you, just-honored intellectuals, will necessarily be occupied for the next years in thinking in a differentiated way, thinking as specialists—as lawyers, businessmen, doctors, scientists, historians, educators. There is vigor and ample creativity involved in all of these professions. But later, if not sooner, you will be pressured from within or from without to think seriously once more about yourself and your relations with women and with men, to think personally and then impersonally, to ask yourself embarrassing questions—knowledge for what? freedom for what? existence for what?—to think, in other words, as a free-lance philosopher, or generalist, about matters of profound and superordinate concern: ways and ends of being and becoming, morals, religion, the human situation, the world's plight. At such times each of you will be, in Emerson's sense, Man Thinking, and your reflections may beget a book or brace of books fitting to your age. Your capacity to write a book—logical, critical, and substantial—has been accredited by the conferring of the Key, symbolic of the fact that learning and transforming what you learn may be the happiest of activities and may, with luck on your side, lead to the solution of crucial problems, turn the lock and open the door to new knowledge.

Today the really crucial problems, as I hook them, are all deep, deep in human nature, and in this country with our long preference for appearances, for tangible, material realities, for perceptible facts, acts, and technics, for the processes and conclusions of conscious rationality, and for quick attainments of demonstrable results—with this native and acquired bent for things that one can plainly see, grasp, count, weigh, manipulate, and photograph, the probability of our solving or even seriously grappling with the strategic problems of our time does not appear to be encouragingly high.

Only if this appraisal is somewhere near the truth can I discern a single reason for your President's election of a depth psychologist as orator for this day. What could his reason be except to have the depth dimension stressed, with the accompanying hint that the key to the more perplexing problems might be lying in the dark. Pertinent to this issue is the old story of the London bobby who, in the blackness of one night, came upon a man half-seas-over stumbling in a circle within the lighted zone around a lamppost. "I am looking for my key," the man explained. "Are you sure you dropped it by this light?" the bobby asked. "No," the man replied, "I dropped it out there in the dark, but I can't see out there and I can see here."

What Freud discovered in the dark of the unconscious was what Puritan and Victorian morality suppressed as Sin, spelt with a capital. But now those floodgates are demolished and sexuality is conspicuously in the open, running loose among the young without benefit of form, grace, or dignity; and what is nowadays repressed, if my reading of the signs is not awry, are all the hopes, yearnings, claims, both dependent and aspiring, which down the centuries were comforted and directed by the mythologies and rituals of religion. Here I leave Freud and stand with Dr. Jung.

That a bent for the ideal is latent in the psyches of men and women of your age is not what I've been told by any confiding undergraduate, and it is about the last conclusion that a reader of modern literature would be likely to arrive at. For certainly most of the best poets, playwrights, and novelists, together with many psychoanalysts, behavioral psychologists, social philosophers, existentialists, and some angry others, seem to be conspiring, with peculiar unanimity, to reduce or decompose, to humiliate so far as they can do it, man's image of himself. In one way or another the impression is conveyed that, in the realm of spirit, all of us are baffled beats, beatniks, or deadbeats, unable to cope as persons with the existential situation.

But tell me, what is the underlying meaning of this flood of discontent and self-depreciation? One pertinent answer comes from Emerson himself. "We grant that human life is mean, but how did we find out that it was mean? What is the ground of this uneasiness of ours, of this old discontent? What is the universal sense of want and ignorance but the *fine innuendo by which the soul makes its enormous claim.*" Yes, surely, "its enormous claim," and in the very midst of this American Paradise of material prosperity. The enormous claim of the sensitive, alienated portions of our society—artists, would-be artists, and their followers—comes, as I catch the innuendoes, from want of a kindling and heartening mythology to feel, think, live, and write by. Our eyes and ears are incessantly bombarded by a mythology which breeds greed, envy, pride, lust, and violence, the mythology of our mass media, the mythology of advertising, Hollywood, and Madison Avenue. But a mythology that is sufficient to the claim of head and heart is as absent from the American scene as symbolism is absent from the new, straight-edged, barefaced, glass buildings of New York.

An emotional deficiency disease, a paralysis of the creative imagination, an addiction to superficials—this is the physician's diagnosis I would offer to account for the greater part of the widespread desperation of our time, the enormous claim of people who are living with half a heart and half a lung. Paralysis of the imagination, I suspect, would also account, in part, for the fact that the great majority of us, wedded to comfort so long as we both shall live, are turning our eyes away from the one thing we should be looking at—the possibility or probability of co-extermination.

In his famous speech of acceptance upon the award of the Nobel prize for literature, Albert Camus declared as follows: "Probably every generation sees itself as charged with remaking the world. Mine, however, knows that it will not remake the world. But its task is perhaps even greater, for it consists in keeping the world from destroying itself."

Were this statement to be made before an auditory of our faculty and students—even by Camus himself, speaking with utter candor out of his embattled deeps of agony—I fear it would be met by a respectful, serious, yet stony silence, an *apparent* silence, for, coming from behind the noncommittal, uncommitted faces, all would be aware of the almost palpable, familiar throb of Harvard's splendid engines of sophisticated demolition.

We are as sick of being warned of our proximity to hell as were the members of Jonathan Edwards' congregation. Wolf! Wolf! How, in heaven's name, does Camus imagine that a league of artists and philosophers could possibly prevent the destruction of the world? The nearest that he comes to telling us is when he states that his "generation knows that, in a sort of mad race against time, it ought to re-establish among nations a peace not based on slavery, to reconcile labor and culture again, and to reconstruct with all men an Ark of the Covenant." These words—"re-establish," "reconcile," "reconstruct,"—suggest that in his mind the prevention of destruction does, in fact, call for a remaking of the world, the building of a new Ark of the Covenant as basis for reunion.

Here, reason might lead us to infer that Camus was thinking of the institution of world government, which as scores of enlightened men, from Woodrow Wilson to Bertrand Russell, have insisted is the only rational answer to global, social chaos, a central government being the sole means that man has ever found of securing and maintaining order. But framing a constitution for world government, as the competent Mr. Grenville Clark has done, is not in line with the special genius of Camus, and, furthermore, it is apparent that the concept of world government, though absolutely necessary, is gaining little popular or federal support. Sanity is overmatched: deep, blind, primitive compulsions which bypass consciousness are towing us with a cable we have no knife to cut and driving us nearer and nearer to the verge of death.

At such a time, when hidden passions are deciding things, a legal scheme, no matter how commonsensical and logical, is not a magnet to large numbers of men and women: it chills them, leaves them frigid, uninvolved. Nor, at such a time, could something like Plato's plan for a republic guided by philosophers arouse enthusiasm. But when Plato, envious of Homer's enormous influence in Greece, banished poets and myth makers from his Republic, he deprived it of the springs of charismatic power, and so, when it came to a showdown with the masses, his beautifully reasoned books were ploughed under by the passionate myths and images of the poet-authors of the Bible. The Bible proved to be *the* fitting book not only for that century but for many centuries to come. It seems highly significant to me that Camus, a firm opponent of the theism of Judaeo-Christianity, should have reached into the fathomless well of the Old Testament to gain a potent image for his hope—Ark of the Covenant. It is there, among those images, that one can find the molds that shaped the deepest passions of the Western World, including Russia.

At this juncture I shall seize, with your permission, the remaining minutes of this proffered opportunity, with its cherished privilege of free speech, to submit a micro sketch of a hypothetical book that I would write if I had been vouchsafed the necessary genius and resources. This hypothetical book would also be a sketch, though a far larger and more detailed sketch, of a book to be composed by other authors, a superpersonal book, a book of books, that might be termed a "testament," a "world testament."

Before submitting this micro sketch of a macro sketch of a book for a new age, I should warn you that this imagined testament will carry us beyond the mythology of dependent and compliant childhood, the same as that of the dependent childhood of our society in colonial days, that is, the authoritarian father-son mythology of the religion we inherited, and also beyond the mythology of adolescence, the same as that of the adolescence of our nation, the mythology of protest, rebellion, independence, rugged individualism. Both of these mythologies are still operative. In fact, the mythology of adolescence, stressing freedom without qualifications or conditions, constitutes our national religion. Please understand and hold in mind that in looking forward to a future that has moved beyond these idealisms of today and yesterday, I am not forsaking them. There is a helpless, suffering child and a frustrated, rebellious adolescent in every one of us, and always will be. I would say, there is a time and place for authority and the founding of character, and there is a time and place for liberation from authority and the development and expression of a self-reliant personality. But, as I see the human situation, we are in need of a mythology of adulthood, something that is conspicuous for its absence in Western literature, a mythology of interdependence and creation, not only on the level of imaginative love, marriage, and the forming of a family, but on other levels, especially that of imaginative international reciprocities. Have we not pretty nearly reached the age when we can well afford to go beyond the glorification of vanity, pride, and egotism, individual and national?

Well, now, to return to my sketch of a sketch. The essential features of the testament that now occupies my mind would be roughly these: it would be the product of the interdependent judgments and imaginations of numerous composers, drawn from different cultures and from different callings. The initial task of these presumably creative and judicious thinkers would be to select from the vast libraries of the world, arrange, and edit whatever past and present writings in poetry or prose were suitable to the appointed purpose. Except for more abundant stores from which to draw their substance, a larger scope and longer span of time, these testament makers would proceed, we may suppose, as did the compilers and editors of the canonical and noncanonical books of the Bible. They would certainly be advantaged by the example of those forerunners. Like the Old Testament, this new one would contain numerous variations of subject matter and of style: narratives, historical and biographical, stories, parables, legends, and myths, songs and poems, psalms of praise, codes and ordinances, premonitions and philosophical reflections.

Most difficult for the testament makers would be the task of loosely integrating, as in the Bible, the selected parts in terms of a philosophy of social evolution—cycles of creation, conservation, decay, or induration—tending, in the long run, toward the fulfillment of that dream of human fellowship which centuries of deep and loving people have recommended to our hearts.

This testament would differ radically from the Bible inasmuch as its mythology would be consonant with contemporary science: its personifications would all refer to forces and functions *within* nature, human nature.

Also, it would differ radically from previous testaments of the Near East and West—the Bible, the Koran, and the Testament of Karl Marx—by describing and praising, with evenhanded justice, forms of excellence achieved by each and every culture. There would be no bowing to special claims, made by any single

387

collectivity, of unique superiority, of divine election, of infallible truth, of salvation for its members and damnation for all others. There would be no ovation for the apocalyptic myth, either in its ancient form—Persian or Judaeo-Christian—or in its modern communistic form; the myth of the inevitable and final Great Encounter between the all-good and the all-evil, resulting in an eternity of bliss for chosen saints or comrades and death or everlasting torments for the enemy. There would be no acceptance of the necessity of inquisitions, persecutions, brainwashings, or concentration camps.

In a sense, the world testament would be a parable, a parable of parables, expressive of the universal need for peace, for interdependence, for fruitful reciprocations among those manifold units of mankind which are still proud and quarrelsome, still locked in clenched antagonisms. Its symbolisms would commemorate on all levels the settlement of hostilities between opposites, their synthesis, or creative union: man and nature, male and female, reason and passion, understanding and imagination, enjoyable means and enjoyable ends, science and art, management and labor, West and East. Its ultimate, ethical ideal would be the resolution of differences through mutual embracement and subsequent transformation. In the words of Henry James, senior: "It is no doubt very tolerable finite or creaturely love to love one's own in another, to love another for his conformity to one's self: but nothing can be in more flagrant contrast with the creative Love, all whose tenderness *ex vi termini* must be reserved only for what intrinsically is most bitterly hostile and negative to itself." In the judgment of America's most profound philosopher, Charles S. Peirce, this sublime sentence "discloses for the problem of evil its everlasting solution."

Finally, in contrast to the unrelieved sociological language of the outmoded testament of Marx, this world testament, heir to the secret of the Bible's everlasting magic, would consist in its best parts of moving and revealing poetic passages. Some devout Christians overlook the fact that the stirring and sustaining influence of the Book they dream and live by depends on the marvelous words, the vivid imagery and figures of speech with which its wisdom is transmitted. This is one of the chief qualities by which a religion can be distinguished from a moral philosophy or system of ethics. If the New Testament, for example, had been written by a modern social scientist in the jargon of his profession it would have died at birth, and Mithraism, or Manichaeanism, or Mohammedanism would have taken possession of the European mind. A religion is propagated by the alchemy of the aesthetic imagination, in striking parables and metaphors that solace, cheer, or channel our profoundest feelings. A code of morals, on the other hand, can appeal only to our intellects and to a few of our more shallow sentiments.

If, perchance, a world testament with the mythic qualities I have mentioned became an invitation to the feelings and thoughts of men and women, it would gain this influence only through its power to enchant, charm, clarify, edify, and nourish. There would be no agents of sovereign authority with threatened penalties to enforce compliance, and, in contrast to the testaments of our established Churches, it would be always susceptible to revisions, additions, and subtractions.

Everybody, I assume—especially on reaching the accepted age for the retirement of his brain—is entitled to a dream, and this is mine, heretical at certain points, but not so visionary as it sounds. Works of the magnitude of this imagined testament have been composed in the past, notably in India. Much of what is needed has been in printed form for years. Ample energy and genius is available—literary critics, historians, social scientists, philosophers, and poets—in different quarters of the globe. Enough money for the effort is in the keep of men who are aware of humanity's dire strait. A provisional first edition of the testament would not be very long in coming. Translated into all languages it might turn out to be the book this age is waiting for.

A war that no one wants, an utterly disgraceful end to man's long experiment on earth, is a possibility we are facing every day. Events are hanging by a thread, depending on an accident, on some finger on a trigger, on a game of wits and tricks, of pride and saving faces. But ours is no momentary problem to be solved by this or that practical expedient. Does a mature nation sacrifice the future for the present? The day will come when small countries will possess enough lethal energy to eliminate a large country. Does a mature nation have the arrogance to believe that it can buy with dollars the permanent good will and loyalty of other peoples? Has our government a long time-perspective, a philosophy of history, a world view to guide its day-by-day and year-by-year decisions? If yes, only a few of us have heard of it.

It is such considerations that have pressured the generation of a vision of something which intellectuals like you and other members of the Phi Beta Kappa Society might have a hand in shaping. Why not? Many times in the past the direction of events has been affected by the publication of a single book. At the very least, the composition of this testament would constitute a brave, farseeing try—no vulgar try—to kindle a little veritable light in a black world.

The one conversion requisite for those who would lose themselves in this demanding enterprise was long ago described in two famous, pithy sentences by a stubborn American patriot, contemporary with Emerson. No doubt many of you have had occasion to saunter down the elm-shaded path in the middle of Commonwealth Avenue and, arriving at the statue of William Lloyd Garrison, stopped to read these words: "My country is the world. My countrymen are all mankind."